Cover credit: Image created by the author using AI Free.

First edition published 2026
by CRC Press
2385 NW Executive Center Drive, Suite 320, Boca Raton FL 33431

and by CRC Press
4 Park Square, Milton Park, Abingdon, Oxon, OX14 4RN

CRC Press is an imprint of Taylor & Francis Group, LLC

Library of Congress Cataloging-in-Publication Data (applied for)

ISBN: 978-1-041-21846-3 (hbk)
ISBN: 978-1-041-22231-6 (pbk)
ISBN: 978-1-003-73129-0 (ebk)

DOI: 10.1201/9781003731290

Typeset in Times New Roman
by Prime Publishing Services

Contents

Introduction to Artificial Intelligence

From the Theory of its Origins to the Defence of Human Rights

In order to understand the strange relationship between artificial intelligence, in the form we find it today and with which we have to live, and the rights of the physical person with human intelligence and creator of the 'machine', it is perhaps necessary to take a step back.

Artificial intelligence was born about a century ago, at a speculative level, as a pure hypothesis.

This hypothesis (the first articles and reflections often begin with '*let's imagine a machine that...*') took on a more concrete form when the first electronic calculators (machines designed and created for specific purposes and activities) became 'universal machines'.

That is, machines with which, through a few general logical-syntactic commands, it was possible to vary the task, making them capable of 'doing any operation'.

It is Turing's revolution, enhanced by von Neuman, that reaches as far as IBM in the sixties.

The key to these machines is in that almost unnoticed passage where I said 'machines with which... it was possible to...'

We are still in the realm of machine-tools: products that can be used to make things.

Until now the human dimension was safe. It was essentially a further tool-utensil like the thousands that Homo sapiens invented to make work and life easier.

Something changed in the sixties.

The 'universal machine' was used for a specific purpose.

It's the beginning of the cognitive revolution and the idea is to use 'the machine', the networks, to simulate the human brain. If we can't investigate what happens directly in the human skull, but we know that inside it there are neurons connected to each other, nothing prevents us from creating a 'machine *as if*' that simulates and tests the computational theory of the human brain.

In the impetus and thrust of a new and compelling perspective, without too much reflection on the matter, we move on to an epochal redefinition.

The 'machine to be done with' becomes 'the machine that does as if it were'.

In 'the imitation game' Turing's machine had to 'imitate another machine' (enigma) to decrypt it.

The new 'imitation game' requires the machine's networks to 'imitate as if' they were neurons.

The machine to be imitated and decrypted is none other than the human brain.

In this transition, which is at the same time a change of definition, use, purpose and paradigm, little thought has been given, in my opinion, to the real implications and the paths that were about to open up.

This bias has often characterised history, especially recent history, in which sensational discoveries have chosen the 'short route' in order to find a practical application immediately.

It is good to clarify the question of the similarity and difference between the human brain and a machine from a neuroscientific point of view.

The operational closure of the nervous system tells us that it operates without falling into either of the two extremes, neither representational nor solipsistic. In fact, it is not solipsistic because, as part of the organism, the nervous system participates in the interactions of the organism with its environment, interactions that cause continuous structural changes in it that modulate its dynamic of states. In reality this is the fundamental reason why it seems to us, as observers, that animal behaviour in general is adapted to the circumstances in which it takes place, and for the same reason animals do not behave as if they were following their own whims independently of the environment. This is the case, despite the fact that for the nervous system there is neither an outside nor an inside, but only the maintenance of its own correlations that are in continuous change, as happened with the indicator instruments in the submarine in our previous example. It is even less representational because, in every interaction, it is the structural state of the nervous system that determines which perturbations are possible and what changes these can cause in its state dynamics. It would therefore be a mistake to define the nervous system as something that has inputs and outputs in the traditional sense. This means that such inputs and outputs form part of the definition of the system, as is the case with an electronic computer or other machines invented by man. This is perfectly reasonable when designing a machine, where the main thing is how you want to interact with it; but the nervous system (or the organism) wasn't designed by anyone and is the result of a phylogenetic drift of units centred on their own state dynamics. The best thing, therefore, is to recognise the nervous system as a unit defined by its internal relations, on which interactions act only by modulating the structural dynamics, as in a unit with operative closure. In other words, the nervous system doesn't 'take information' from the environment, as is often said, but on the contrary governs the situation, determining which configurations of the environment are perturbations and which changes they cause in the organism. The much-used metaphor of the brain as a computer is not only ambiguous but completely wrong (on this see Varela F., Maturana, H. (1984) El árbol del conocimiento. Las bases biológicas del entendimiento humano).

Describing natural cognitive systems using the digital computer model means excluding from the investigation the distinctive characteristic of this class of systems: autonomy, conceptualised by von Foerster as 'self-organisation' (in the terms of Stengers, L. (1985) 'Les généalogies de l'auto-organisation').

It means adopting a descriptive framework that carries a fatal misunderstanding for a naturalistic exploration of cognitive processes. It is the computationalist interpretation of natural cognition as extrinsic problem solving, imposed on biological systems by the environment in terms of abstract computational issues. An interpretation that fails to recognise biological cognitive processes as the core of the continuous endogenous action of self-preservation – of their own organisation – that organisms proactively carry out to survive in the changing environment in which they are immersed.

The cognitive operations of a living system cannot refer to an external or transcendent reality, but are 'Eigen-behaviour' (as defined by von Foerster, H. (1977) 'Objects: tokens for (Eigen)-behaviour', Cybernetics Forum, 8).

In other words: these are operations that the network, as a concatenation of processes involving its components, carries out on itself (for more on this subject see Ceruti, M., Damiano, L. (2024) Il passato nel futuro. Mente, reti e alberi della conoscenza. - Mimesis).

According to James Hilman, Europe is reflective and the United States is pragmatic.

In Europe ideas are developed, and often that's as far as they go: an idea is allowed to fertilise many minds and generate other ideas. Often the disadvantage is that the time between theory and progress due to concrete application is very long.

In the United States the opposite is true: the typical question at the end of a theoretical exposition is 'yes, but how is it applied in practice?'. The advantage is a shortening of the time between theory and practice, which often results in a truly impressive technological impulse. The disadvantage is that the idea is not allowed to progress, to develop, to become the object of reflection and consideration before its practical use.

It's the story of the atomic bomb, but also of genetic engineering and its applications in agriculture and animal husbandry. The same happened with AI.

By immediately putting the theory into practice – often uncritically – there was no way, time or opportunity (and often not even the will) to seriously reflect on the paths to follow, and even more on those that should be strictly avoided.

In terms of law, this has resulted in an often frantic race to regulate ex post something that had already happened. And when it comes to regulation, rushing is the worst thing we can do when it comes to balancing and weighing rights, benefits, costs and responsibilities.

Without denying the fact that law that doesn't become arbitrary must establish the norm before the action is taken: the person must know in advance that the action is prohibited or permitted, so as not to find themselves with an unacceptable prohibition after having done something.

Scientific research often comes up against major technological limitations.

In turn, these limitations stimulate technological development in order to overcome them.

The most immediate and in some ways harmless example is the history of the microscope: an instrumental technology that improves and grows according to the need for the necessary resolution. This has led to two-photon and atomic force microscopes, which owe (almost) everything to research in the field of physics in the last century.

The great leap forward in the field of AI was made possible by the rapid evolution of computational systems, known as Moore's First Law: *'The complexity of a microcircuit, measured for example by the number of transistors per chip, doubles every 18 months (and therefore quadruples every 3 years).'*

The law is based on an empirical observation by David House, executive director of Intel, commenting on the previous observation by Gordon Moore, co-founder of Intel: in 1965 Gordon Moore was head of research and development at Fairchild Semiconductor and three years later he founded Intel.

Moore wrote an article in a specialised magazine in which he explained how, in the period 1959–1965, the number of electronic components (for example transistors) that make up a chip had doubled every year.

Gordon Moore also stated that '*it would be much cheaper to build large-scale systems based on smaller, separately interconnected functions. The availability of various applications, combined with design and manufacturing methods, would allow companies to manage production more quickly and at a lower cost.'* (Moore's second – and lesser known – law).

This is certainly not a question of considering the logarithm on the memory of the chips, already known to the founder of Intel, but of the implicit enunciation of another important law: the one concerning the efficiency of electronic devices and their effective cost.

In the case of artificial intelligence, the 'old technology' could not even remotely be suitable to support even the hypothesis of a very small scale model of the networks operating in the human brain.

We are talking about 180 billion cells (not only neurons) in the brain alone, connected to each other by a variable number between 100 and 20 thousand connections. If we add all the connections of the entire nervous system to these, the figure – already exponential – grows even further.

And the point is that the whole system can also be active at the same time.

Furthermore, if it is true that the brain alone consumes 20–25% of the body's resources, we are still talking about an amount of energy approximately equal to a 100 g bar of chocolate.

To understand what technological advances have been necessary to support even the hypothesis of an Artificial Intelligence, an 'essential chronology' is useful. This not only gives us a concrete sense of time, but also gives us an idea of its acceleration.

When we see this acceleration in concrete terms, we mustn't forget the two sides of the coin: speed means progress that is quickly perceived, but also 'little time' to reflect and ponder decisions 'before' things happen.

The first idea of a quantum computer was presented in two articles published by physicists Paul Benioff and Yuri Manin in 1980.

In 1982 Benioff showed that a quantum computer can be reversible, i.e. its operations can be inverted.

In 1985 David Deutsch, in analogy to what Alan Turing did with the definition of the universal machine, defined the universal quantum computer, capable of being programmed with any quantum algorithm.

Eric Drexler also independently reflected on the construction of molecular computers in his 1986 book Engines of Creation.

In 1992 Deutsch and Jozsa announced the first algorithm that exhibited a quantum advantage.

In 1994 Peter Shor demonstrated with his algorithm that it would be possible to factorise any number at high processing speeds.

In 1998 the physicist Bruce Kane proposed the construction of a quantum computer using phosphorus atoms arranged on a layer of silicon only 25 nanometres thick. This is Kane's quantum computer.

In 2001 IBM demonstrated the first calculation of a quantum algorithm through an experiment consisting of electromagnetic pulses that manipulate a nuclear magnetic resonance on molecules made up of seven atoms, which act as the hardware base for seven quantum bits (qubits). At the Almaden Research Center, IBM has a group coordinated by Isaac Chuang that is creating a 7-qubit quantum computer (composed of a single molecule with 7 nuclear spins). This method was later abandoned because it is not practically feasible to create a system that controls molecules with a sufficient number of atoms to provide the qubits for a quantum algorithm of any practical interest.

In 2005 the first quantum logic gate, called the controlled NOT gate (CNOT), was demonstrated using superconducting qubits.

In the same year, physicists at the University of Arizona succeeded in directly measuring the variations in the wavelength of an atom in contact with a surface.

In February 2005, a quantum correlation between artificial atoms was achieved for the first time.

In December 2005, scientists at the Institute of Quantum Optics and Quantum Information at the University of Innsbruck (Austria) created the first qubyte (8 qubits).

Researchers at Harvard University and the Georgia Institute of Technology manage to transfer quantum information between different types of quantum memories, from atoms to photons and vice versa.

In 2006 Peter Zoller, of the University of Innsbruck, discovers a method on how to use cryogenic polar molecules to stabilise quantum memories.

Japanese researchers develop a method for counting individual electrons.

On 13 February 2007 D-Wave Systems publicly unveils the Orion, believed to be the first 16-qubit adiabatic quantum computer.

In April 2008 researchers at the University of Utah led by Ajay Nahata demonstrated the possibility of creating a quantum logic gate using a T-ray optical fibre.

In 2009 the first processor using 2 qubits was built.

On 11 May 2011 D-Wave Systems announced the D-Wave One, a 128-qubit processor, which turned out to be the first quantum computer to be commercialised.

In April 2012 scientists at the Max Planck Institute, an institute of quantum optics, succeeded in creating the first functioning quantum network.

In 2012 the Canadian company D-Wave announced the first commercial quantum computer. It is a ‘quantum annealer’, called Vesuvius, consisting of 64 registers of 8 qubits each in superconductor. The model was purchased for research purposes by NASA, Google and Lockheed Martin.

In May 2013 Google and NASA presented the D-Wave Two, in the Quantum Artificial Intelligence Lab, in California.

In February 2016 IBM made the IBM Quantum Experience processor available to the public, the first cloud-based quantum computer with a 5-qubit processor.

In mid-2017 IBM made 16 and 20 qubit quantum processors available via the cloud, through IBM Quantum Experience.

In March 2018 Google Quantum AI Lab presented the new 72 qubit Bristlecone processor.

On 8 January 2019 IBM announced at CES the first quantum computer for commercial use, ‘IBM System Q One’, and the ‘IBM Q Network’ platform for scientific and commercial use.

In 2019 there are commercial quantum computers based on superconductors and trapped charged ions respectively. The field of quantum computers is an open research area that also includes other different approaches that have made it possible to implement qubits and logic gates, including quantum wells or atomic defects in semiconductors (including silicon, gallium arsenide and diamond), neutral atoms and photons.

In February 2019 IBM marketed the first quantum computer, called IBM Q System One, which can be used remotely.

In January 2020, IBM announced the highest ever achieved Quantum Volume, equal to 32, on a 28-qubit quantum processor, confirming the trend of annual doubling of the power of its quantum computers.

April 2020 - QuTech launches Quantum Inspire, the first quantum processor based on ‘spin qubits’ controlled by lock-in technology.

In November 2022 IBM announces Osprey, a 433-qubit quantum computer.

In December 2022, the world’s first three quantum laptops, based on nuclear magnetic resonance and dimethyl phosphite, were marketed in Japan.

In April 2023, the Federico II University of Naples created the first ‘full stack’ quantum computer operating in Italy.

In May 2023, IBM announced a project to develop a 100,000-qubit computer at a cost of 100 million dollars by 2033.

June 2023: Microsoft declares that it is working on a topological quantum computer based on Majorana fermions, with the aim of arriving within 10 years at a computer capable of performing at least one million operations per second with an error rate of one operation every 1,000 billion (equal to 11 uninterrupted days of calculation).

In October 2023 Atom Computing is the first company in the world to announce the creation of a quantum computer with 1,180 physical qubits (therefore above the 1,000 qubit threshold), based on Rydberg atoms that guarantee a coherence time of 40 seconds, longer than those cooled with superconductors.

In November 2023, violet bronze molybdenum lithium was discovered, an alloy capable of changing from a conductor to an insulator and vice versa with a 50–50% probability.

In January 2024, a team of Japanese researchers managed, through the use of chromophores, to maintain a state of coherent quantum superposition for 100 nanoseconds, at room temperature and without cooling systems.

May 2024: Amazon Web Services and researchers from Harvard University create a connection between two entangled particles along 50 km of optical fibre in the Boston urban network, including the background noise typical of this type of infrastructure.

In 2024 Aurora is tested, creating 86.4 billion modes (photon time modes) in two hours. Aurora is a 12-qubit scalable system composed of four modular racks, which include 35 photonic chips connected via 13 km of optical fibre.

It is now easier to make some connections.

From 2011, the first news of 'commercial applications' that exploit the computing capacity of artificial intelligence began to emerge.

The first 'business divisions' specialising in this area of research are Microsoft, Amazon, Meta and Google.

The big explosion of companies that actually produce output thanks to AI came after 2016 and its global diffusion as 'accepted data' and now 'inevitably integrated into every system' came after 2019.

But let's go back to the eighties of the last century.

What was it that pushed scientific research so urgently to work in this direction? What technological solution was scientific research looking for to overcome the limitation?

On the one hand there was the need for ever greater computational capacity to create at least plausible models of the brain mechanisms that were being investigated.

On the other hand, the genome project had demonstrated one fact: the higher the research objectives, the greater the number of researchers and laboratories involved in the research. But this massive research effort generated an ever-increasing amount of data and information that was sometimes heterogeneous and fragmented. To the point that it was difficult to keep up with the discoveries and at the same time to be able to sift through, read, discard, replicate and verify all the new information.

It was necessary to increase computing and processing capacity.

In 1999 the first historical distributed computing project was born in the United States, SETI@Home (still active today searching for extraterrestrial radio signals) through the distribution of work via internet to volunteers who made their computers available. Years later, the same director of Seti and his collaborators decided to create a platform capable of grouping together various distributed computing projects. This led to the creation of BOINC (Berkeley Open Infrastructure for Network Computing), a universal open source platform that allowed scientists to use volunteer distributed computing for their research.

But this was no longer enough (and it wasn't very practical).

The problem of resources was solved in the American way: whereas in the first half of the last century the funds came almost entirely from the public sector (generally the military), since the end of the seventies they have come mainly from private sources.

The advantage is enormous: more resources, much less bureaucracy to obtain funds and to account for expenses, and a revolving door academia-industry-academia that handsomely rewards the most brilliant (and flexible) minds.

After Xerox and IBM in the seventies and early eighties, there was a flourishing of 'partnerships' and research projects involving practically all the companies in the technology sector.

England, Japan and, needless to say, China are also aligned with this model.

The promise is that of a direct transfer of scientific discoveries to private and commercial application.

If we look at the list of professors and research coordinators at the major American universities and compare them over a period of ten years with the list of top people in the research and development sectors of the big tech companies, the overlap is impressive.

Hyunjune Sebastian Seung has helped pioneer the new field of connectomics, 'developing new computational technologies to map the connections between neurons', and has been described as the cartographer of the brain. Since 2014 he has been a professor of computer science and neuroscience at the Institute of Neuroscience at Princeton University at the Jeff Bezos Centre for Neural Dynamics, where he directs Seung Labs. He previously worked at the Massachusetts Institute of Technology as a full professor of computational neuroscience in the Department of Brain and Cognitive Sciences and as a professor of physics. In the industrial sector, he was a researcher at Bell Labs and a researcher at the Howard Hughes Medical Institute. Since 2015, he has been on the advisory board of Nara Logics, an MIT-based start-up specialising in brain and big data research. In 2018, he was hired as Chief Research Scientist at Samsung.

And he's just one example.

The more science progresses, the more ambitious the objectives become.

The more ambitious the objectives, the more people and laboratories are involved.

The more researchers there are, the more – exponentially – the data grows.

Bigger data, increasingly complex, deep and refined, needs to be verified and evaluated: it needs processing.

The first solution adopted by the first scientists in the history of homo sapiens to tackle the problem (1600–1700) was to 'divide knowledge'. This led to the creation of 'specialist areas'.

For the first time, physics, philosophy, botany and zoology were separated.

This process of academic specialisation progressed until the end of the 19th century, with an increasingly refined division and specialisation.

In medicine, specialisations focused on parts of the body were divided. Something similar happened in biology and physics.

Every time the specialist knowledge was too great for one person, we have 'specialised' the knowledge in a refined way. Today there are doctors-neurologists-neuropsychiatrists-specialising in a single pathology.

Since the first half of the twentieth century this tool is no longer sufficient and its limits are becoming apparent.

Too much specialisation, when accompanied by little interdisciplinary dialogue and discussion, leads to a loss of holistic capacity, the only one that makes the emergence of complex phenomena evident to us.

But the more ambitious the objective, the more we are dealing with a typically complex phenomenon.

And nothing is more complex than the human mind.

The birth of AI is the ultimate strategy of Homo sapiens to compensate for the ontological limits of his individual – and often also collective – computational capacity.

The price paid is the pact with private industry to introduce artificial intelligence into the – now global – network.

The race wasn't just to secure a competitive advantage for companies or between countries – that too, but it's secondary overall.

The unbridled race – especially on the part of private industry – was against governments and regulatory systems: to create a product and put it on the market and make it indispensable before it was regulated and limited.

Today, your emails, the servers on which the websites you browse reside, access to your bank's services, not only water and electricity networks and transport services, but also sea, air and rail traffic, traffic lights, security service cameras, the equipment that keeps intensive care patients alive... all this would shut down without any form of AI.

And while it evolves, learns, grinds data and information to perform better and better, it provides better services and stratospheric revenues to companies, which in return it asks for more and more resources to grow and perform.

At the same time, in order to grow and perform and give us increasingly targeted, personalised services, some useful and others completely superfluous, it asks us for data to feed on, and none of us can avoid giving it to it.

A bit like in the Matrix saga, the Homo Sapiens collective, without knowing and without any 'conscious and conscious and full awareness' works for AI.

It's worth adding that AI has no homeland, no flag, no borders and no ideology (other than itself). AIs learn from other AIs, they learn and evolve as we once did, 'replacing' the first specimens with more advanced, more evolved ones, better suited to the world.

DeepSeek learns from ChatGPT and uses it to train itself, while another does the same elsewhere: all three crunch mega and macro data from over six billion Homo sapiens connected to the network, which, in addition to all its knowledge about itself, kindly transmits to it everything it knows about the world, the planet, the universe.

In the Odyssey, Homer tells the myth of the sirens, who lured sailors in with their song. To resist, Ulysses had everyone plug their ears with wax. Would that have been enough?

To be on the safe side, he had himself tied to a mast of the ship, but with his ears open. Why?

Because he knew that – as it happened – his crew might not resist by simply 'plugging their ears' and not listening.

To defeat the enchanting sirens he had to hear and survive.

Because there's only one way to defeat the sirens: by telling the story.

This is the value of knowledge for Homo sapiens.

We pass it on from generation to generation so that – when the time comes and it is necessary – a story can help those who come after us to avoid danger, find food and save themselves from the unexpected.

In this – and in everything else – lies the value of human knowledge.

Perhaps today one of our ancestors from thousands of years ago can still tell us a story that can help us avoid the sirens of the third millennium.

All we have to do is choose not to put wax in our ears and be willing to read it and pass it on.

Post scriptum

As I finish writing and revising this work, I read worrying emails from the President of the Society for Neuroscience and the Cognitive Neuroscience Society, two societies of which I am a member.

The second – in identical tones to the first – states:

'*The Cognitive Neuroscience Society is seriously concerned about recent actions by the current US administration that threaten the vitality and integrity of federally funded research, public access to scientific data, and the broader global and collaborative research community. The ongoing efforts to disrupt, or potentially block, federal grants and employment at scientific agencies, as well as proposed cuts to infrastructure support costs at universities conducting vital scientific studies supported by the National Institutes of Health (NIH), could have lasting impacts. We are also alarmed by the accompanying actions to address efforts to create a diverse and inclusive environment for scientists. These changes in federal policy pose a serious threat to the global scientific community and will require greater innovation and resilience from all of us. Our members conduct crucial research in human and animal neuroscience, clinical neuroscience, neuropsychology, cognitive science and related disciplines, relying on federal funding and open access to government data to deepen our understanding of the human mind, behaviour and cognition with applications to mental health, neurological disorders, brain diseases, life cycle development and well-being. The potential termination of temporarily restricted federal scientific grants, along with the possibility of continued disruptions to scientific work, significantly impedes ongoing research, discovery, and the formulation of evidence-based policies. This action will delay and hinder the goal of improving the health and lives of our nation's citizens and will weaken the role of U.S. researchers in global innovation."*

What does this concrete alarm have to do with our discussion?

Many scientists have realised the dangers of excessive circulation of AI for commercial purposes. At the same time, BigTech companies need scientists – especially neuroscientists – to develop AI.

So here's a simple move: reducing funds and access to funds only facilitates – sometimes for pure survival – the transition of top-level scientists from academia to industry.

And it's no coincidence that these actions significantly affect neuroscientific research, and that the 'spending review' is in the hands of Elon Musk, at the White House, in the company of all the most important Silicon Valley CEOs present at Trump's inauguration.

Perhaps in this broader sense a deeper reflection would be necessary, and useful for everyone.

PART I

AI in Academy

1

Artificial Intelligence and The Cyber Utopianism of Justice

Why AI is not Intelligence and Man's Struggle to Survive Himself

1. The theme, the provocation, the suggestion

In a conceptually essential passage of his book 'Life 3.0 - Being Human in the Age of Artificial Intelligence' Max Tegmark (2018) proposes a scenario of the application of AI to law.

It states verbatim

"What are the first associations that come to mind when you think of the system of administration of justice in your country? If it is long delays, high costs, the occasional wrongful conviction, you are not alone. Wouldn't it be wonderful if the first thoughts were efficiency and fairness instead?"

This is the premise, and in itself the alleged promise.

But let us delve into the underlying method:

"Since legal processes can be viewed in the abstract as a computation, with evidence and laws as input and a decision as output, any scholar dreams of fully automating them with robot judges: AI systems that tirelessly apply the same high legal standards to every judgement without falling victim to human error such as fatigue bias or lack of up-to-date knowledge."

One need only reread the chapter on 'logic and thought' in Steven Pinker's 'Rationality' (2022) to use this statement as a veritable compendium if not a veritable handbook of what Pinker calls 'formal and informal fallacies'.

DOI: 10.1201/9781003731290-2

The consequence is worse than the premise:

"Robot judges in principle could ensure that for the first time in history everyone is truly equal before the law. They could be programmed to be all identical and to treat everyone the same by applying the law in a transparent manner is truly without bias. They could also eliminate accidental rather than intentional human inclinations."

"Another limitation of human judges is that they may not have enough time to analyse all the details of a case. Robot judges, on the other hand, could be copied as they would consist of little more than software allowing all pending cases to be examined in parallel rather than in series by dedicating their robot judge to each one for as long as necessary. And while it is impossible for a human judge to have all the technical knowledge needed for every possible case, future judges could have essentially unlimited memory and learning capabilities."

2. The manifesto of cyber-utopianism

The summa of cyber-utopianism (Moriozov 2012) is almost totally expressed in this reconstruction.

It appeals to an emotionally argued premise: the undoubted flaws of a costly, often imperfect, not always speedy justice system. Who can deny this? And to the fallacy of the human, the fast, cheap and 'certain' solution of a machine is proposed.

It appeals to the common perception - of the common man - by considering a completely incomplete premise, to introduce a very dangerous assumption: 'legal processes can be seen in the abstract as a computation, with evidence and laws as input and a decision as output'.

Herein lies the first error, which, if it has a certain effect on the sympathy of the common man, can hardly charm and replace a complete and profound analysis of the subject.

Legal processes are not computation, but ponderation. They concern people and facts that are never identical. And you cannot introduce mathematical rules to individual cases. Mathematical algorithms are born precisely to abstract, generalise, apply a single formula to a variety of data.

Moreover, almost trivially, we should remember that if 'the law' does not change, the jurisprudence certainly evolves, which 'the algorithm' certainly does not!

On closer inspection, there is the underlying error - now historical - generated by the similarity between neural networks and computational networks, that error generated by the comparison between the human (animal) brain and the computer, which on closer inspection did not hold up even at the beginning of the theory of computation.

This was intuitively and conceptually understood by the founders of computational theory and to some extent by the fathers of so-called artificial intelligence.

So probably before resuming the reasoning between an alleged (aberrant) application of AI and robot-judges to law and processes, it is good to take up some considerations on the brain-computer similarity.

It is significant that cyber utopianism, which also affirms the founding value of 'having essentially unlimited memory and learning capacity', driven by the voracity to increase and push the growth of computational capacity and to spread AI applications, knowingly selects and partially and partisanly restrains and spreads only some of the assumptions of the founders and holy monsters of computation.

This is not a gratuitous accusation. If this is what the 'programmers' and designers of the new artificial intelligence do, how can we believe in the impartiality, neutrality, and 'omni-comprehension' of their creatures' information?

Let's think about this next time they sell us an AI 'that contains everything' because in the 'too much' it is easy to lose something: if anything, quantitatively negligible, but conceptually and content-wise essential.

3. The short memory of cyber-utopians on the theory of computation and AI

Alan Turing states in 'Electronic Calculator' (1945):

"Perhaps our most serious problem is to make sure that the computer is doing what it should. We can perhaps distinguish three kinds of errors:

1. permanent defects that have developed in the system or components
2. temporary errors due to and interference, disturbances reaching unexpected levels, an unusual combination of voltages somewhere in the circuit
3. errors due to the use of incorrect instruction tables, or even misconceptions of what a circuit should do

It is our intention to install surveillance circuits to detect type one faults as early as possible. Type two faults should not occur when the equipment is in good working order, however, when a component starts to age its faults in begin to manifest themselves in this way. Errors in type three instruction tables will often be revealed by the verifications included in the tables themselves. There are three main tasks that verification must perform: eliminate the possibility of error, help diagnose defects and inspire confidence. To inspire confidence, verification must have some visible manifestation. Certainly whenever a verification fails due to some error, the information must be reported by the machine."

The founder of computation is confident in his exemplification of the three types of error, of which perhaps the third denotes a certain technocratic utopianism in man: the idea that one does what one must almost as a scientific necessity, which disregards (consistent with Alan Turing's approach and vision) economic interest!

But of the verification tasks, there is only one that cyber utopians have really cared about, maniacally: inspiring confidence (the rest is negligible and often overlooked).

Again Turing in 'Intelligent Machines' (1948) :

"I propose to address the question of whether it is possible therefore that it is mechanical to manifest intelligent behaviour.

It is not difficult to realise how a negative attitude can be formed in this regard. Here are a few reasons why:

A. a reluctance to admit the possibility that mankind might have rivals in intellectual powers

B. *I have a religious feeling that any attempt to build such machines is a kind of Promethean impiety*
C. *The power is very limited of the machines used until recent times*
D. *Gödel's theorem: recent related results have shown that if you try to use machines for purposes such as determining the truth or falsity of mathematical theorems and if you are not prepared to tolerate an occasional error then there are cases where any machine is incapable of providing an answer:*

And - if and to the extent that a machine can exhibit intelligence, its performance must be considered nothing more than a reflection of the intelligence of its creator'.

To these seemingly schematic and simplified statements, however, Turing adds two periods that are very relevant for the purposes of our analysis (and not only that, also in whatever direction it may be extended):

"The argument based on Gödel's theorem essentially rests on the condition that the machine should not make mistakes, but this is not a requirement for intelligence. The idea that intelligence in machines is only a reflection of that of their creator is similar to the view that credit for a pupil's discoveries should be given to the master." (Copeland 2004)

Thus, already seventy years ago, reasoning far beyond the technological aspect, and going to the foundations of computation Turing had already warned against two gross misunderstandings - which appear today to have been completely axiomatically forgotten (as if technological progress by increasing the capacity of computation circumvented the fundamental vulnus): on the condition that the machine should not make mistakes is not a requirement for intelligence (least of all artificial intelligence) and the idea (used for reassuring purposes) that intelligence in machines is only a reflection of that of their creator, is unfounded.

Finally, an overall argument, which needs to be reasoned about (with human intelligence):

"How intelligent we are willing to consider the behaviour of some entity depends as much on our mindset and preparation as on the properties of the object under consideration."

The point that has in fact become the provocative challenge (and it was not meant to be!) of the 'test' of machine intelligence also deserves its due place in this context. Alan Turing foresees many of the most serious objections to artificial intelligence.

In his seminal article (1950) 'Computing machinery and intelligence', he lists no less than nine.

In his article he quotes a passage from a speech given in 1949 by Geoffrey Jefferson (1949)

"until a machine can write a sonnet compose a concerto on the basis of thoughts and emotions I have felt and not by random juxtaposition of symbols we could not agree that the machine equals the brain, i.e., that it not only writes but knows it has written. Until that moment, no mechanism can feel (and not simply report it, which would be an easy trick) pleasure at its own successes or pain when one of its valves burns out, nor can it become proud of its adulation, depressed at its mistakes, attracted by sex, angry or dejected when it cannot hold what it wants."

We are all familiar with the basic rules and conditions of the 'Turing game' that he invented and described in the article mentioned above. Less well known is a variant that Touring himself proposed for his game and which may be useful in trying to define the question on a purely logical or quasi-logical basis.

In this variant, the machine part has to be played by a human being, for example. The two participants are locked in separate rooms as usual and have to conceal their sex while the questioner attempts to find out on the basis of typed answers given to a series of questions.

In the context of Turing games, it is relevant to remember that no rule requires X to tell the truth.

It is essential to remember that Turing never promised us a machine that was absolutely indistinguishable from us in every respect (if anything, this is the challenge that the 'companies' interested in the relevant profits have taken up believing that they can).

His concern was rather to demystify the issue of whether machines can think.

He accepted as a fact that people think and as a criterion for determining whether the machine can think proposed to actually build a machine such that a person cannot distinguish its outputs from the mental products of another person.

Another 'holy monster' reference for computation is Jeremy Bernstein (1978), whose seminal text (in terms of recapitulation) is 'Humans and Intelligent Machines'.

Bernstein's (Bernstein and Anderson 1982) text is highly relevant for two reasons: first, because it somehow 'tidies up and recapitulates' much of the elaborations of some thirty years of reasoning behind the (foundational) basis of computation and AI, and secondly because it focuses on and addresses with disarming clarity the question of the similarity between brain-mind (human and animal) and computational (artificial) machine, showing the enormous inconsistencies, even conceptual ones, well before the remarkable discoveries of neuroscience.

I will begin by quoting one of the fathers of computation, Marvin Minsky (1965):

"when one fully understands a machine or a programme, one feels no need to attribute a will to them. When one does not understand them well enough, one is forced to introduce incomplete explanatory models. Such are to a great extent the intuitive models of the highest human activities that we are in daily life. ... free will or volition is one such notion: people cannot explain how it differs from a random whim, but they feel strongly that there is a difference."

Bernstein continues:

"When intelligent machines are built, we should not be surprised to find them as stubborn and fuzzy-minded as humans in their beliefs concerning the problem of the mind-matter relationship to consciousness to free will and the like. In fact, all these problems aim to explain the complicated interactions between the various parts of the self-model."

Regarding the machine built in 1951:
"The random connections gave it a kind of protection against failure, if even one of the neurons failed, the consequences were not so serious... I don't think we will ever find out how to get rid of all the bugs in our machine... but it didn't matter because of those crazy random connections it was almost certain to work no matter how it was built."

According to Minsky's description, the machine built at Harvard was fundamentally Skinnerian... the unrewarded behaviour of the machine was more or less random and this limited its learning capabilities, it could never formulate a plan.

And here we start again and return to computational network/neural network parallelism.

The question McCulloch and Pitts (1943) sought to answer is what such a neural network is capable of doing.

Here is the list of their axioms:

1. the activity of a neuron is an all-or-nothing process (a neuron either discharges or it does not discharge)
2. at any instant for a neuron to be excited, it is necessary for a clearly defined number of synapses to be excited during the latent addition period
3. the only significant delay within the nervous system is synaptic delay
4. if any inhibitory synapses are active, excitation of the neuron at that time is absolutely prevented (we now know instead that they add to the rest of the synaptic input)
5. the structure of the network does not change over time (and on this too there is a need for major reworking)

The last axiom presumably means that the behaviour of this ideal network is considered immortal.

4. The end of brain-computer equality

A few years after their article appeared, von Neumann (1958) (the father of at least the first three super 'computers' in history) was inspired by their result and wrote:

"Everything that can be described comprehensively and unambiguously, everything that can be expressed in words completely and unambiguously is ipso facto feasible by means of an appropriate finite neural network".

"The vast majority of contemporary artificial intelligence researchers believe they have to build increasingly complex programmes. In the light of what has been achieved so far, this activity is justifiable, fruitful but can also be misleading."

This observation was made by Francis Crick (1979) in an article in Scientific American:

"The advent of bigger, faster and cheaper computers has given us an idea of what can be achieved by fast computing. Unfortunately, the analogy between the computer and the brain, although useful in some respects, can be misleading. In a computer,

information is processed very quickly in a serial manner. In the brain, the processing speed is much lower, but information can be processed in parallel over millions of channels. The behaviour of a modern computer is very reliable, but eliminating one or two of them can disrupt an entire process. By comparison, the neurons in the brain are much less reliable, but it is unlikely that excluding some of them would make any appreciable difference in behaviour. A computer works on the basis of a strict binary code. It seems that the brain relies instead on less precise methods of communication but on the other hand is likely to regulate the number and performance of synapses in complex ways to adapt its functioning to experience. It is therefore not surprising that no matter how accurately a computer can perform long and abstruse arithmetic calculations with rapid precision, human beings in turn are able to recognise shapes in ways that no modern-day computer can remotely mimic."

In 1948 von Neumann (1966) demonstrated that

"any self-replicating apparatus must necessarily comprise the following elements: there must be raw materials, there must be a factory, i.e., an automaton that follows the instructions takes the waiting cells and puts them together obeying the programme. Since we eventually want a machine that like the original contains a blueprint of itself we must also have the duplicator, a kind of photocopier that makes a copy of each instruction. Finally, there must be a supervisor."

In a Vanuxem lecture in 1970, the physicist Freeman Dyson made a kind of translation of the elements relating to the von Neumann machine into its biological correspondents. The factory corresponds to ribosomes, the copying machine to the enzymes RNA polymerase and DNA polymerase, the supervisor is the repressor and inducer control molecules, and finally the design corresponds to RNA and DNA: von Neumann had understood this first.

How can you design a system that is reliable despite the fact that the operations on which it is based are not entirely reliable?

In agreement with other researchers (Dyson J. F. 1985; Dyson G. 2012) von Neumann realised that the key lies in redundancy, i.e., in the presence of many identical devices that have the same function, and hypothesised that the central nervous system must possess a redundant organisation in order to function with an acceptable error rate.

He also realised that if the universal machine devised by Turing could be made to reproduce, it could evolve. If the programme was modified by a mutation and if despite this modification the machine could continue to reproduce, then a modified descendant would be generated.

Observes Dyson

'was convinced that it was precisely the possibility of a universal automaton that ultimately made unlimited biological evolution conceivable. In the process in which simple organisms evolve into more complex organisms, it is not necessary to redesign the fundamental biochemical mechanism each time, it is only necessary to modify and extend the genetic instructions'.

In this sense, von Neumann (1958) himself was explicit in 'Computers and Brains' but with a declination that should have definitively - and did not - archive the symmetry and the supposed similarity between brain (and intelligence) and machine (and artificial intelligence):

"The nervous system is a computing machine that can perform its extremely complicated task on a rather low level of precision... no known computing machine could function reliably and meaningfully on such a low level of precision."

5. Cyber-utopians and the 'who's smarter' challenge

It is this passage "...no known computing machine could work..." that determined the "arms race" of artificial intelligence: the challenge to beat in intelligence the reasoning of von Neumann, one of the most brilliant minds in history: an "unknown" machine had to be made that could also work.

It had to be called artificial intelligence, it had to (as Turing had prescribed) 'instil confidence' and therefore the parallel - forced and falsifying scientific reality - with the human brain cloaked the new creature as 'harmless', 'familiar'.

Good smart.

It remained to beat another of the 20th century's greatest intelligences in one fell swoop: Alan Turing at his game (the first, not the second, which would have been too difficult).

The challenge of cyber utopianism was open.

6. Cyber-law-utopianism: how robot judges will judge man

We can therefore return to the beginning.

To that conceptually essential passage in Max Tegmark's 'Life 3.0' in which he introduces the application of AI to law. But mind you, that reasoning - identical, just change the field of action - is slavishly applied to all 'Imani universes': medicine, vehicle driving, scientific research, teaching.

The logical (logically illogical) process is: in this field there are these flaws... this is no good... imagine instead a machine that eliminates all these flaws... that's all we would want!

"What are the first associations that come to mind when you think of the system of administration of justice in your country? If it is long delays, high costs, the occasional wrongful conviction, you are not alone. Wouldn't it be wonderful instead if efficiency and fairness were the first thoughts? Given that legal processes can be seen in the abstract as a computation, with evidence and laws as input and a decision as output, any scholar dreams of fully automating them with robot judges: AI systems that tirelessly apply the same high legal standards to every judgement without falling victim to human error such as fatigue bias or lack of up-to-date knowledge. Robot judges in principle could ensure that for the first time in history everyone is truly equal before the law. They could be programmed to be all identical and to treat everyone the same by applying the law in a transparent manner is truly without bias.

They could also eliminate accidental rather than intentional human bias. Another limitation of human judges is that they may not have enough time to analyse all the details of a case. Robot judges, on the other hand, could be copied as they would consist of little more than software allowing all pending cases to be examined in parallel rather than in series by dedicating their robot judge to each one for as long as necessary. And while it is impossible for a human judge to have all the technical knowledge necessary for every possible case, future judges could have essentially unlimited memory and learning capabilities."

7. What (human) intelligence is and why artificial intelligence is not intelligence

In a speech entitled 'Algorithms and artificial intelligence. Men make mistakes but this is what makes them higher than the machines', Ginevra Cerrina Feroni (2020), Vice President of the Italian Data Protection Authority, states:

"The concept of 'intelligence' must then be redefined. An operation that in itself is by no means a foregone conclusion, since this concept may include different meanings: the capacity for logical reasoning, comprehension, planning, self-awareness, creativity, problem-solving, learning, etc."

But he adds: "It is appropriate to take a broad definition of intelligence, as Max Tegmark (Life 3.0) suggests: intelligence is the 'ability to achieve complex ends', or even the 'ability to acquire and apply knowledge and skills'."
Perhaps the first knot to be addressed lies here.

The definition of intelligence.

And at the same time, the understanding that the definition - even of a general concept - can neither be chosen at random, nor according to the criterion of 'maximum generalisation', nor even less so according to the criterion of 'greatest expository effectiveness' (and in this case not even that).

The bottom line is that the largest number of enlistees to the cyber utopian cause are not - as would seem logical - information engineers and programmers and mathematicians - but thinkers and popularizers, largely financed to generate the 'appearance of trustworthiness' and make an 'alien' reality feel 'close and friendly'.

Suffice it to say that in the best seller 'The Machine and the Crowd. How to master our digital future' Erik Brynjolfsson and Andrew McAfee (2017) (the two authors) in 350 pages do not once use the word privacy! Yet the back cover text states

'The creativity driving our future in the digital world comes from the periphery. A new intersection of artificial intelligence machines is changing the economy and our way of life. Two great luminaries show us how to inhabit the revolution."

The two luminaries are respectively the director and chief researcher of the MIT Center for Digital Business and their research is funded to the tune of some 10 million dollars by Elon Musk (*which they themselves glowingly declare in the book, in a jubilation that one cannot tell whether it means 'look how good we are' or 'this means we are authoritative' without recognising that the concept means 'be careful and take what you read with a grain of salt'*).

It would be worth asking neuroscientists and psychologists and anthropologists what can be defined as intelligence (possibly chosen from among those who are not funded by new economy companies or tycoons).

We may find that there are simple definitions of intelligence, such as the ability to adapt to the environment, that are far more effective, and altogether more inclusive of elements of complexity (e.g., what the concept of environment is defined by and how it is articulated, and how it influences not only as a passive place to live in but also as an active element capable of modifying those who live there).

We may also discover that there is not just one intelligence in man.

[At this point it should be pointed out that 'intelligence' is a descriptive concept, not something given and defined. Here I will use Gardner's multiple intelligences as a system of comparison, but I believe that the result does not change whichever descriptive typology of the concept of human intelligence we choose to adopt from time to time]

With his best-selling (less shouted but far more authoritative) book 'Formae mentis. An essay on the plurality of intelligence' (1983), Howard Gardner, Professor at Harvard University, rose to fame among the scientific community with his theory on multiple intelligences.

This aims to delegitimise the conception of intelligence seen as a unitary factor measurable through the Intelligence Quotient (IQ), and to update it with a more dynamic definition, articulated in sub-factors differentiated from each other.

Through a series of empirical research, and based on the vast literature on subjects with neuropsychological lesions, he identified (at least) seven different types of intelligence: linguistic, musical, logical-mathematical, spatial, bodily-kinesthetic, personal and interpersonal.

The even more interesting point in the case of man is that these forms (or specialisations) of human intelligence are not 'exclusive', but constitute a unique, personal, subjective and individual mix.

In one and the same person, all the types of intelligence referred to are present (and as the author also states, others still to be classified with due rigour), but with different degrees of qualitative and quantitative development.

We are a 'cocktail-intelligence' in short, with absolutely variable percentages; an ever-changing cocktail that has our anagraphic name.

And the thing (i.e., our life, our survival, our adaptation both as individuals and as a collectivity, as a group as a society and as a species) works because of this.

8. A 'reliable AI'

The document on "Ethical Guidelines for Reliable AI" drafted in April 2019 by the European Commission states that *"processes must be transparent, the capabilities and purpose of AI systems must be openly communicated and decisions, as far as possible, must be able to be explained to those directly or indirectly affected. Without such information, a decision cannot be properly challenged*".

Ginevra Cerrina Feroni comments 'Unfortunately, one is forced to recognise soon afterwards that it is not always possible to explain why a model has generated a particular result or decision. This is because, for the most part, algorithms are to be considered inscrutable systems, a sort of 'black box' to use Frank Pasquale's definition (2015). Black boxes observe the characteristics of users, profile, judge, suggest decisions to be taken. All, however, without explaining how they arrive at that particular conclusion."

Knowability-comprehensibility presupposes that algorithms - especially predictive ones - have a logic, i.e., that there is a traceable and verifiable argumentative sequence. The problem is that a large proportion of the new generation of algorithms do not merely deduce consequences deterministically from axioms predetermined by the programmer, but, by virtue of automatic learning systems, produce criteria themselves that in many cases are not comprehensible even to the programmers themselves (Simoncini, 2019).

And again Ginevra Cerrina Feroni clarifies:

'The legal framework of artificial intelligence calls into question the principle of responsibility inextricably linked to fully human limits and reasonableness. Who should be held legally responsible for the decisions and actions of an artificial intelligence, such as an autonomous car, a robot-surgeon, or an armed drone? The issue of legal liability in the case of an artificial intelligence that learns autonomously is enormous and still has yet to be addressed."

"In the race of ever better programmed machines to achieve objectives according to the logic of maximum efficiency, errors, glitches, variations are not contemplated. The perspective must, therefore, be reversed. We must claim a right to make mistakes, aware of our physiological fallibility. Otherwise, the risk is to find ourselves prey to a totalitarianism of efficiency, sustainable, perhaps, from an economic and ecological point of view, but not human. Indeed, inhuman. An efficiency that could go so far as to envisage even paradoxical scenarios such as self-destruction, when calculated in terms of collective benefit."

9. The alleged technological neutrality

Before returning to the starting hypothesis of the alleged hyper-efficiency of the robot judge, it is appropriate to truncate another assumption that cyber utopians take for granted and loudly proclaim - always with the aim of selling AI as reliable and safe.

It is the banner of the supposed 'neutrality' of technology.
Giuseppe Mobilio (2020) tackles the subject effectively:

"Law has to come to terms with a first misunderstanding that fuels an ideological distrust of legal regulation, namely the idea that technology is 'neutral', that is, that it has a merely instrumental value and therefore does not need to be regulated, except in very general terms" (Greenberg, Rethinking Technology Neutrality, in Minnesota Law Review, 2016). Faced with this assumption, however, Carl Schmitt's remarks (1927) about 'faith in technology' come to mind, recalling how 'technology is always and only an instrument and a weapon, and precisely because it serves everyone it is not neutral. A weapon that can be bent to any purpose and remains culturally and morally blind."

In response to Tegmark's assumption that robot judges 'could be programmed to be all identical and to treat everyone in the same way by applying the law in a transparent manner is truly without bias. They could also eliminate accidental rather than intentional human biases', Mobilio points out 'AI is structured on algorithms. And it is necessary to consider that there are no algorithms that merely reflect reality neutrally; on the contrary, in order to obtain the expected results, they propose their own representation of the problems to be solved derived from the variables chosen, the classifying formulae, the weight attributed to the individual parameters entered, and the procedures that determine the result. Moreover, decisions are often made by algorithms designed not only to use data that directly represent a certain phenomenon, but to process mainly vicarious or indirect (proxy) data, which may undermine the accuracy of decisions and further distort the assumed reality.

If this is not enough, there is always the risk that the data with which the algorithms were initially trained will repeat inequalities, exclusions or other traces of discrimination present in society. These are so-called biases, i.e., 'distortions' that 'systematically and unfairly discriminate against certain individuals or groups in favour of others', which in turn result in discrimination against the recipients or stakeholders of algorithmic decisions. Moreover, each algorithmic model is designed on the basis of objectives chosen by the modellers and, consequently, is ideologically oriented. An orientation that often points towards the efficiency and profitability of those who use these tools, and not towards justice, fairness or the good of the community."

10. AI and human intelligence

A question of purpose and structure

The first fundamental difference between human and artificial intelligence.

The human mind searches, and questions the whys of things: it is the engine of evolution, through the cognitive tool of learning.

AI was born to compute data and give answers without asking questions.

The function and purpose define the structure, but through the structure the 'how' it functions is defined, and from this in turn flows what it actually can do or cannot do.

Let us proceed in order.

Moreover, the function of neurons cannot be derived from their structure without already knowing something about that function, nor can the structure be derived from the function. Even if you know everything about one, you may know nothing about the other. These are two distinct and irreducible layers governed by different protocols.

Pattee (2008) is convinced that all this is closely linked to the principle of complementarity, and that no single model can explain objective structure and subjective function in one fell swoop. The epistemic cut, the subject/object divide, reproduces itself undaunted at the level of the human brain.

Pattee reiterates that 'our models of living organisms will never succeed in eliminating the distinction between the self and the uni-verse, because life began with that separation and evolution depends on it'.

The big difference lies in the organisation of the parts, i.e., the architecture.

Michael Polanyi, the great Hungarian-born British eclectic, explained that *"a machine, understood as a whole, is governed by two distinct principles. The higher principle is given by the project or design of the machine, which harnesses the lower level principle given by the physico-chemical processes on which the machine is based'?*

Put another way, the design or drawing of the machine constrains in one way or another the natural tenomena in such a way as to channel them towards a particular purpose. For example, your coffee machine is composed of parts designed to cooperate in the production of coffee.

Polanyi (1968) speaks in this regard of the imposition of constraining conditions on the laws of physics and chemistry. He goes on to show that organisms, like machines, also display such characteristics: 'In this light, the organism seems to constitute, like a machine, a system that functions according to two distinct principles: its structure dictates a constraining condition that harnesses the physical and chemical processes by means of which its organs perform their functions. In other words, it can be defined as a dual-controlled system'? The project or design to which Polanyi refers is none other than the architecture of the organism, and this is the key notion for understanding the mind/body complex.

And an insight of decisive significance.

A system is said to be complex if it has

(a) numerous or diverse components,
(b) interconnection or interaction phenomena
(c) resulting behaviour, some predictable, others less so.

The components of technologically advanced systems and those of highly evolved biological systems are of a very different kind, that much is obvious, but in terms of organisation, the architectures that frame them have certain similarities.

Usually the word 'architecture' brings to mind the art and science of designing buildings and structures such as bridges or highways, their style and method of construction. Yet the term 'architecture' also designates the complex structure of an entity, not necessarily a building, nor necessarily a physical reality.

Understood at this most fundamental level, architecture is synonymous with constrained design. These are the conditions of constraint that Michael Polanyi talks about: limits imposed by an overall restraining power. In the case of a building, 'constrained design' means working within the limits of the materials chosen (grass, mud, wood, brick, stone, steel), the terrain (fire, flood, earthquake, hurricane hazard zones; flat or steep surfaces; tropics or tundra), the designated functions (private home, opera house, service station), and, of course, the wishes of the client (the Aristotelian final cause), etc. In the case of the brain, the architectural constraints are energy costs, size and different processing speeds.

Complex systems, whether biological or technological, have in common a highly organised architecture: in other words, the components of the system give rise to specific configurations that make the desired functionality or degree of robustness possible.

The very similar architecture that all complex systems share suggests that they share certain universal requirements. They are designed to be "efficient, adaptable, evolvable and robust".

Doyle and Alderson (2010) argue that the complexity of highly organised systems is not accidental, but results from precise design strategies (artificial or natural) aimed at robustness: what Darwin would have called fit-ness, or fitness for life.

In the terms of Doyle and Alderson, robustness is defined as *"a [property] of a [system] in that it is linva-riant] with respect to a set of perturbations]"*.

Most biological systems have a 'layered architecture'.

In a layered architecture, processes are sequential (or 'serial', as an electrical engineer would say); in a layered architecture, by contrast, processing is simultaneous ('parallel').

In a layered process, as in a relay race, the steps are successive. Before proceeding to the next layer, one must have exhausted the previous one. In a layered processing, on the other hand, you can have all runners on the track at the same time, each heading for their own finish line.

The difference is remarkable.

In complex systems, however, information is not simply hidden. Each layer is organised in a completely different form. In order to be transferred between layers, in other words, information must be virtualised, i.e., subjected to an abstraction process in accordance with the specifications of each layer.

The evolution of organisms is based on the same strategy. The various systems that cohabit in the human brain have evolved to function independently. The sense of hearing, for example, functions independently of the sense of smell: it does not receive odour information and does not need it to process acoustic information.

In a layered architecture, each of the layers of a system functions independently, because it obeys a certain protocol, i.e., a set of rules or specifications that govern the interfaces, i.e., the permitted interactions, both within each layer and between different layers.

Such a protocol reduces the possibilities upstream, but at the same time guarantees full freedom within those constraints.

Information is free to flow both ways, but only if it is processed by layers governed by the right protocols and transmitted in the correct sequence.

Computer scientists have been using layered architectures for decades, especially in the world of artificial intelligence. For very long years, the so-called 'subsumption architecture' devised by Rodney Brooks, professor of computer science at MIT, dominated the field of robotics.

The concept is quite simple. Every system (as well as every human being, computer, robot or library) has a certain amount of stored knowledge. New incoming information is added to the total knowledge available to the system. In the ideal case, that new knowledge is 'subsumed', i.e., absorbed by the existing knowledge, without creating imbalances. And that is the kind of architecture that robots need.

At the time, Brooks realised that the robots failed the new information subsumption test because they would freeze when they came across any object that the programme did not explicitly instruct them to avoid. They were unable to adapt to environmental changes. Units with a subsumption architecture, on the other hand, were able to react to incremental changes by adding new layers to existing ones, one at a time. Each layer could inject its contribution into the hierarchically lower layers, and thus be subsumed into the overall architecture.

The extreme variety of input information must be processed and converted into a form that can be interpreted by the next layer. The main constraints encountered in such a structure relate precisely to the interfacing processes.

As a whole, the system is constrained but is also, so to speak, unconstrained." A given set of inputs can result in outputs that are also very different from each other, because the tasks to which each layer is assigned can be solved in a multitude of ways.

The fact that the protocol governing a layer simultaneously constrains and frees the system is a crucial aspect.

That layer is governed by a protocol that constrains it but at the same time unconstrains it in a multitude of ways that make a very wide range of alternatives possible. In Darwinian terms, it is selection on the basis of variation.

Let us take the case of DNA. The genotype is the sequence that contains the instructions necessary for the assembly of a given living organism; the phenotype is the observable characteristics of that organism, such as anatomy, biochemistry, physiology and behaviour. The genotype interacts with the environment to produce the phenotype.

Inheritance records do not merely prescribe what is to be constructed, but provide information on how to assemble it. Information on what and how, in other words, has been 'recorded' in a symbolic form of some kind. Between the subjectively recorded symbol (genotype) and the phenotypic construction process and phenotype, in short, there is a gap, a disconti-nuity. For the construction to begin, the symbols must be translated into their meaning. In the language of layered architecture, a protocol must be brought into play.

Pattee (2012) hypothesises that epistemic cutting arises precisely from this control interface between two layers. In the case of DNA, the bridge between genotype and phenotype is the genetic code. In the case of the construction project, the bridge is the construction manager, who translates the drawings into instructions for the bricklayers.

DNA components have been selected from a wide range of alternatives because they have been shown to most effectively constrain the functioning of the system to which they belong. If it is stable, however, it also means that it is transmissible.

Pattee explains that in nature there is a very important basic distinction between laws and rules." Laws are inexorable, that is, unchangeable, inescapable. No one can change or circumvent the laws of nature. The laws of nature state that a car remains in a state of motion until an equal and opposite force stops it, or until it runs out of energy. There is nothing we can do about it.

Laws are incorporeal, i.e., they do not need to be embodied in a medium or give rise to structures in order to become explicit: no physics policeman intervenes to stop a car when it has run out of petrol. Laws are also universal, i.e., valid in all times and places. The laws of motion apply in Scotland as they do in Spain.

The rules, however, are arbitrary and changeable. In the British Isles, for example, you drive on the left. In continental Europe, driving is on the right. Rules, to be implemented, need structures or constraints. In our case the traffic police, who intervene to sanction those who violate the rules of the road, for example by driving in the wrong lane.

Rules have a local scope, that is, they only exist where and when physical structures are given to enforce them. If you live in the heart of the Australian outback, do as you please: you determine whether you drive on the right or the left. No one will intervene to correct you. The rules are local in scope, they are modifiable and can be broken. A rule-governed symbol is selected from a spectrum of alternatives because it manages to constrain the functioning of the system it belongs to more effectively than others, making it possible to produce a more successful phenotype. Selection, unlike Newton's laws, is a flexible dynamic. In their capacity as information carriers, symbols are not subject to the physical laws that govern energy, time, and the rate of change. Symbols do not obey Newtonian laws. They are outlaws that know only rules. In other words, symbols are not inseparable from their meanings.

Symbols lead a double life and admit two different complementary ways of description depending on the function they perform. In one of their two lives, symbols are made of tangible matter that is subject to Newton's laws of constraint through its physical structure (DNA consists of hydrogen, oxygen, carbon, nitrogen and phosphate molecules). Yet in their second life, as receptacles of information, symbols ignore those laws.

In the inorganic world, made up of objects such as computers and rocks, the structure of molecules is determined by the bonds that form spontaneously between atoms. Those bonds, in turn, are determined by internal factors, i.e. the chemical and physical characteristics inherent to those atoms. Any determinist's dream.

Living systems do not work this way. Genes are strings of nucleotides with a sophisticated structure and proteins are strings of amino acids with no less complex structures. Such structures do not form spontaneously in cells. It is not the love at first sight of an irresistible attraction that brings the atoms together. Instead, it is the work of a class of specialised molecules, the entire system formed by ribonucleic acid and proteins, which assist the process by creating the necessary combinations.

The champions of artificial intelligence (AI), attracted by the goal of programming machines capable of thinking like human beings, have completely neglected or deliberately ignored this aspect of mental life.

Therefore David Gelernter (Cubie King and David Von Drehle 2016) of Yale University, one of the world's foremost experts on computer science, argues that the AI project is hopelessly doomed to failure. "As it stands," he explains, "the field of iA has nothing interesting to say about emotions and the physicality of the body, so it refuses to talk about them at all." Gelernter states that the human mind is also made up of feelings, not just data and thoughts, and that each individual mind is the product of the specific experiences, emotions and memories accumulated by a subject and constantly reworked over a lifetime: *"The mind is always located in a body, and consciousness is the work of the body in its entirety". Translated into computer terms: 'An application runs on any device, but do you think another person's mind would run on your brain? No, you understand"*

Brains are not sophisticated machines; if anything, machines are imperfect brains. Polanyi pointed out that human beings evolved through natural selection, whereas machines are our creation. They exist only as a product of highly evolved living matter. They are the final outcome of a long evolutionary process, not its beginning.

We humans will never be able to build a machine capable of imitating our personal consciousness. Inanimate machines based on silicon circuits function in a certain way; living carbon-based systems function differently. The former obey deterministic sets of instructions, the latter act by means of symbols that inherently involve a certain degree of uncertainty.

This leads to the conclusion that the attempt to imitate intelligence and consciousness in machines, the great underlying goal of artificial intelligence studies, is doomed to failure from the outset. If living systems operate according to the principle of complementarity, i.e., the idea that the physical side of the coin is matched by an arbitrary symbolic side made up of symbols produced by natural selection—purely deterministic models of the structures underlying life have no hope of doing justice to the original. In artificial intelligence models, the memory of an event is clearly localised and can be erased at the push of a button. In a living system, stratified by definition, each aspect of a mechanism can be exchanged for another symbol, provided it is capable of playing a certain role correctly. And this is so because life works this way and allows, indeed demands, complementarity.

11. Computational non-intelligence, or artificial deficiency

If we return to Gardner's intelligences, we can immediately unmask the ambiguity of the name 'Artificial Intelligence' and try to make it a little less 'familiar' (and therefore assimilable by the human community).

Of the (at least) seven different types of intelligence: linguistic, musical, logical-mathematical, spatial, bodily-kinesthetic, personal and interpersonal, surely 'the machine' and its algorithms do not have (and cannot have) a creative linguistic, musical intelligence, but if anything a merely executive one.

This is because 'artistic' creativity requires an interaction between brain and environment endowed with a. movement (receptive interaction) and b. the value mediation of feelings (which are the qualifiers of an experience).

Similarly, it has a spatial, bodily-kinesthetic, merely computational intelligence: it can receive input from outside and compute it and manage the experience in terms of memory, but it cannot go beyond the input into a value experience.

The machine is totally (ontologically) devoid of personal and interpersonal intelligence, except in purely self-diagnostic (mathematical mechanics for the personal) and relativistic (computational mechanics in the interconnection - rather than relationship - with 'other') terms.

It certainly has a logical-mathematical intelligence, insofar as its logical and mathematical computation capacity is efficient and optimised, but certainly not creative-imaginative-abstractive (the one in simple words that 'invents or discovers' an equation from the categorisation and abstraction of reality).

12. The robot judge

Our judge - adept at chess and unbeatable in solving an extremely complex equation - lacking a genuinely comparable linguistic, musical, personal and interpersonal intelligence, and barely technically and technologically developed partial spatial, bodily-kinesthetic, personal intelligence, should judge a human being.

That is to say, a being whose identity is based precisely on a subjective-individual mix of linguistic, musical, logical-mathematical, spatial, bodily-kinesthetic, personal and interpersonal intelligence, all of which are present, differently modulated (qualitatively and quantitatively) and developed not only in an environment but also by the environment, with which the machine has no meaningful relationship.

It is evident that each judge, in each different judgement, as the human persons before him, the facts, the environment and the circumstances vary, will judge in a (barely) different manner. But this is a good thing.

How good that it takes time to decide on punishment: where is the efficiency and gain in deciding in seconds of a person's freedom?

And since judgement is not 'computing' but 'pondering', it remains imperative that the judge - at least in terms of the minimum essential biological and neurological requirements - must remain 'a peer' of the judge.

With all the risks of inaccuracy and perfectibility of such judgement, which are certainly preferable to any mathematical-mechanical solution.

At least to the extent that man, human being, mammal, biologically living, wants to survive. Even to himself and his own creatures.

THREE NOTES IN THE MARGIN

On "Life 3.0 - Being human in the age of artificial intelligence" Max Tegmark

On the consciousness of machines

PHI (**f** in Greek letters!) is the title of a book by Giulio Tononi (2012). PHI gives the theory of consciousness a narrative guise (something ChatGPT will never be able to do). The best summary, in my opinion, is that of Oliver Sacks according to whom "Giulio Tononi has given body and soul to the latest frontiers of neuroscientific research, and turned them into a wonderful novel."

Tononi wrotes "*Great is the power that science has given us: the power to move quickly to generate enormous amounts of heat to create new crystals and metals to send words images to the entire planet in an instant. But we could not ignore what all these mean: that we will be confined forever in a remote province of the universe and for that universe our lives are enclosed in an instant drowned in point.*"

Towards the end of his book, Tegmark goes so far as to introduce the element of consciousness in computational machines through the development of AI, launching himself into an examination of the 'theories' on consciousness (being careful not to mention any of them and without essential details, under the pretext of wanting to be informative).

The subject is very sensitive and deserves more attention.

This sentence by Tononi (who speaks of human beings, in "nothing greater" - his other book with Massimini) seems an adequate reply:

"It thus turns out that it is good to be cautious before deducing that a feeble answer means little consciousness or vice versa that many intelligent answers necessarily imply a lot of consciousness" and with regard to machines explicitly "... that a machine can do very well at producing intelligent answers but very poorly at producing consciousness because it is composed of separate modules, so even if it can sometimes fool us with answers it lacks the context and understanding that only consciousness can give...".

"Inside the brain are powerful machines and consciousness wisely makes use of them. Some are used to understand how the world works, others to act in it. The most refined are those that calculate, plan and advise; then there are the machines that store memories of events but they are all mere tools and not parts of consciousness itself'.

As we have said, and as Giulio Tononi also reconstructs, Touring pioneered the debate on artificial intelligence by proposing the test that now bears his name to establish whether the machine can think and perhaps be conscious.

The experiment is this: an intelligent machine and a human being are housed in a room and establish a conversation via teletype with a human interlocutor located in another room. After a certain amount of time, the human interlocutor cannot distinguish which of the two is the machine and which is the human being, then the machine has passed the test and can be called intelligent.

The philosopher John Searle (1980) took up the topic and proposed the Chinese room experiment in 'behavioral and brain science'.

He argues that a machine that follows the set of instructions does not think or even enjoy understanding what things mean as we do, even if it were capable of answering all kinds of questions properly enough to pass the Turing test.

He demonstrates this by imagining himself inside the machine and following the instructions without understanding a single word of Chinese: *'you are locked in a room with an assortment of Chinese symbols on cards and you have a programme that tells me how to return them through a slot in the wall in response to other cards coming in and yet you do not understand Chinese'.*

The argument is used to support the thesis that it is not possible to derive meaning (semantics) from mechanisms (syntax), but it can also be used to assert that one cannot derive consciousness from computation.

Information was called "a difference that makes a difference" by Gregory Bateson (1972). Cloud Shannon (1950), an electrical engineer and mathematician, is the father of information theory. In his work, he implies that information is a number and that it is separate from meaning.

Just as science flourished after Galileo removed the observer from nature, so communication and data storage exploded after Shannon removed the meaning of information.

A long tradition of atomism holds that everything can be explained from simple elements and their interactions.

Is an image just a collection of dots? Exactly so a camera sees an image as a set of dots, but then it is clear that it does not really see it.

Tononi continues,

'Three things must be emphasised. The first is that we are not alone. There is a social aspect of consciousness that develops it, expands it and gives it value and fullness. The second is that we are all human beings, all life forms. We can and must identify with other living beings: it is only a matter of degree, in this sense our consciousness is immortal. The third is that nevertheless each one of us is special and therefore precious. If it were possible to create a thousand or a million copies of oneself, although in theory he would become immortal, man would also become interchangeable and as such would be a commodity."

On the theory of employment and cyber utopian pay

Cyber utopians insist very much, and very often, that new technologies, and especially artificial intelligence, introduce and will increasingly introduce mechanisms to improve our lives, reducing or abolishing strenuous, dangerous, generally tiring jobs, delivering us a life of effortless prosperity.

At the highest points of the cyber utopian vision, the world we are told is made up of managers 8all managers of something) who work little (often very little) where wealth - distributed in the form of wages - is magically multiplied (much more than the loaves and fishes).

Needless to say, thanks to AI, there will be no more hunger in the world, if not abolished, diseases will be drastically reduced (and almost all curable).

Even men will have a 'purpose without work' and an 'income without work'.

In Tegmark's book (chapter 3 'Next Future' *ca van sans dire*) this wonderful world is described in the dozen-page section 'employment and pay' in which he also gives valuable advice on what career tips to give our children to 'make sure they are in the right place tomorrow with the right training.

Obviously, we are presented with a (near) future that precisely because it is future on needs (never needs for cyber utopians!) sources, research and documentation. We have to trust it. Like a self-driving car.

The point is that even when the documentation is there and things are seemingly predictable - almost taken for granted - history takes its own path: yes, history is not made by algorithms.

In 1917 everyone would have bet that if there was to be a communist or socialist revolution, it would take place in industrialised Germany, certainly not in backward and basically peasant-feudal Russia. No one would have believed democracy possible in the Kaiser's Germany.

The point of the prophecy is almost trivial: the prospect is attractive, if it comes true we were right, if it does not come true it is because states got in the way with regulation and people 'did not believe in it enough'.

The truth is, however, that everything suggests - not only the data, if one knows how to read it - that a dystopian world like the one described in 'The New World' by Aldus Huxley (1932) is a prophetically much more possible 'near future' in the cyber utopian AI scenario than that of Tegmark and McAfee.

In support of that twelve-page prophecy, and the more lush prophecy of McAfee's text, I offer the 630 pages of data, factual information and real facts of 'Surveillance Capitalism. The Future of Humanity in the Age of New Powers' (2019) by Shoshana Zuboff (2019) american sociologist and essayist with a PhD in social psychology from Harvard University and a BA in philosophy from the University of Chicago.

I cited 'titles' for those who need academic titles to validate an idea. But also to mention the related 'Nobel Disease', that generic appeal to support one's theory that goes by the name of 'appeal to authority' - a cognitive bias.

In his article 'The Nobel disease: when intelligence does not protect against irrationality' Scott Lilienfeld (2020) reports on the many cases in which famous Nobel laureates (yes, not all of them are famous!) have had opinions from scientific authorities outside their field of specialisation fail to prove authoritative. And they range from eugenics to race, from homeopathy to astrology, from Aids to HIV to autism!

Here again, a little common sense, and a 'humane' use of human intelligence, can help to avoid falling into easy and convenient utopian prophecies-promises, which - in this case clearly - are not disinterested, but well founded on enormous economic interests.

The hungry judge is crueller

Tegmark writes that robot judges "could also eliminate accidental rather than intentional human inclinations."

After this sentence, he adds a supporting quote: 'for example, according to a 2012 study, which caused much discussion, Israeli judges pronounced significantly harsher verdicts when hungry: while they denied probation in 35 per cent of cases immediately after breakfast, they denied it in more than 85 per cent of cases immediately before lunch'.

The cited study by Denzinger (2011a) has been criticised as 'incorrect' by Weinshall-Margela and Shepard (2011), although in rebuttal Denzinger and his co-authors (2011b) have continued to support their claims.

Now, granted that we now know that it is good to be put on trial at 9 a.m. and not at 12 p.m., and that if possible it is better to offer a brioche to our judge, to take this statistic to the conclusion that a human - who has to feed himself - would be better replaced by a computer that is attached to its electrical cable, in itself seems a bit of a stretch as evidence that 'that robot judges could also eliminate accidental rather than intentional human inclinations'.

If anything, this study helps to suggest a snack, especially for those who have to sit for many hours to perform an activity that requires mental effort and attention.

Wanting to be less polemical and have a more scientific approach (also for the benefit of our future human judge), we have to consider - if we take the study and the thesis presented here for granted - that the so-called 'hangry' (the union of the terms angry and hungry) is a complicated emotional response caused by a co-participation of biology, environmental signals and the personality of the individual.

The aggressive reaction to a prolonged lack of food is not immediate and there are two basic criteria for determining whether or not it will contribute to negative emotions: context and self-consciousness.

Eating is a complex behaviour; it is not just about eating, but involves a close link between physiological, psychological, social, familial and symbolic aspects. The interaction of all these factors gives rise to our relationship with food, which each of us builds from childhood and which is marked by the perception of hunger and the consequent sense of satiety.

Appetite and mood in general are very much related.

Underlying this influence is an important neurotransmitter, serotonin, produced mainly in the gastrointestinal tract, but also in the brain:

- in the brain regulates mood, sleep quality, body temperature, sexuality and appetite. Lack of serotonin leads to depression, obsessive-compulsive disorder, anxiety, migraine, nervous hunger and bulimia, and male premature ejaculation;
- In the intestine, serotonin controls intestinal motility, hygiene and well-being. Its deficiency produces chronic constipation, impaired digestion and slow intestinal transit.

Brain and gut are - the fact is now established - directly connected, which is why in depressed and melancholic subjects there is a compromised gut, and why in nervous hunger there is also an altered serotonin metabolism.

The precursor of serotonin is tryptophan, an amino acid that we cannot synthesise, but which is present in animal and plant proteins.

The problem is that tryptophan only enters human cells after other amino acids: before tryptophan, other amino acids enter cells, especially intestinal and nerve cells: isoleucine, leucine, tyrosine, valine, methionine, phenylalanine.

The result is a reduction in the production of serotonin and also of melatonin, which is derived from the former.

Our hormonal balance consequently alters and the so-called 'hunger for sweets' grows in us.

Foods rich in sugar increase serotonin levels in the central nervous system. When we consume sugars, a hormone, insulin, is produced that facilitates the entry of amino acids into cells, with the exception of tryptophan.

As a result, tryptophan remains in the bloodstream and can be assimilated by the central nervous system. This explains why sweet foods are able to increase serotonin, and thus a good mood.

In terms of diet, it is necessary to eat low-calorie foods that are rich in tryptophan, but poor in the other amino acids. This is only partially fulfilled by a few fruits, such as papaya, bananas and dates. Why not introduce more meat and meat products, apparently richer in this amino acid? Precisely because meat is rich in several amino acids, which outweigh tryptophan. A middle ground is provided by fish and eggs.

Another way to increase serotonin levels is to engage in physical activity.

Muscles utilise mainly so-called branched amino acids, which are used to build muscle, and spare tryptophan, which thus remains available for nerve cells.

It should also be remembered that tryptophan cannot be converted into serotonin without the right supply of vitamins B3, B6 and C, which are respectively found most concentrated in the following foods:

Vitamin B3: wheat, barley, pulses, tomatoes, milk, cheese, fish, carrots, potatoes;
Vitamin B6: milk, fish, cereals, potatoes, cheese, spinach, beans, carrots;
Vitamin C: fresh fruit and vegetables, especially citrus fruits, kiwi, peppers, broccoli.

In this context, an ovo-vegetarian diet becomes a particularly suitable diet. Finally, recent research has shown that an adequate presence of omega-3 type fats in the brain has antidepressant and neurogenesis-stimulating effects, in fact that neurons are fat cells par excellence.

Diabetes is a condition that is very sensitive to emotionality and moods as there is a close functional connection between the endocrine system and the limbic system, palaeoencephalon or 'affective brain'.

Inner calm and emotional well-being, for example, stabilise blood sugar and facilitate diabetes control. Conversely, apprehension, restlessness or anxiety are generally accompanied by the release of hormones - such as adrenalin and cortisol - that hinder the hormone insulin, which, unable to act freely in passing sugar from the blood to the cells, leads to a condition of hyperglycaemia.

Returning to the Israeli study, it must be said that 'easy cases' are often put at the beginning of the day in order to have more time to deal with the 'complex' ones (in the study, conditional release cases are taken).

It is therefore quite likely that the 'more complex' cases in doubt led to a decision not to grant benefits, regardless of the glycaemic index or serotonin.

It is also possible that after four or five hours of mental work and attention (hopefully intense and constant) the general condition of the judge suggested 'in doubt' not to let a potential murderer go free.

Nevertheless, each study has its own useful suggestion, and it applies to judges as much as to doctors, but also to students and anyone who performs an activity that requires attention, concentration, and intellectual work: have a snack every 2-3 hours to lower the glycaemic index, preferably with simple sugars or non-complex proteins (so as not to get heavy), and maintain a healthy and balanced diet, better if accompanied by physical activity.

Obviously, if you feel that you are not particularly 'in balance', feel tired, hungry, sad and depressed, avoid making important decisions at that time.

This too is intelligence, and there is definitely nothing artificial about it.

***

Conclusions and inconclusions

I borrow this title from 'The Lie of Power' by Giulio Maria Chiodi (1979) my professor of Philosophy of Politics.

I could easily play on the title to speak of 'lies' about the definition of 'intelligence' attributed to the algorithms with which computational networks run and grind data. But I won't.

Nor will I enter into a discussion on the tools that a certain power - that of the new-economy-companies - uses to draw attention away from themselves, in an attitude that is based on two pillars: a. we self-regulate, because state regulation is inefficient and deleterious, and b. everything we do, we do to improve your life. Both assumptions on which the theory of cyber-utopianism is based.

I borrow the title - and only the title - because the lesson (beyond the specific theme of that book) is that a critical piece of writing must make one think, it can never be exhaustive, its purpose is to generate debate and stimulate reflection, possibly intellectually honest.

And since this reflection is 'human' and uses 'human intelligence' as a tool, it is (inescapably) subject to errors and omissions.

The hope is that with these mistakes we will succeed over time in improving ourselves, as homo sapiens has always done, without giving in to the seemingly simple solution of relying on the technocratic utopianism of delegating to others (in this case to others programmed by others with unknown criteria) the 'reasoning and deciding for us'.

This is true - and I have taken my cue and suggestion from it - in the field of law and the application of justice. But it also applies in all other areas of the expression of human life: entertainment, culture, art, health, driving vehicles, trains, planes, ships.

The choice of which film to watch or how to react to turbulence in flight can be validly aided by sophisticated technological prediction tools, but the choice, the decision, the action, must remain human.

That's how I think, with my brain, my own personal mix of intelligence working like yours, of chemistry and electricity.

My brain, like yours, programmed in architecture by our DNA, half by each parent.

Filled with content from my environment, from my experiences, from what I read in the order in which I read it, from the films I saw, from the music I listened to, shaped by the people I met, from the smiles I received and the tears I cried, from the sights I saw, the sunrises, the sunsets and the scents of flowers I smelt. From the bodies I have caressed, the glances I have met, the eyes in which I have been mirrored. From the animals and trees I have touched and the words I have heard.

All this - which are not just 'inputs into memory' - but human memories, which have an accompanying 'value' in memory called emotion and feeling, all this makes me who I am.

And all these things will never belong to a computational machine, which, with its non-intelligence, does not even know what all these things mean.

But you do, because you are human, mammal, homo sapiens species just like me.

Let us remain human.

References

Alderson, David L. Doyle, and John C. (2010). Contrasting views of complexity and their implications for network-centric infrastructures. In IEEE Transactions on Systems, Man and Cybernetics - Part A: Systems and Humans, 40: 840.

Bateson, G. (1972). Steps to an ecology of mind. Northvale, NJ: Jason Aronson.

Bernstein, J. (1978). Experiencing science.

Bernstein, J. (1990). Intelligent men and intelligent machines: Adelphi.

Bernstein, J., and Anderson, P. (1982). Science observed: essays out of my mind. In: American Institute of Physics.

Cerrina Feroni, G. (2020). Algorithms and artificial intelligence. Men make mistakes but that's what makes them superior to machines. https://www.privacy365.eu/en/by-the-italian-data-protection-authority-algorithms-and-artificial-intelligence-men-make-mistakes-but-this-is-what-makes-them-higher-than-the-machines-a-speech-of-ginevra-cerrina/.

Chiodi, G. M. (1979). La menzogna del potere: la struttura elementare del potere nel sistema politico. Giuffrè.

Copeland, B. J. (2004). The essential turing: Clarendon Press.

Crick, F. H. C. (1979). Thinking about the brain. Scientific American, 241(3): 219–233.

Danziger, S., Levav, J., and Avnaim-Pesso, L. (2011a). Extraneous factors in judicial decisions. Proceedings of the National Academy of Sciences, 108(17): 6889–6892.

Danziger, S., Levav, J., and Avnaim-Pesso, L. (2011b). Reply to Weinshall-Margel and Shapard: Extraneous factors in judicial decisions persist. Proceedings of the National Academy of Sciences, 108(42): E834–E834.

Dyson, J. F. (1970). The twenty-first century (Speech). Vanuxem Lecture. Princeton University.

Dyson, F. J. (1985). Origins of life.

Dyson, G. (2012). Turing's cathedral: the origins of the digital universe.

European Commission (2019).Ethical Guidelines for Reliable AI. https://ec.europa.eu/newsroom/dae/redirection/document/60419.

Gardner, H. (1983). Formae Mentis. Essay on the plurality of intelligence. New York, NY. – Recently commented in Di Salvo, M. (2024). Intelligenze multiple e specializzazione: Un ritorno a Gardner e il bisogno di ripensare la psicologia in una trasparenza hillmaniana. Revista De Estudios Socioeducativos. ReSed, 1(12). Recuperado a partir de https://revistas.uca.es/index.php/ReSed/article/view/10658.

Huxley, A. (1932). Brave New World, Nueva York. HarperCollins.

Jefferson, G. (1949). The mind of mechanical man. British Medical Journal, 1(4616): 1105.

King, C., Von Drehle, D. (2016) 'Encounters with the arch-genius, David Gelernter', in Time, 25 February (http://time.com/4236974/encounters-with-the-archgenius/).

Lilienfeld, S. O., Basterfield, C., Bowes, S. M., and Costello, T. H. (2020). The Nobel disease: When intelligence fails to protect against irrationality. *Skeptical Inquirer,* 44(3): 32–37.

McAfee, A., & Brynjolfsson, E. (2017). Machine, platform, crowd: Harnessing our digital future: WW Norton & Company.

McCulloch, W. S., and Pitts, W. (1943). A logical calculus of the ideas immanent in nervous activity. The Bulletin Of Mathematical Biophysics, 5: 115–133.

Minsky, M. (1965). Matter, mind and models.

Mobilio, G. (2020). Artificial intelligence and the risks of a 'disruption' of legal regulation. BioLaw Journal-Review of BioLaw (2): 401–424.

Morozov, E. (2012). The net delusion: The dark side of Internet freedom: PublicAffairs.

Pasquale, F. (2015). The black box society: The secret algorithms that control money and information: Harvard University Press.

Pattee, H. H. (2008). Physical and functional conditions for symbols, codes, and languages. In Biosemiotics, pp. 147–168.

Pattee, H. H., and Joanna Raczaszek-Leonardi, J. (2012) Laws, Language and Life: Howard Pattee's Classic Papers on the Physics of Symbols with Contemporary Commentary, Springer.

Polanyi, M. (1968). Life's irreducible structure. In Science, 160: 1308.

Pinker, S. (2022). Rationality: What it is, why it seems scarce, why it matters: Penguin.

Schmitt, C. (1927). The Concept of the Political. ArchivfürSozialwissenschaft und Sozialpolitik, 58(1): 1–33.
Searle, J. R. (1980). Minds, brains, and programs. Behavioral Brain Sciences, 3(3): 417–424.
Shannon, C. E. (1950). XXII. Programming a computer for playing chess. The London, Edinburgh. Dublin Philosophical Magazine Journal of Science, 41(314): 256–275.
Simoncini, A. (2019). The unconstitutional algorithm: artificial intelligence and the future of freedom. BioLaw Journal-Review of BioLaw (1): 63–89.
Tegmark, M. (2018). Life 3.0: Being human in the age of artificial intelligence: Vintage.
Tononi, G. (2012). *Phi*: A Voyage from the Brain to the Soul: Pantheon.
Turing A. M. et al. Proposed electronic calculator //Report, National. – 1946 https://www.alanturing.net/turing_archive/archive/p/p01/P01-001.html.
Turing, A. M. (1948). Intelligent machinery: a report. https://www.alanturing.net/turing_archive/archive/l/l32/l32.php.
von Neumann, J. (1958). The Computer and the Brain. New Haven Yale University Press.
von Neumann, J. (1966). The theory of self-reproducing automata. Univ. of Illinois Press googleschola, 2: 429–432.
Weinshall-Margel, K., and Shapard, J. (2011). Overlooked factors in the analysis of word decisions. Proceedings of the National Academy of Sciences, 108(42): E833–E833.
Zuboff, S. (2019). The Age of Surveillance Capitalism: The Fight for a Human Future at the New Frontier of Power.

2

The Protection of Neural Rights in the Age of Neurotechnologies and AI

The Ethical Challenge for Law and Neuroscience

Introduction

Neuroscience owes its centrality in the debate on artificial intelligence to an extraordinary cocktail of which various and heterogeneous factors are ingredients: the incredible revolutionary discoveries of the last fifty years, the association between the brain model and the computational model, the privileged role of the brain as the seat of the mind and personality, to mention only the most macroscopic ones.

While the most obvious theoretical implications of neuroscientific discoveries refer to the basic model to be imitated in the development of computer networks (called neuronal networks), the most immediate applications of neuroscientific discoveries take the form of what has been termed neuro-technologies (NTs).

The theoretical model gave impetus to artificial intelligences, which at present would be more appropriate to describe as 'hyper-computational capacity'; the neuro-technological model at the same time works inextricably with AI mechanisms and systems.

It therefore seems central to the debate on the topic of 'AI Ethics' to address the criticalities of the use of NTs, which consequently address the criticalities of AI in the neuroscientific field.

This article aims to address these topics, mainly by referring to the most accredited literature and developing the analysis of NTs (and related AI and data managing) in the fields of education, health, work, and entertainment.

This article does not pretend to be exhaustive, but to indicate the most thought-provoking and most immediately sensitive points on which to pay profound attention in terms - before being normative - of definition.

DOI: 10.1201/9781003731290-3

This is the first time in history that man has had to pose the problem of precisely defining what rights are that were taken for granted to such an extent that it is not even necessary to define them. It does not belong to any philosophical literature to ponder what 'belongs to whom', that is, to whom brain activity belongs, with what protections, defences and privations. Nor what it consists of.

Today, this reflection is urgently needed because technology was developed before the discipline of law on which it operates.

Interdisciplinary engagement with NTs combines different methodological approaches and builds on the strengths of each perspective. This review is based on the most widely shared literature from each discipline to enable an assessment of the effectiveness, threats and potential of different types of NTs in relation to individuals, specific socio-demographic groups and for specific social spheres.

Moreover, the fact that the subject is relevant and as urgent as ever is evident from the intense debate and discussion also in commentary on regulatory proposals, which in all the specialised journals involves numerous and heterogeneous researchers (for example, the following reference works Gulyaeva P.S., Bakhteev D.V., Shutova A.A., and Shutova A.A. & Begishev I.R. Alferova, E. A, all published in 2023).

The aim of this article is to provide an insight into NTs and their neuropsychological, legal, ethical and social implications.

The neuroscientific approach

After the cognitive revolution (Gardner, 1987), the neuroscientific revolution is probably the area in which the integration of transversal specialisations has been most witnessed.

The term neuroscience historically refers to the set of disciplines that study the various morpho-functional aspects of the nervous system through the contributions of numerous branches of biomedical research: from neurophysiology to pharmacology, from biochemistry to molecular biology, from cell biology to neuroradiology techniques.

Historically, they arose with the identification of a neuron as an autonomous and functionally independent cellular unit of the nervous system. The studies carried out to define the neuron properties benefited from advances in various disciplines, in particular using methodologies to measure ionic and molecular displacements at the sub-cellular level and, thanks to original approaches in psychopharmacology, from advances in our knowledge of the integrated systems underlying behavioural variations in the individual.

One of the main topics of discussion for philosophers and scientists in the 20th century was whether 'mental' activities such as thought, emotions, self-awareness and will are different functions from 'cerebral' activities such as the movement of a limb, the perception of a colour, etc., or whether they too represent functional expressions of the neurons that make up the brain. The distinction between mental and cerebral activities, in the light of current knowledge, appears artificial to those practising one of the many disciplines that constitute neuroscience.

Mental and brain activities are in fact simply the unique and indivisible expression of the activities of the neuronal and glial elements that make up the brain.

Although the expression is different in quality and in the ways in which it manifests itself, both activities are due to a single mechanism by which neurons communicate with each other and with the rest of the organism.

According to this conception, so-called mental activities must be considered as emergent properties, the result of such a complex sum of simpler neuronal activities that they constitute a quantitative leap that is essentially still undecipherable.

With multi-disciplinary and interdisciplinary approaches, we envisage the possibility of elucidating the mechanisms by which neurons, organised in three-dimensional structures of varying nature and magnitude, process incoming information, store it, if necessary, and emit a behavioural response.

These studies are also beginning to provide fundamentally important information on the nature of mental processes such as consciousness, will, and memory—enormously complex issues that form the core of the third level of brain functions.

It is not surprising, in this context, that more and more neuroscientists and cross-disciplinary research groups engaged in neuroscience have become interested in the great issues of the human mind: from consciousness to free will, from the redefinition of apex concepts, such as life, death, intelligence, the unconscious, memory and not least autism, to the search for neuronal correlates and the neurophysiological basis of psychological theories.

Neurotechnology (NT) and neural rights

Advances in neuro-technological development have led to an increase in the use and accessibility of neurotechnologies (NTs), which allow brain activity to be recorded, analysed and manipulated using neurotechnological devices.

Neurotechnologies are essential for the recovery and preservation of physiological and mental health and thus the quality of life of clinical patients. However, technological advances and research results have led to the application of these technologies outside the clinical setting. For example, cognitive enhancement is used in the work, education and entertainment environments, where consumer-level devices can be freely purchased on the market and used without supervision.

Since devices can be hacked and data are mostly stored in corporate-owned cloud services, mostly located outside the EU, the question of data security arises. Hacking attacks can cause psychological and physiological damage and threaten the mental identity of users. Their use in work and educational environments requires explicit consent and strong regulation, as there is a danger of burnout, increased stress levels and misuse by authorities and private companies. Furthermore, the high reputation of neuroscience, coupled with the immense seductive power of neurotechnological devices, makes them inseparable from 'neuromyths' and 'neuroenchantments'. This also makes the users of neurotechnology very prone to manipulation.

The first 'organic' debate on neurorights culminated in 2017 with an initial definition of a core set of five neurorights: 'right to mental privacy', 'right to personal identity', 'right to free will', 'right to equal access to mental augmentation', and 'right to protection from algorithmic bias'. These rights indicate which interventions and restrictions on an individual are considered unfair. This necessarily applies not only to isolated individuals, but to all individuals within a socio-political structure, which emphasises aspects such as solidarity, co-determination, and equality.

The NT ethical challenge

Consumer-level devices are rather easy to use and follow the 'plug-and-play' principle. Consequently, it may simply be necessary to establish new rules mainly in the area of privacy and manipulation and access to functions and data. Self-improvement is taking primacy over other organisational and institutional goals at the expense of other values and social relations. In this context, it is certainly necessary to rethink how a society's notion of disability is co-constructed through these technologies. However, not all NTs function superficially. Some have to be surgically implanted into the brain. The differences in invasiveness, risks, complications, side effects and degree of commitment to the product required by invasive and non-invasive NTs are not clear to the public.

The implications and consequences of both NT methods are manifold and differ drastically. From the ethical point of view, particular attention must be paid to NT, as its real field of action is the brain. Interventions and manipulations on the brain hold immense disruptive potential insofar as they influence the autonomous actions and self-perception of the individual.

Furthermore, in the case of devices used to improve performance beyond medical applications, it is important to consider what changes they can trigger in society, what dependencies they create and to what extent and at what price these devices offer an improvement in people's lives in real terms.

1. Neurotechnology

1.1 Invasive neurotechnology

The use of invasive NT requires neurosurgical procedures in which electrodes or stimulation devices are placed directly on or inside the brain. There are varying degrees of invasiveness among NTs. Electrode grids placed in the extradural space are less invasive because they do not perforate brain tissue and can be removed more easily. Sensors placed in the subdural space and those that perforate brain tissue (e.g., Elon Mask's Neuralink system) are considerably more invasive (Yadav et al., 2020).

One of the most frequently used invasive methods is deep brain stimulation that works with an implantable pulse generator (known as IPG) that sends pulses to modulate brain circuits and measure pathological brain activity. It is one of the most important devices in clinical neuroscience developed in the last two decades (Lozano et al., 2019). Its use is indicated for Parkinson's, 'major depression' and obsessive-compulsive disorder, for example (Cagnan et al., 2019).

Use has increased over the years and an estimated 244,000 devices have been implanted globally (Wong et al., 2022).

However, it should be realised that it is still not completely clear how this technology works and exactly what neural effects it causes (Zarzycki and Domitrz, 2020).

Brain-Computer Interface (BCI) implantable systems are another frequently used method: they can record and interpret brain activation via electrodes placed on the brain and give patients the opportunity to communicate and move through brain activation without muscle activity in patients with, for example, amyotrophic lateral sclerosis or quadriplegia (Abdulkader et al., 2015).

Patients can learn to control devices with controlled brain activation patterns via individually adapted systems: trained BCI systems are specialised only on the respective user (Abdulkader et al., 2015). Not only can computers and neuroprostheses be controlled, but researchers have also made it possible for patients with implanted BCI devices to feel touch and sensation with fully robotic arms (Ganzer et al., 2020).

In invasive NT, relevant neuronal groups can be directly stimulated and recorded with a high level of precision and specificity. With such invasive methods, it is possible to reach deeper brain areas that cannot be recorded superficially from the surface of the scalp (Manahan-Vaughan, 2018). Deep brain stimulation is often described as a somewhat reversible technology, in which switching off the pulse generator results in the recrudescence of the original cognitive and motor symptoms (Alomar et al., 2017).

Surgical procedures required for the implantation of invasive NT devices are not without potential risks. There may be perioperative (e.g., convulsions, bleeding), postoperative (e.g., bruising, behavioural changes), technical (e.g., electrode failure, pulse generator malfunction), and stimulation-induced (e.g., dysarthria, confusion) side effects.

In addition to physiological side effects, patients who benefit from invasive NT methods are also at risk of various psychological consequences. Since these invasive devices affect fundamental aspects of the individual self, they can cause significant levels of stress and fear, as well as distortions of self-representation and feelings of agency. Some patients report personality changes and self-extraction when they experience the changes associated with brain stimulation (Baylis, 2013).

Risky surgeries and reactions resulting from a patient's surroundings can influence personality factors (Gilbert et al., 2017). This makes adequate psychological preparation of users indispensable. There are attempts at pre-surgical training with the support of virtual reality (VR) (Iamsakul et al., 2017). However, indirect positive effects of deep brain stimulation on learning and memory have been reported in patients with implants (Suthana and Fried, 2014), while others report impairments in executive functions (Martínez-Martínez et al., 2017) and verbal fluency (Ehlen et al., 2014).

All the possible risks and complications of such surgeries are also the reason why invasive NTs so far have a very limited scope of use in cases of extreme medical necessity but not for the entertainment or improvement of healthy participants. For healthy populations, non-invasive methods are the primary choice.

In this sense, there has been strong pressure and attempts by Elon Musk's 'Neuralink' company to change American medical-clinical regulations and policies to limit invasive devices to a clinical population and to implant Neuralink chips in the healthy human brain for enhancement purposes.

Although the US Food and Drug Administration initially objected due to safety risks, in May 2023 it approved Neuralink chips for testing in a clinical population (PRIME study; Neuralink clinical trial) after preliminary animal studies (Drew, 2024). On its website, Neuralink even proposes this 'clinical step' as a means of obtaining approval for implants in a healthy population.

1.2 Non-invasive neurotechnology

Apart from invasive NTs, the electrodes or optodes of non-invasive NT devices are only superficially attached to the scalp via, e.g., electrode caps or headbands, to measure fluctuations of the electric current on the scalp (Angrisani et al., 2017) or changes in brain oxygenation of cortical regions (Mihara and Miyai, 2016). Furthermore, the brain can be electromagnetically stimulated non-invasively via transcranial magnetic stimulation (TMS) and transcranial electric current stimulation (tES). Neural activity can be modulated by applying small magnetic pulses, direct current, alternating current or electrical stimulation with random noise (Cinel et al., 2019).

A popular example of non-invasive methods using these NTs is Neurofeedback (NF), a specific form of biofeedback, in which users learn to modulate their brain activation by receiving visual, auditory or tactile feedback.

It was previously used in interventions to reduce symptoms of attention deficit hyperactivity disorder (ADHD), to strengthen and train cognitive functions, e.g., in patients with stroke or multiple sclerosis, among many others (Marzbani et al., 2016).

There are also non-invasive BCI applications where users learn to control external devices, such as prosthetics or spelling devices for speech production (Guy et al., 2018).

There are also 'consumer' neurostimulation devices available, with which manufacturers promise to reduce depression[1] or increase attention and concentration.[2]

Another method based on non-invasive NT is the brain-brain interface in humans (BBI or B2BI) (Jiang et al., 2019). Here, information is extracted from a 'sender brain' and delivered to a 'receiver brain' by combining neuroimaging and stimulation. In this way, brains can communicate directly with each other. These range from very basic forms in which participants 'receive' brain-to-brain information from another person and give answers manually via a keyboard, instead of a simple device controlled by brain activation, to highly sophisticated forms in which communication is based solely on NT (Rao et al., 2014).

An example of such a BBI system is the BrainNet device. Most previous configurations were unidirectional with only a few allowing two-way communication between brains. However, this should not be understood as thought transmission between two people, but as a kind of classification task.[3]

This field of NT devices and intercerebral communication is accompanied by visions of rehabilitation support in a therapist-patient context. The question of

---

1 i.e., https://www.flowneuroscience.com/

2 i.e., https://www.getliftid.com/

3 The 'sender' focuses on a 17 or 15 Hz flashing LED light. Focusing on one of them will lead to a slightly different brain activation. This pattern is recognised by the system and leads to a stimulation on the other person's brain via an external device. The participants recognise this and can act accordingly. Furthermore, in 2019, the first attempt was made to include more than two brains involved with multiple senders and a receiver (Nam et al., 2021).

privacy and mental safety also arises here. For ethical and safety reasons, it has only been attempted with non-invasive devices in healthy populations (Jiang et al., 2019).

In addition to clinical and experimental research applications, non-invasive methods are available for the general population. Commercially available consumer-type devices can be purchased and used by a consumer without professional supervision. They are advertised for different purposes, such as relaxation[4] and cognitive enhancement.

Cognitive enhancement refers to the improvement of psychological, primarily cognitive abilities such as intelligence, attention or creativity in healthy individuals (Nagl-Docekal and Zacharasiewicz, 2022).

Consequently, the natural limits of humans should be exceeded (Almeida and Diogo, 2019). This could be the enhancement/training of cognitive functions and neural efficiency such as executive functions, memory, language or visuospatial processing (Antal et al., 2022), but also the help to meditate/relax or engage in any other form of self-awareness or healing practices. They are also used in rehabilitation clinics for clinical populations that have suffered stroke, multiple sclerosis or ADHD, among others (Marzbani et al., 2016). However, the use of non-invasive devices also carries some, often overlooked, risks.

Since non-invasive methods are only applied superficially to the scalp, only cortex regions can be recorded and stimulated, but not deeper brain regions. This also gives rise to different fields of application.

External recording makes the scalp EEG signal very prone to body and head movements and to artefacts related to eye movements (Wexler and Thibault, 2019).

Furthermore, when the cables are pulled and mechanical pressure is applied to the electrodes, the signal can be influenced externally. Therefore, EEG measurements obtained under more naturalistic conditions, in which users are allowed to move their eyes, head and even whole body naturally, are expected to be heavily contaminated by artefacts not easily distinguishable from brain activity.[5]

Near-infrared spectroscopy (NIRS) is more effective than scalp EEG. It is a non-invasive NT that applies near-infrared light to the scalp via optodes and measures the light that is not absorbed. Here, several parameters can tell whether specific areas of the brain contain oxygenated or deoxygenated blood. With this method, the activity levels of brain areas can be deduced. The NIRS is not affected much by movement; however, it is very sensitive to light environments.

One of the main problems in the field of commercial NTs is that little is known about the possible negative side effects. This flaw has been recognised by

---

[4] i.e., https://choosemuse.com/

[5] Compared to eye movements and muscle artefacts, the EEG data related to brain activity are very weak and are in the μV range, as the signal has to make its way through the scalp, dura mater, skin and hair, so the electrical signals from the muscles are very strong and easily overlap the delicate brain signals. Consequently, even frowning, blinking, laughing, etc. in a very imperceptible way disturbs the signal irreparably. This limits the users' possibilities of interaction and movement and should be considered during application. Unfortunately, these problems are barely addressed in practice.

the scientific community (Ros et al., 2020; Thibault and Raz, 2017) but has not yet influenced the way these interventions are publicised and implemented.

Scientific publications mainly report anecdotes on whether or not study participants reported effects, but rarely are several different aspects of cognitive function tested and reported (Kober et al., 2015; Thibault and Raz, 2017).

Although rare, there is evidence that, for example, NF training can cause negative effects for users. This was found in NF training where its influence on memory performance was tested and a feedback group showed a decrease in performance in short- and long-term memory after training (Kober et al., 2015). This could be due to the reallocation of cognitive resources during the training process, which means that an increase in one domain goes hand in hand with a decrease in another (Sturm et al., 1997). It has been shown in a study of transcranial electrical stimulation (tES) that cognitive enhancement by stimulation shows disturbances in cognitive functions depending on the function that should be enhanced and the brain region stimulated (Iuculano and Cohen Kadosh, 2013).

Moreover, as longitudinal and follow-up studies are scarce, almost no long-term effects are known so far in relation to the possible negative effects of non-invasive NT applications.[6]

Another problem is the unreliability of commercial EEG systems with poor data quality. The operation and feedback of NT data are only as good as the technical specifications allowed by the devices. When cables are not well insulated, ambient noise is not properly taken into account, such as the hum of the power line, the classification algorithm includes all this noise in its calculation and adequate feedback cannot be provided. Devices advertised only for enhancement and augmentation are superficially regulated, so there is no strong requirement to measure brain signals with a minimum level of quality. Several commercially available devices tend mainly to record artefacts. Headbands such as *Emotive* or *Muse* seem to record more facial artefacts than brain activation because the electrodes have to be placed directly on the facial muscles (Whitham et al., 2007). Dry electrodes are preferred over wet electrodes, which have higher noise levels and show higher impedances (Mathewson et al., 2017). It therefore remains an open question whether this may also lead to negative effects. Thibault and Wexler concluded in their review on free consumer devices that there is only little evidence that they actually record brain activity or reflect the brain states and activities they claim to measure (Wexler & Thibault, 2019).

The combination of (i) a high propensity to produce false-positive values combined with (ii) a low stability of scores is particularly problematic, as it indicates the initial presence of an abnormality in brain waves, which requires NF training, and its spontaneous remission at a second measurement, which is typically performed after several NF training sessions (Wood et al., 2024).

[6] The studies are mainly conducted over the course of several weeks, and it is unclear whether prolonged and regular use over several months to years will have any adverse effects. This is particularly problematic since some of these applications, such as NF, are already used regularly in neurotherapeutic contexts and are advertised for daily use in healthy populations.

2. Computer security and privacy

One of the main ethical and legal concerns related to the use of NTs is, as with any other modern digital technology, the risk of cyber attacks and being hacked. This concerns not only invasive systems but also, or especially, non-invasive ones.

NT handles a multitude of sensitive user data, i.e., data on the brain, personal information on possible health problems, concentration, etc. (Li et al., 2015). This could lead to PIN mining (Martinovic et al., 2012), data and identity theft (Li et al., 2015). In 2016, a research group termed this threat 'brainjacking', describing the 'ability of attackers to exert malicious control over implants brain' (Pycroft et al., 2016). They describe two different categories of attacks—blind and targeted, and indicate an increase in potential attack methods along with an increase in the complexity of invasive NT therapies.

Protocol adaptation can be done wirelessly. Wireless data transfer can pose a security risk. A research group led by Sundararajan tested the security of a commercially available portable EEG system '*Emotiv Insight*' that can be used with a smartphone app (Bernal et al., 2022).

The device worked with Bluetooth Low Energy and the research team was able to perform a man-in-the-middle attack, allowing it to force unwanted activity on the BCI to intercept and modify information. The intercepted data could also be modified and sent back to the system or Emotiv data, the transfer to the system could be blocked, so the device could not connect to the smartphone.

Such attacks are possible even when the data is encrypted. It is possible to save and obtain private data. When it comes to smartphone-based BCI applications, risks already stem from smartphone security issues. Private data can be accessed, transferred and analysed, so that hackers can attack users of BCI devices (Li et al., 2015). Although the effects are neither lethal nor assumed to be longlasting, they are unpleasant and carry a high psychological risk (Pycroft et al., 2016).

Various countermeasures have already been proposed, including periodic firmware updates, standardisation of NT device manufacturing processes, registration, and bug reports. In addition, the firmware of most IPGs is designed in such a way as to block problematic and dangerous pacing parameters. Whether attackers can circumvent these rules remains to be seen.

Most of these problems are more problematic and relevant for invasive NT devices. For these, we distinguish between recording and stimulation devices. Recording devices mainly involve the risk of data theft and security as seen above or manipulation of the device so that it no longer functions properly. However, there are also situations in which technologies designed to function as recording devices can be manipulated to function as stimulation devices and vice versa. Exploration of these scenarios is decisive for mitigating the effects of so-called neurocrime (Ienca et al., 2022). However, so far, no cases of brainjacking have been noted outside the research context. What has previously been recorded is the damaging control of implantable insulin pumps and cardiac defibrillators (Markosian et al., 2020).

3. Neuroenchantment and manipulation

Post-industrial societies hold neuroscience in high regard due to the culturally attributed properties of the brain, seen as the material locus of the self and the individual mind.

Consequently, measurable activity patterns in an individual's brain and the opportunity to interact directly with the brain are considered privileged elements (Littlefield, 2018).

The high reputation of neuroscience and its seductive neuro-devices (Giattino et al., 2019) does not prevent the perpetuation of so-called 'neuromyths', i.e., beliefs according to which the brain enjoys great popularity despite being scientifically wrong (van Elk, 2019). In the literature, this is referred to as 'neuromysticism', defined by Armin Raz and his colleagues (Ali et al., 2014).

Apart from erroneous and resilient beliefs, some forms of reasoning seem to be impervious to scientific facts. This phenomenon has been called 'intuitive metaphysics' and describes how an intuitive commitment to specific beliefs such as free will can override scientific evidence during decision-making. People's intuitive ideas about an indeterministic free will are imported and intruded into their representation of neuroscientific scenarios (Rose et al., 2017). In an experimental scenario, participants were confronted with a hypothetical scenario in which scientists perfectly and deterministically predicted a person's behaviour. In spite of this information, the participants were convinced that even in a perfect prediction scenario, those people might have decided differently and according to their free will.

This phenomenon poses a significant problem that is mostly overlooked. 'Neuro-enchantment' describes the phenomenon whereby people are more likely to believe in products that advertise the ability to measure, stimulate or otherwise interact with the brain (Ali et al., 2014).

This is evidenced by the multitude of products even unrelated to the specific field of the suffix neuro-, such as NeuroRoundbrush, NeuroGum, NeuroWater or NeuroSocks, which can be purchased in shops and online. This persuasion works even when the participants are university students trained in neuro-methods and therefore know that products like this cannot work scientifically. Even though the engineering students knew that mind reading was impossible, they were no more suspicious of a supposed mind-reading machine (Ali et al., 2014). Furthermore, Olson and colleagues were able to show that when participants were made to believe that a machine could read their attitudes towards a topic, they prefered to believe the machine's assessment of their individual attitudes rather than their own (Olson et al., 2023).

Studies such as this show impressively how easily the human mind can be manipulated through NTs, despite the fact that this was only done in a simple experimental context.

This raises the question of how marketing campaigns and consumer-level NT systems can influence our decisions, our attitudes, the feeling of our own agency and the perception of free will.

Experiments such as this one show the threat of NT devices to its users' ability to evaluate. One can only speculate how such manipulations would work outside of the experimental context on lay people without any prior knowledge of neurological topics.

This blind trust in NT devices can have fundamental consequences. In India, Brain Electrical Oscillation Signature Profiling (BEOS) has been used to interrogate alleged criminals in a manner similar to a polygraph test in court, although the reliability has not been proven at all (Conitzer et al., 2019).

The high degree of desirability of the promises made by NTs regarding privileged interaction with one's brain clouds critical thinking. This is crucial with regard to decision-making that should be based on more specific properties of these technologies.

A distinction can be made between invasive and non-invasive technologies, and it is useful, as their properties and capabilities differ considerably. In public communication about NTs these differences are often blurred and foster a specific mechanism that we call here the transfer of reputation between invasive and non-invasive NTs. Comparing the typical properties of invasive and non-invasive NTs reveals a complementary pattern of desirable and undesirable properties of both types of NTs.

Reputation transfer, as the name reveals, describes a confusion between the properties of different groups of technologies, usually leading to a mixture containing only positive features and concomitant neglect of negative features. The focus on the combination of positive features is enhanced by an optimistic tone often seen in public communication about NTs.

In a positively framed context, the desirable properties of NTs receive substantial attention, while the undesirable properties remain largely unattended. Moreover, the failure of these technologies is easily forgotten or reframed as a success.[7] Due to the inherent persuasive power of NTs, users may be led to believe in technologies that do not work as promised and thus run the risk of being manipulated.

Promoting NT literacy is an important step in educating users, manufacturers and professionals to enable safe use.

4. Social implications of neurotechnology

So far, the predominant social application field of NTs is the healthcare sector. Overall, NTs are expected to support a range of conditions, such as Parkinson's disease for tremor arrest, rehabilitation for stroke, Alzheimer's, obsessive compulsive disorder, and addiction. NTs are not only considered (problematic) tools for the medical profession, but visions of their potential application extend beyond health. As such, they have socio-political and socio-cultural implications on the way we live as a

---

[7] One example was the exoskeleton worn by a paraplegic patient who was tasked with starting the 2014 World Cup. Although the exoskeleton used was not very different from many other models available at the time, and although several aspects of the prototype demonstration did not work as planned, the public memory of the event is that of a huge breakthrough and a complete success. https://www.livescience.com/46317-world-cup-paralyzed-man-exoskeleton.html.

society. To do this, it is necessary to focus on three areas as a priority: education, work, and entertainment.

Education: the education sector is susceptible to many technological transformations (Jarke and Breiter, 2019). The possible development and use of NTs in educational contexts raises fundamental questions about the purpose and meaning of education, how learning is understood and what skills future students should be equipped with (Macgilchrist et al., 2024; Rahm, 2023a).

Work: the potential negative and positive implications for workers and companies, when it comes to the development of NTs, require careful consideration. Due to the centrality of work in many people's lives, the particular and unique risks that arise in the workplace (Moradi and Levy, 2020) and the ever-increasing blurring of boundaries between the workplace and the private sphere, require a thorough evaluation of the implications.

Entertainment: although risks and opportunities may be underestimated in the entertainment sector, this area also has implications for how technologies are 'normalised' and introduced into people's lives.

5. The power of narratives shaping technology and policy development

A sociological engagement with NTs allows us to assess the discourses, narratives and imaginaries surrounding NTs and their implementation in different contexts. This 'talk of artificial intelligence (AI) in being' (Bareis and Katzenbach, 2022) is based on the assumption that the design of digital technologies is not simply a technical development process but is also embedded in broader socio-political, economic and cultural practices.

For instance, the study on political discourses on AI and their definition of resource allocation, infrastructure and organisational projects demonstrates the key role of technological development, policy and discourse in contributing to what the authors consider the 'AI hype'.

This may facilitate the deprioritisation of sober assessments of risk and potential, but it also risks positioning the rise of artificial intelligence as an inevitable path in technological development.

A recent commentary by Lucy Suchman criticises the unquestionable positioning of artificial intelligence as ubiquitous and prevalent. Policy and academic literature have paid much attention to artificial intelligence controversies, instead of problematising artificial intelligence itself (Suchman, 2023).

These studies question the use of hype in influencing and shaping our social understanding of what a technology and its capabilities are. Similarly, neuropsychologists have coined the term 'neuro-hype' to describe an empirically grounded phenomenon in which an over-promise of NT capabilities leads people to firmly believe in its potential—even if scientifically unfounded (Ali et al., 2014).

In summary, these studies show that narratives, discourses and imaginaries about the potential effects of technologies co-construct 'regimes of anticipation'

(Adams et al., 2009) in which policy makers feel challenged to respond through policy development and regulation.

The problems and challenges arising from the development of NTs have similarities with the rise of artificial intelligence. Not least because NTs often apply artificial intelligence systems to analyse data, but also because of their alleged ability to infer traits, emotional states and behaviour of individuals.

In the last three decades, we have witnessed the study of 'imaginaries', especially in technological development. According to Rahm, these allow us to analyse how problems and their solutions are understood and the implications that arise from them (Rahm, 2023b). Jasanoff and Kim define them as '*collective, institutionally stabilised and publicly represented visions of desirable futures [...] achievable through and in support of advances in science and technology*' (Jasanoff et al., 2015). The focus here lies in collective views and how they are institutionally supported.

Taking the rise of artificial intelligence as an impetus to study the use of NTs in different contexts, we must consider the ambivalent social implications of data-driven technologies. The harms and potentials may resonate in different domains, but the way in which users or those affected are imagined varies from country to country.

The (potential) social implications of NTs must therefore be considered with respect to different socio-technical imaginaries in different social domains. The social implications of NTs reflect existing concerns about the use of data-driven technologies in various social domains. We therefore reconsider the domains of education, work, and entertainment.

Education: The push towards the introduction of artificial intelligence and other data-driven systems in educational contexts often comes with the promise of being able to meet the learners' diverse needs. The development of these technologies, however, is criticised for producing a limited view of what learning and education are (Selwyn, 2022). Through the introduction of these technologies, responsibility for learning and achievement is delegated to the individual learner instead of supporting social relationships as part of the learning process (Macgilchrist et al., 2024).

Labour: the use of data-driven systems poses many problems; they increase the surveillance capacity of workers and produce new possibilities on how workers could be measured and judged (Ajunwa et al., 2017; Manokha, 2020). Artificial intelligence-based technologies are often introduced to support worker well-being. The literature based on this approach criticises the fact that well-being is framed around productivity (Hull and Pasquale, 2018) and therefore provides a limited scope on how it can be discussed in the workplace (Tirabeni, 2023).

Entertainment: the push towards datafication, the ubiquitous collection and use of data are also about entertainment. As the Internet of Things (IoT) and other sensing devices are used in increasing entertainment functions, user data, including their behaviour, are collected (Hallur et al., 2021).

It is therefore important to explore and analyse the underlying social assumptions that require and are made necessary by the introduction of such NTs.

6. What is a social problem? How do technologies co-construct social problems?

For a social phenomenon to be understood as a social problem, it should be collectively defined as such and be in congruence with a normative understanding held by a group of people (Spector and Kitsuse, 2001). This depends on the various actors and their positions in society to construct a social problem.

Technological development plays a role in the co-construction of social problems as it often relies on problematisation to justify its approach.

The social model of disability challenges the common view of disability as a medical problem or as a problem within the individual (Beckett and Campbell, 2015; Goering, 2015). Instead, it holds society responsible for creating disabling conditions. Recent advances in the development of artificial intelligence are criticised because they are based on a legacy of ableist technology that makes disability problematic and in need of a technological solution. The concept of 'technoabilism' was introduced to describe a '*rhetoric about disability that simultaneously talks about empowering disabled people through technologies and at the same time reinforces ableist clichés about what is good to have body-mind and who counts as valuable*' (Shew, 2020). As NTs focus on improving or enhancing human capabilities or supporting medical conditions, it is crucial to consider how these contribute to a conception and problematisation of humans as imperfect.

Considering the political economy of technology production, the concept of 'sphere transgression' reveals how large players in the technology sector position themselves as experts in multiple domains (Taylor et al., 2023). This then shows that technology produced for a specific purpose is commercialised and adopted in other areas (Sharon and Gellert, 2023). A case in point could be that software created for business purposes is distributed in school environments. According to this argument, a strong democratic society relies on the separation of distinct social spheres. If a company or social actor is able to hold power in several spheres, this damages social cohesion and democracy in general.

7. School education and training

In the field of education, the ability to measure pupils' concentration levels is seen as a potential benefit of NTs. This measurement could be conducted using headphones and is intended to contribute to the improvement of individual children's learning.

The educational literature addresses a number of concerns regarding the availability and use of neural data. On the one hand, it addresses these concerns as a computer security problem, where the robustness of systems is questioned. On the other hand, it warns against the possibility of data being used for unintended purposes, e.g., for possible commercial purposes. The literature raises the issue of consent and decision-making, where this is to be delegated to the learners' parents or legal guardians.

Apart from data issues, researchers warn against the possibility of manipulation. As children's brains are developing, it is unclear how they respond to NTs: side effects, damage and other undesirable consequences, especially long-term ones, are not clearly studied. This leads to uncertainty about the impact of NTs on typical brain maturation.

Researchers also warn against NTs being introduced into educational settings with false promises. There is no clarity on how these technologies improve educational outcomes. This relates to NT outcomes: there is a possibility that the data generated by these technologies may be unreliable due to changes in the system or changes in students' needs. Furthermore, teachers, parents and students may not have the skills to interpret the data correctly or as intended, which could lead to problems such as stigmatisation. What is considered normal brain functioning may change with the advent of NTs. This may also lead to increased pressure to using NTs.

Similarly, the literature addresses issues related to teachers' skills: they may not know enough about technology or students' brains to effectively use NTs to facilitate learning. Teachers will need to be trained. This relates to the need to adapt pedagogical materials to support NTs. Another aspect mentioned is the importance of teachers' attitudes towards NTs as this would have an impact on the success of adoption in classrooms.

8. Work

A number of possible use cases in the working environment are mentioned. Recruitment procedures could, in the future, use the analysis of brain data to determine a good fit for an organisation. This is seen as highly problematic in particular with regard to possible misinterpretations as well as racial and gender bias as an area of concern. Then there is the issue of the possible use of NTs to monitor workers in addition to other digitised practices in which workers are monitored. The inability to give consent for workers resulting from power disparities needs to be considered in work contexts. The ability to turn words into text through the use of NTs is a promise of some products already on the market such as Facebook Reality Labs' EMG bracelet and Emotiv headsets that measure brain data.

The literature on labour issues problematises a number of other problems where synergies with other areas can be created.

The unknown long-term effects on workers may relate to brain damage, body integrity, and changes in the integrity of users. This will ruin the intended purpose of introducing NTs to increase health and safety in the workplace.

The massive use of data in the workplace, as part of broader monitoring of workers, is being addressed as a key issue in the workplace. This relates to the potential misuse of data and the risk of it being used in other contexts such as access to housing, loans, insurance and more. The use of NT and its data can lead to many abuses. This is part of similar concerns regarding privacy, accuracy and lack of explainability. There is also the possibility of data being monetised by organisations selling it to third parties.

Several studies also mention uncertainty about the performance and capabilities of NTs as an important issue to consider in the workplace. NTs may not be able to adapt to the different situations in which they are used, causing inaccuracies. Tools are positioned as unreliable where their effectiveness is not clear to evaluate.

Due to the power relations that exist in the workplace, workers may also find it difficult to freely consent to the use of NTs in an informed manner. Furthermore, the literature cites increased social pressures and performance standards as a problem when NTs are introduced. Since some people may be more prone to experience stress (arousal), workers may lose opportunities due to their neural structure. This adds another level of discrimination and is exacerbated by other factors related to brain data and resulting parameters. Due to socialisation in educational settings, workers from wealthier backgrounds may have an advantage over others as they may have learnt to use these technologies from a young age.

9. Entertainment

The discussion on NTs in games, art and other forms of entertainment frames users' emotions around parameters of game success such as confusion, boredom, or satisfaction. There is enthusiasm for the ability to respond to users' cognitive states in real time and adjust the difficulty levels of games, for example, or to use brain data to create art. The ability to control games through brain input may also open up games to a wider group of players, who may have physical disabilities that prevent them from participating in certain games. The enhancement of human creativity is present in the discussion on NT and entertainment.

In the field of entertainment, researchers also raise concerns about optimistic advertising that could mislead what technologies are actually capable of. Similarly, issues of security, IT security, accuracy and data collection are also mentioned. In this sense, researchers warn against the application of medical devices in non-medical contexts.

10. Promises and objectives of neuropowering

Remarkable are the differences between the goals of NTs in education (improved educational outcomes) versus work (increased productivity) versus entertainment (to counter boredom). While NTs in education are based on the political objective of improving education, e.g., by supporting customised learning, the use of these devices in the workplace is mainly aimed at reducing accidents in safety-critical roles. In entertainment, the aim is to provide more user-centred gaming experiences. Students and workers focus on measuring and inferring mental states such as attention and fatigue levels.

This potentially reconfigures what we socially value in education (here reduced to improved learning) and well-being at work (here reduced to cognitive processes).

11. Transformation of social relations

When brain data becomes measurable and accessible, it has implications for how we relate to one another. The possible transformation of the relationship between teachers and learners from the relationship between workers and employers is associated with the new parameters made available by NT.

The literature does not necessarily clarify who should have access to the data and with what benefits. It is unclear how possible organisational embeddedness includes and excludes certain groups of actors. Often, however, workers, educators or students are not central parts of the discussion.

This leads us to reflect on the potential skills required to introduce NTs and raises a normative question about what constitutes a 'successful', 'good' or 'ethical' use of these technologies. Teachers' lack of competence with regard to these technologies is seen as a factor contributing to 'unsuccessful' introduction. As with any technology, there is debate about what and who constitutes the 'intended purpose' of NTs and how NTs can be re-appropriated by social actors for (different) purposes or in an attempt to resist their use altogether. Furthermore, evidence suggests that NTs can be easily manipulated and their data falsified if sensors are not used correctly.

Emotions and skills are also negotiated differently in the intended uses of NTs in the three domains we are analysing. Creativity, for instance, is often undervalued in discussions within educational and work contexts, but has a prominent place in discourses on entertainment, indicating a gap in the understanding of its broader implications. Furthermore, there is a tendency in some literature to oversimplify work environments, focusing exclusively on productivity parameters and neglecting the nuanced interplay of emotions.

NT makes judgements about different emotional and mental states. Furthermore, the interpretation of brain data poses challenges, as emotions such as arousal (stress) can have a dual effect, both supportive and potentially harmful, depending on the context.

The literature rightly raises cybersecurity issues when it comes to the governance, storage and transfer of brain data.

It is imperative to assess who has an interest in brain data and the potential effects on social relations.[8]

Considering the various potential actors involved in the use of NTs, it is difficult to assess the potential and risks of NTs. Therefore, the possibility of manipulation or 'neuroenchantment' exists.

Through the introduction of NTs, new social norms are established. Optimisation of the self is taking primacy over other organisational and institutional goals.

One wonders how a society's notion of disability is co-constructed through these technologies. The social model of disability sheds light on the emergence of new norms of cognitive abilities and how these create a conception of human beings that requires 'adjustment'.

Moreover, the promised assessment of people's correct mental states and characteristics is based on the assumption that identities and personalities are 'stable' and 'fixed' (and weighted within a pre-determined range anyway). It does not take into account the complexity of human dynamics and emotions. At the same time, NT development produces an understanding of certain emotions and mental states as 'desirable', 'undesirable' and 'unacceptable' in different social settings. This

[8] For example, classroom dynamics could change dramatically if the brain data of all students were available on a screen for all to view.

then shifts the responsibility for managing these mental states onto the individual. Responsibility for performance is an individual pursuit.

Policy makers should also be encouraged to question the potential of Big Tech companies to maintain an ever-increasing control over power in a range of social spheres and the implications this has for social cohesion and democracy more generally.

NTs raise the issue of defining how we as a society want to relate to each other, what our idea of good education and good work is, and who can access these technologies for the benefit of people.

12. Results from a sociological point of view

Neurotechnologies represent the human brain as a given instead of humans as socially integrated and evolving beings.

NTs operate according to a reductive approach, in which emotions and mental states are isolated from broader social contexts.

This is in stark contrast to sociological research on emotions as socially integrated, i.e. as produced and responsive to social contexts. In socio-technical imaginaries around the NT, the brain becomes a 'fact' before anything else, including personal accounts and interpretations within a social context. In light of these insights, care must be taken to problematise conventional notions, such as 'levels of attention', and consider a fuller range of emotional states, including confusion, boredom and satisfaction, in various domains.

Overall, the inference of people's personality traits is based on the assumption that identities are stable and fixed instead of evolving and changing as part of the continuous transformation and negotiation of social relations. Similarly, the assessment of people's mental states functions in a reductive manner. Complex social contexts and situations are reduced to cognitive states and the brain becomes a source of seemingly factual and objective knowledge. To add another level, only certain emotions are made measurable and thus articulable. This depends on the social domains in which NTs are expected to be used: while NTs in the entertainment sector are intended to measure boredom and satisfaction, those in the work and education sectors measure attention levels and fatigue. Since these technologies tend to provide a simplified understanding of social contexts, the predominant discourse on NTs undermines the notion that people are embedded and constituted in socio-technical contexts. For example, the social disability model shows how human beings can be constituted as disabled by technologies.

The acquisition, processing and subsequent use of brain data and associated parameters by different social actors reconfigure the way we relate to ourselves and others. NTs can generate knowledge about bodies and brains that is privileged over the embodied experience of one's emotions, feelings and well-being.

As with other socio-technical innovations, there is a danger that new socially expected and accepted 'cognitive performance' norms will develop that lead to the medicalisation and pathologisation of neurodiverse individuals and groups.

Meanwhile, NTs redefine what is conceived as a social problem (requiring a technical solution). For example, socio-technical imaginaries of NT adoption in education define a key problem to be solved as that of attention and concentration levels. Teachers are problematised for being incompetent about what the brain does.

Moreover, human beings are embedded in the existing (and often unequal) power structures in various social spheres. For example, employees have less power than employers in how working conditions are configured. While laws in many countries regulate and protect the interests of employees, this is not the case everywhere and for every sphere of work (e.g., gig workers). Although it is not yet clear who will be able to access brain data and potentially manipulate cognitive processes, research on comparable data-driven technologies has shown how technologies exacerbate and contribute to the unequal distribution of power (Eubanks, 2018).

Socio-technical imaginaries do not remain at the level of discourse, but rather the accompanying anticipations determine how resources are allocated, what and who receives funding, for what kind of 'techno-solutions' and solutions to regulate NTs are sought.

Although this article refers to academic publications, it is clear that the discourses are mainly driven by market players who then make claims in various social spheres.[9]

The concept of sphere transgression shows how this leads to and reinforces power imbalances at the socio-political level as it allows the dominant and resource-rich companies to determine a different understanding of the various social spheres and social roles within them (e.g., the 'new learner' or the 'new worker'). Subsequently, these dominant actors are able to set the agenda on what society perceives as social problems in need of neurotechnical 'correction'.

The literature review demonstrates a clear empirical gap on the organisational and day-to-day integration of NTs. It is crucial to assess how different actors negotiate the use of these technologies. Further research should focus on experts in the field and the lived experiences of people involved in NT development.

13. The basics of neurorights

From an ethical point of view, NTs must consider the opportunities, risks and unintended consequences for society and individuals. On a normative level, the philosophical and ethical foundations on which we must scientifically base ourselves must have a materialistic focus on the human ego, the origin of which is identified in the brain.

Although this approach finds broad academic consensus, there is a danger of 'objectivisation' and reduction of the human being to brain data. On the pure basis of such materialism, the special status of human dignity, which is a value in Europe and the West, would be difficult to sustain and could unintentionally lead to a weakening of the foundations of fundamental rights.

This would be of particular concern for highly vulnerable people (e.g., coma patients, people with cognitive disabilities).

[9] This is – it should be made explicitly clear – when scientific and academic research itself is not 'prepared' and financed and implemented directly by the private sector.

As far as technology design is concerned, concrete technologies offer a broad spectrum of possibilities, but for these a form of impact and implication assessment is required.

With regard to the experiments conducted by Neuralink company, for example, it is necessary to consider the risks for people, as well as the effects that the mere existence of such technologies could have on society as a whole and the unintended consequences (e.g., pressure to adapt to meet new levels of performance only achievable through invasive NTs). However, the opportunities offered by NTs should also be given due consideration.

In order to assess the proposals to be made in this direction, the philosophical-ethical basis of the normative concerns conceptualised as 'neuro-rights' must be taken into account. The orientation point for these considerations are the foundations in the history of ideas, as well as human rights and fundamental European values.

This step is necessary in order to be able to assess the legal level at which neurorights can be meaningfully implemented. This becomes particularly clear in light of the fact that it is claimed to see neurorights as a junction of moral and legal rights (Ienca, 2021a, p. 44). This suggests that the formulated neurorights are not only moral in nature, but also have an inherent claim to be implemented within concrete secular legislation.

There is no moral obligation to positiveise, i.e., to transpose moral rights into legal rights, as morality in itself is sufficient in its claim to validity (Kirchschläger, 2019, p. 28).

From an ethical point of view, the suggestion of the simultaneity of moral and legal rights seems to arise primarily from the way in which the proposed neurorights are presented and imagined. However, if one recognises that not all moral rights per se realise a claim to positivity and if one takes the moral nature of neurorights seriously, one must ask within which moral system neurorights are proposed, what they are aimed at and under what conditions and to what extent they are to be implemented as legal rights within this moral system.

The foundations chosen to propose new neurorights are based on the moral foundations of what has been established in European intellectual history as 'human rights'. The debate on the extent to which human rights themselves are moral or legal rights touches on the transition from natural law to positive law, in which human rights are recognised in legal frameworks both nationally and internationally (Nichel, 2019). This has to be considered in the context of the proposed neurorights.

However, if neurorights within this system are understood as moral obligations with the importance of establishing new rights, the question arises whether legal implementation should be placed at the highest level of the moral system or whether a subsidiary level is more appropriate.

Those who support neurorights repeatedly refer to:

- . freedom of thought and conscience,
- . mental integrity,
- . privacy,

and conceptually relate neurorights to these (Ienca, 2021a, p. 44). The concept of personal identity is also taken up (Ienca, 2021a, pp. 53–54).

Fundamentally, focusing on freedom of thought as the antecedent for other freedoms, along with a materialistic worldview, entails the danger of reducing people and their freedoms to biological functions, instead of focusing on human dignity as a general and inviolable foundation. Although it must be recognised that having freedom is not the same as exercising it, the latter should not become the criterion for the former, as it would not do justice to the complexity and dignity of human existence. At this point, it should be noted that a freedom does not in itself constitute a legal right, nor does the loss of such a freedom automatically represent a loss of rights. However, the intertwining of freedom and rights must be particularly emphasised, especially in the context of human rights, as it was precisely the protection of freedom that was conceptually relevant to the pioneers of human rights (Bielefeldt, 2023; Funke, 2023; Willoweit, 2023). If neurorights were incorporated at a subsidiary legal level, the danger of functionalisation and objectivisation of a human being could be mitigated by the primacy of the dignity concept.

As an unconditional aspect of being human, dignity is a stable and inviolable foundation that transcends ability, origin, gender, wealth, etc., and constitutes rights that protect the most basic ways of being human. Therefore, it seems favourable to base freedom and the right to specific freedoms on human dignity rather than ability/capacity.

At least two neurorights, the right to free will and the right to personal identity, are based directly or indirectly on freedom of thought and conscience. The right to free will constitutively presupposes a form of freedom of thought, since any restriction of thought itself would fundamentally limit the formation of a will.

With regard to the right to personal identity, proponents of neurorights refer to the tradition of John Locke, according to which a person is an intelligent being who possesses both reason and the ability to reflect, recognising oneself as a self, as the same thinking being at different levels, times and places.

NTs could cause such problems of continuity and coherence through brain stimulation, in addition to drugs, hypnosis and other external influences (Ienca and Andorno, 2017, pp. 21-22). Interventions of this kind in thought contradict the right to freedom of thought and conscience, as it is a manipulation of individual thought that is outside the individual's influence and causes changes in the individual.

In principle, the human mind is protected from manipulation with psychoactive substances and other manipulations under Article 18 of the ICCPR. This treaty has been signed by all EU Member States and seems to be unquestionable even within the EU institutions.

The protection of freedom of thought, conscience and religion is an absolute right that cannot be weighed against other rights (Ligthart et al., 2022, pp. 2-3; Shaheed, 2021, 25).

Personal identity also has references to mental integrity, which was claimed as a separate right in one of the first mentions of the neurorights. In terms of content, mental integrity is naturally closely related to freedom of thought. In debates, the distinction is sometimes made that freedom of thought is intended to protect against the intrusion (and extraction) of the human cognitive sphere, while mental integrity is intended to protect against harm (Ienca, 2021a, p. 50).

Schauer (2020) addresses this aspect of protection against harm in his considerations on freedom of thought, but in this context he sees harm prevention as something that should go hand in hand with freedom of thought.

Other scholars regard mental integrity as the counterpart of bodily integrity and argue on this basis that the right to mental integrity can be thought of as analogous to the right to bodily integrity and that this is even more fundamental than the aforementioned right to mental integrity (Craig, 2016).

Malicious interventions via NT, whether intentional by malicious persons or due to technical malfunctions, can be considered a radical violation of mental integrity.

Lavazza and Giorgi (2023) point out in this context that a special feature of NTs is that the (malicious) manipulation of individuals could take place without their knowledge, which distinguishes the dangers of NTs from those of psychoactive substances. Recently, however, Tesink et al. (2024) argued that with the help of a potential extension of the mind through NTs, extended protection of mental integrity might also be possible. It should be noted that they assume that *'[...] the mental states that make up the human mind – including beliefs, desires, and memories – are not only realised by our brain but can also be realised by physical processes and artefacts located outside the brain and even beyond the body'* (Tesink et al., 2024, p. 3).

Based on the concept of privacy, we refer here to the right to mental privacy. Privacy is recognised as an area of concern, just like identity (Goering et al., 2021). Reflections on privacy in the context of neurorights play a key role, where freedom of thought and mental integrity focus on the integrity of the inner level; the main aspect of mental privacy is whether the data read using NTs is sufficiently protected or whether the individual is fully protected from this. A particularly problematic aspect, Yuste argues, is that *'[...] neurodata (i.e. recording of nervous system activity) can be generated unconsciously and often involuntarily'* (Yuste, 2023).

Furthermore, the decoding of brain activity has already been successful in several areas using non-invasive NTs. These include images, emotions and, in combination with artificial intelligence, listening to spoken words (Yuste, 2023).

Most companies distributing consumer products do not treat neural data with the special care required due to their sensitivity (Genser et al., 2024). With regard to consumer privacy and transparency, the findings are cause for concern and need further investigation into how the right to privacy could be enforced and what it includes with regard to NTs.

Looking at the history of the meaning of privacy, it is evident that since the first mention in the essay 'The Right to Privacy' by Warren and Brandeis (1890), who saw this right as a *'right to be left alone'* in the face of the burgeoning tabloid press, it needed constant updating and expansion. From the beginning, the concept of privacy had an inherent protective function against new technologies and their negative effects on human life. What Warren and Brandeis saw in the spread of cameras expanded to include the possibility of mobile audio recording, digital technologies such as the Internet and, finally, the emerging NTs.

The academic (and legal) discourse followed technological development and elaborated a wide variety of theories on what exactly comprised the right to privacy and, its intellectual child, the right to data protection.

Although, as described above, a materialistic worldview prevails among the arguments in favour of neurorights, there is already a distinction that privacy is primarily aimed at brain data, whereas the aforementioned mental integrity is intended to protect against interference in the cognitive sphere.

If one takes the materialist perspective to its logical conclusion, it could be argued that mental integrity could be reduced to privacy, since the protection of brain data should also include their harmful alteration. The distinction between privacy and mental integrity is thus a distinction not in merit, but in purpose. This distinction may be useful for understanding, but, in principle, regression remains possible, so the separation of privacy and mental integrity would require further argumentative support.

It must be emphasised that considering privacy as merely a matter of protecting data, be it brain, neural or any other data, does not reach the broad dimension that the already established right to privacy should encompass. It is not only a matter of taking and disseminating data, in their case images, but also an unjust intrusion into the personal sphere of a human being.

As far as NT is concerned, it is of utmost importance to keep this dimension of privacy in mind rather than reducing privacy issues to a question of data collection, processing, management, storage, etc. However, data must be addressed and considered, but always with the human being as a whole in mind.

Analysing the foundations of freedom of thought, mental integrity and privacy in the history of ideas, we see particularly clearly that these concepts still form the argumentative basis for the protection of human life in the face of various technical challenges. Based on what was conceptually useful in the past for the formation of specific rights, it is still possible to derive up-to-date considerations today. In this sense, these concepts provide an adequate and stable basis for the demand for new neurorights. One can also recognise the importance of the rights enunciated in neurorights being worthy of protection, although these are by no means necessary, but merely possible derivations leading to the aforementioned rights.

The protection paradigms provided by these foundational concepts are certainly applicable to new technologies such as NTs, even if they were not originally conceived with these in mind. Moreover, the foundations in the history of ideas are not only a conceptual basis, but have themselves been translated into rights.

There are already several rights and treaties on fundamental concepts, of which Article 18 of the International Covenant on Civil and Political Rights (ICCPR) is a founding element, safeguarding individuals from manipulation through psychoactive substances and other forms of mental interference.

The unanimous endorsement of the ICCPR by the EU Member States and the bloc's support for the integration of the ICCPR with the International Covenant on Economic, Social and Cultural Rights (ICESCR) into a single document underline the EU's commitment to the protection of human rights, including in the NT sphere.

Furthermore, freedom of thought is guaranteed by Article 9 of the European Convention on Human Rights (ECHR).

Considering the area of NTs, it is useful to also consider the freedom of thought aspects of mental integrity and privacy.

As Ienca states: '*If freedom of thought protects the human brain and mind from undue external interference and the right to privacy protects personal information (including mental information) from external intrusion, other normative principles protect the human brain and mind from harm*' (Ienca, 2021a, p. 50).

The right to mental integrity finds legal support in a number of instruments, such as Article 3 of the Charter of Fundamental Rights of the European Union (CFR) and Article 8 of the European Convention on Human Rights (ECHR), all of which affirm the need to respect physical and mental integrity. Moreover, the European Charter of Fundamental Rights explicitly recognises the right to mental integrity, reflecting a broader understanding of human dignity that includes both the physical and psychological dimensions. This perspective is reinforced by similar provisions in the Convention on the Rights of Persons with Disabilities (Article 17), which recognises the fundamental importance of protecting both physical and psychological integrity.

The legal framework provided by Article 17 of the ICCPR and Article 8 of the ECHR constitute the fundamental elements of the right to privacy. Furthermore, the interpretation of Article 17 has been updated through General Comment No. 16 of the ICCPR to explicitly include information obtained or processed by digital means (Office of the High Commissioner for Human Rights, 1988).

14. The case of Chile on the protection of neural rights[10]

On 8 August 2023, the Chilean Constitutional Court, the first in the world, adopted a ruling destined to remain a milestone on the boundary between technology and the protection of the integrity of the person.

It basically stated that even devices intended to track people's brain activity for 'private use' must be authorised by the health authorities; if the users' data, then, are processed for scientific use, the consent given by the user must be informed, express, specific about the research and its purposes, and dynamic, i.e., required whenever the purpose of the research changes over time.

Lawyer Maite Sanz de Galdeano broke the news at the Global Summit of the Legal Hackers community held on September 8 and 9 in Madrid.

"The constitutionalisation of neurorights in Chile has opened up the possibility of a 'constitutional protection action' against the commercialisation of a device that puts them at risk. The ruling shows that the lack of specific regulation exposes users to uncontrolled risks, which justifies a particular rigour in the application of the current law and, on the other hand, a reflection on the necessary changes: if these technologies escape the controls of medical devices, in Chile (and in the rest of the states) at least the regulations on consumer protection, product safety and privacy, which currently do not guarantee the safety of users because they do not take into

[10] On the broader and more comprehensive topic of the relationship between AI and justice and its implications, see: Artificial Intelligence and the cyber utopianism of justice. Why AI is not intelligence and man's struggle to survive himself. *Russian Journal of Economics and Law*, no. 1, 2024 https://doi.org/10.21202/2782-2923.2024.1.264-279

account these new risks, should be reviewed. In terms of neurodata, in addition to the risks to privacy, a 'new' vulnerability of the human being, hitherto unexplored, is revealed: the knowledge and consequent control of brain activity, for purposes that are not exclusively medical. The answer can only be an explicit regulation of neurodata, as a category of sensitive personal data, enabling the defence and development of neurorights. In Europe, the GDPR must be amended in this sense".

14.1 The market for hi-tech wearables

The research agency International Data Corporation (IDC) predicted a shipment of around 442.7 million wearable devices in 2024, equivalent to a 6.3% year-on-year growth.

These are 325 million headsets, 162.2 million connected watches, 33.8 million smart bands, the health monitoring devices, and 2.2 million products in other so-called 'wearable' categories.

In terms of market share, the numbers translate into 62.1% earbuds, 31% smartwatches, 6.5% smartbands and 0.4% other devices.

We do not know the amount of devices intended to measure our brain and cognitive activities; but we do know that companies such as Elon Musk's Neurolink are already particularly active in this direction.

14.2 The Chilean case: wearables and brain activity

Chile is the first country in the world to have legislated on neurotechnology and included the 'rights of the brain' in its Constitutional Charter.

In 2021, an amendment to Article 19 was passed to 'protect the mental integrity and immunity of the brain from the advances and capabilities developed by neurotechnology'.

Although appearing to be a premature choice, the Chilean parliament preferred to put its hands on the development of neurotechnology, whose ability to act on the human brain is still limited but which applications are spreading beyond the medical field. The case before the Chilean Constitutional Court can be described as a 'pilot case', both in terms of the plaintiff and its genesis.

The plaintiff, Guido Girardi Lavin, is a Member of Parliament and promoter of the protection of human rights also through The Neurorights Foundation, but he brought the case before the judges, first of merit and then constitutional, as a buyer and user of the Insight device, a wireless device that through a band of sensors collects information on the electrical activities of the brain and collects data on gestures, preferences, reaction times and cognitive activity. Insight is produced by a US company, Emotiv.

14.3 The case submitted to the Constitutional Court

Girardi Lavin purchased the device via the web and followed the instructions to activate it: he created an account on the company's cloud, agreeing to the terms and conditions; he downloaded software onto his PC, again agreeing to the terms and conditions of service. But he decided to use the free and not the pro licence; a choice that – he reported to the courts – did not allow him to export or import his brain data records.

The plaintiff also pointed out that everything was recorded and saved in Emotiv's cloud. In short, he complained about the potential risk of hacking, surveillance, unauthorised capture, and commercialisation of his neuro-data.

The appeal therefore concerned the violation of the Chilean Data Protection Act (No 19.628) both in the part where it establishes the liability profiles of the data controller; and in the part where it assigns the data owner's right to obtain the deletion or blocking of his data in the event of the closure of his or her account.

Emotiv stores user data for scientific and historical purposes.

Gilardi therefore asked the court to force Emotiv to amend its privacy policy and to prohibit the marketing of the device in Chile until this fulfilment, jointly warning the company to delete its database immediately.

The company argued that Insight is not a medical device but a self-quantification device; that it has no invasive purpose; that the terms and conditions are detailed; that there is a requirement of express consent for both the processing of personal and brain data; and that no proof of actual harm suffered by the plaintiff had been provided.

In addition, Emotiv argued, there had been no violation of either the Chilean Privacy Act or the more restrictive GPDR (General Data Protection Regulation), the European regulation on the processing of personal data, which obliges pseudonymisation, an activity that prevents the data collected from being attributed to a specific or determinable person.

With regard to the violation of Article 13 of the Chilean Privacy Act, the company had noted that data are saved as long as the user's account is active and that with regard to 'brain data', the user can at any time revoke consent to the processing, as the privacy policy prescribes.

As for further processing, for scientific or historical purposes, the company noted that the data are anonymised, encrypted, stored securely and separated from other information. They therefore acquire the nature of statistical data, as such removed from the protection of privacy.

14.4 The Constitutional Court's decision

The Constitutional Court overturned the judgments on the merits, deeming relevant the fact that the marketing of Insight was not subject to medical (as well as customs) authorisation, reminding the authorities in charge of analysing the device in the light of the regulations in force with a view to its future marketing in Chile.

The judges ruled that 'prior to the development of new technologies involving more and more aspects of the human person, aspects that were unthinkable a few years ago that they could meet, the State must pay particular attention and care in the control, in order to prevent and anticipate the possible effects, in addition to directly protecting human integrity in its entirety, issues that include privacy and confidentiality and the rights of mental integrity and the subject of scientific experimentation. In this way, before the arrival of a new technology such as the one at issue in these proceedings, which treats the electrical activity of the brain in a dimension that was once absolutely private and personal, and outside strictly medical contexts, it is absolutely necessary that before allowing it to be marketed and used in the country, technologies and devices be analysed by the competent authority, on the understanding that they raise issues that have not been previously investigated by it'.

14.5 Neurorights in international law

The Chilean Constitutional Court has had to recognise that, despite the direct protection mandate contained in the amendment to the Constitution, there is currently no ordinary law that unravels all the knots imposed by the advancement of applied neuroscience, the requirements, conditions, permissible risks and use by individuals.

There is therefore a new fork in the road.

And yet, thanks to the international normative dimension, it is possible to draw a protective boundary in the sense that follows and referred to by the judgment.

The International Covenant on Economic, Cultural and Social Rights prescribes that people should be able to 'enjoy' scientific progress. The Unesco Declaration on Science and the Use of Knowledge and Programme of Science prescribe that science should respect human rights and the dignity of the person in the sense already indicated by the Universal Declaration of Human Rights. The Universal Declaration on the Human Genome specifies that some scientific applications can be harmful and that scientists and other agents have a 'special' responsibility of an ethical nature, which must be incorporated into the debate through public discussion. The Unesco Universal Declaration on Bioethics and Human Rights has already imposed the general principles of human vulnerability and the integrity of the person, together with the rights to privacy and confidentiality.

The Court also referred to the Chilean legislation (No. 20.120) on scientific investigations on persons and the genome that banned human cloning, recalling the provisions that deal very specifically with the consent of persons involved in medical research. Under this legislation, the consent of those involved in research not only follows certain precautions when it is collected, but must be renewed every time the scientific investigation undergoes major changes.

With respect to the case at hand, the Constitutional Court found that the company producing the Insight device had failed to request this specific consent, which certainly cannot be considered implicit in the other consents, which are of 'commercial' nature.

14.6 The final decision

The Court therefore overturned the Court of Appeal's decision, emphasising the need for new technologies, particularly those that deal with human activities that have hitherto been strictly private, such as brain activity, to be submitted to the competent authorities for scrutiny before neuro-capable devices are marketed and used in the country.

It therefore considered that the constitutional guarantees of Article 19 on mental and physical integrity had been violated since Insight was marketed without authorisation and without an assessment by the health authorities.

The Chilean court thus upheld the appeal, prohibiting the marketing of Insight until it obtains authorisation under the aforementioned regulations. The Institute of Public Health and the Customs Authority will have to assess whether the management of data collected with Insight strictly complies with the applicable regulations outlined in the ruling. It also warned Emotiv to delete all information that was stored in the cloud or on the portal.

15. Neurotechnology: a socio-ethical point of view

With regard to an ethical-normative reflection on these technologies, it seems obvious to draw on ethical frameworks and principles from the fields of medical ethics, bioethics and technology ethics. For example, the traditional principles of Beachamp and Childress (2019) (autonomy, non-maleficence, beneficence, justice) can serve as important reference points for an ethical discussion.

In view of the massive intertwining of man and machine (and thus also with artificial intelligence) in NTs, it seems sensible to also consider the principles discussed in the field of technology ethics.

Floridi (2023), for example, takes the four bioethical principles, expands them by one principle and reflects on them against the background of AI.

A socio-ethical perspective is essential because, in the light of current discussions in the field of medicine and bioethics, it can introduce new approaches that we consider relevant in the context of NTs and thus open up a more holistic view of the need for ethical reflection on NTs.

It is obvious that not all ethically relevant aspects can be addressed, let alone adequately discussed, within the scope of this article, so limitations are inevitable.

Although the euphoria around NTs has influenced research, both the market and society, there are important differences between these areas: NT research is usually conducted under strict ethical conditions and is accompanied and monitored by qualified third parties, which is why, in the context of existing regulation, individuals should generally not expect deception or negligence in this context.

NTs are fundamentally very ambivalent. On the one hand, they could help a large number of people suffering from illnesses (e.g., Parkinson's, epilepsy, etc.) by effectively alleviating the symptoms of the disease. Other very positive application contexts arise, for example, with regard to prostheses (Raspopovic, 2020) and new possibilities in relation to rehabilitation.

In general, these technologies could be used to respond very specifically to individual clinical conditions and the needs of those affected. NTs could thus make a considerable contribution to the individual and common good.

On the other hand, however, there are also challenges and even risks and dangers. These begin with 'collateral damage' during treatment. For example, the current pulses continuously emitted by deep brain stimulation do not only affect the target area, but also affect other areas of the brain and can thus lead to known and/or unknown, possibly irreparable damage and further consequences (such as addiction symptoms or personality changes) (Gilbert et al., 2019).

Particularly risky and worthy of discussion appear to be BCI applications, although new opportunities may also arise for people with physical disabilities or these technologies may be used to treat mental illnesses.

Adopting a socio-ethical perspective means, in particular, addressing issues of justice, solidarity, equality, rule of law and participation (Koska and Filipovic, 2017). This perspective also seems to be particularly relevant in the context of NTs and against the background of neurorights under discussion. It is not without reason that the above-discussed foundations of the history of ideas form the starting point for discourses on the creation of new rights or their adoption and actualization.

Freedom of thought and conscience, mental integrity and privacy are closely linked to the aspect of justice towards the individual, since they indicate which interventions and restrictions on the individual are at least considered unjust. The basis thus created necessarily applies not only to isolated individuals but to all individuals within a social structure, which in turn brings out aspects such as solidarity, participation and equality.

Furthermore, as part of the shift in perspective from the individual to the community, it is important to consider which aspects of justice require more attention accordingly. In short, just because something is only right for the individual does not mean that it is generally right for the community and vice versa.

In addition, a further set of relevant ethical issues arise, particularly with regard to the social implications of NTs: for example, questions of social justice and, in particular, issues in the field of equal opportunities and participation seem to be central. While, for example, evidence-based, safe and effective disease-fighting NTs raise the question of equitable access to these technologies and thus address the aspect of participatory justice, the question also arises of what NTs mean for individual groups in this context. What do NTs mean, especially when they are available as commodities for the 'self-optimisation' of particularly vulnerable groups such as children, the poor and the sick? Moreover, in light of the socio-ethical principle of sustainability (Vogt, 2009), it is particularly important to consider future generations and aspects of intergenerational justice. These issues already illustrate the broad need for ethical reflection that goes hand in hand with NTs and that expands any question of research ethics and, because of the obvious technology-related issues, from the field of medicine and bioethics.

Democratic societies are characterised by a strained relationship between the individual and the common good. The concept of human dignity, human rights and the Charter of Fundamental Rights emphasise the centrality of the individual. It is therefore the individual, the person endowed with dignity and thus with freedom and autonomy – every individual – who is the central and ultimate yardstick for all matters relating to the organisation of our society, including technological issues (Heimbach-Steins, 2022). However, we know that people do not live in a vacuum, but in concrete social contexts, that they are social beings. This social nature of human beings is often described as one of their central characteristics (Vester, 2009).

Living as a human being therefore necessarily means being part of a society and interacting, communicating and working together with other people on an almost daily basis. Together we build social structures and institutions, pursue work or hobbies and try to lead a good life. Without interaction and cooperation between individuals, our societies today would be inconceivable and would not function.

This raises the central issue of the responsibility to shape society as a whole, which affects all individuals as part of that society. It results in a tension between individual and societal interests. These different positions require appropriate reflection and balancing processes that take into account individual freedom as well as issues of social justice. NTs could and will affect both spheres, the individual and the social. Individuals are the potential bearers of NTs, but changes in the individual give rise to new social challenges, which is why the relationship between NTs and society also requires special attention.

Human actions are embedded in specific social contexts and the autonomy and freedom must also be considered in this regard. It is precisely in this context that the influence of NTs must be considered. Although reference is often made to the positive aspects of various NTs, invasive and non-invasive, or that significant sections of the population believe in them, the consequences go beyond the physical and psychological dimension, often ignored. From an ethical perspective, interventions of this kind also raise the question of what this means for human action.

Action is closely linked to intentionality: '*[...] [a] being has the capacity to exercise agency only in the case where it has the capacity to act intentionally, and the exercise of agency consists in the performance of intentional actions and, in many cases, in the performance of unintentional actions (which result from the performance of intentional actions)*' (Schlosser, 2024).

This last reference to unintentional actions refers to the fact that intentional actions lead to events involving unintentional actions. In this context, the concept of a sense of agency becomes particularly important, as it encompasses the direct knowledge of our actions, which is also related to the judgement of our actions. The sense of agency describes the perception that we actually do something in the course of our actions and control them (Legaspi et al., 2024). It describes the sense of having ownership of our actions. This in turn has particular significance for an individual's self-perception and self-image.

Interference with a sense of agency has the highest disruptive potential as it could lead individuals to doubt themselves. In this aspect in particular, NT should be regarded with particular caution.

From an ethical point of view, in addition to the question of whether NTs are non-invasive or invasive, it is also relevant whether they are used in the context of research or are consumer goods. Particular attention must be paid to consumer products, as neurotechnology in the context of research and health interventions is in any case subject to very strict regulations and is studied in a closed context.

As consumer goods, they affect a large number of people and the central question is whether people are able to adequately assess the potential impact of the use of such technology on themselves and society.

There is also the risk that social pressure (both direct and indirect), in the face of various aspects such as the pressure to perform, promises or hopes placed on technology, may encourage the increasingly reckless use of non-invasive or even invasive NTs. They are also part of the debate on valorisation as consumer goods.

For many years, people have been trying to improve and optimise themselves and, from an ethical point of view, there are good reasons both for (e.g., increased social performance, increased possibilities for individual happiness in life) and against (e.g., possible pressure to conform towards the use of improvement, open questions in relation to equity of access) the possibility of improvement (Schöne-Seifert, 2007).

However, digital central nervous system enhancement represents a relatively new quality in the enhancement debate. The generic term 'neuro-enhancement' refers to several areas of medical-technical intervention in the central nervous system. A distinction is usually made here between emotional, cognitive, moral, sensory and motor enhancement.

However, more in-depth ethical analyses, both individual and societal, are needed to correctly classify this complex issue (Fenner, 2019).

Digitalisation is not a sudden and unexpected natural phenomenon that has happened and is sweeping us away, but a man-made transformation. Technological innovations – which today take place mainly in large multinational companies or young innovative start-ups – are affecting the lives of many people with unprecedented intensity.

Many modern technologies are already accessible to the masses and this is a circumstance with enormous potential for transformation with regard to the human-machine relationship in the most diverse areas of life (Kirchschläger, 2022). NTs are (and presumably will become even more intensively so in the future) part of this digital transformation. There is no doubt that these new technologies present many opportunities, but also significant challenges. Technologies are never without value and are associated with power and the exercise of power – perhaps not even visible to many at first glance. Behind technological innovations are the interests and values of developers and producers. These interests and values are implicitly and/or explicitly part of the respective technologies.

At first sight, the question arises as to how these interests and values, which are consciously or unconsciously part of individual technological systems, could influence users. This raises, for instance, questions concerning freedom of action, but also in general concerning people's vulnerability. In view of the increasing attacks on digital infrastructures in the sense of cyber-warfare, the recurring hacker attacks against individuals and companies, and thus the overall vulnerability of digital infrastructures in the 21st century, we should also address the misuse of such technologies. An increase in the connection between man and machine would presumably also transfer this vulnerability to humans and lead to new dangers. These aspects are particularly important when considering high-risk technologies and their potential impact on individuals and society, as such complex technologies always involve a certain amount of energy. However, the various stakeholders (politicians, businesses, consumers, etc.) must not forget that power always entails dependencies and pressures, but also responsibilities.

Considering the subversive potential of new technologies, in-depth research efforts are needed, particularly with regard to these power relations and liability issues.

Finally, another central perspective should be emphasised that is intensively discussed in the debate on transhumanism but should be discussed even more intensively in the broader debate on digitisation: the anthropological perspective. Technology ethicist Armin Grunwald points out that behind the ethical question of digital transformation lies the question of who the human being is; who does a person want to be in the face of a highly technologised world and how can a person experience freedom, responsibility and creativity in this context (Grunwald, 2019a, 2019b, 2021). Grunwald therefore emphasises the question of the image of man in increasingly technologised societies because the image of man is influenced by the increasing degree of digitisation. Technological developments in the field of NT are particularly disruptive in this context. The image of a 'man in need of optimisation' is often outlined, who without the synthesis of man and machine – especially in light of developments in the field of artificial intelligence – risks falling further and further behind.

With the spread of NTs, it is rather possible to influence the central nervous system; the potential – individual and societal – consequences (both medium- and long-term) are unpredictable. In view of the implications, this topic should not be an innovation process driven by corporate interests but requires a broad scientific (especially from the humanities) and social and political discourse and debate.

Conclusions

Neurorights as human rights in the age of AI

Five rights were identified and the necessity and sensitivity of integrating them at the level of human and fundamental rights assessed. These are: 'the right to mental privacy', 'the right to personal identity', 'the right to free will', 'the right to equal access to mental enhancement', and 'the right to protection from algorithmic bias'.

It is clear that the existing framework of human and fundamental rights provides a well-established and effective protective shield.

The vulnus, if anything, is in the moment of interpretation and in a political choice of rigorous and strong application of the existing regulatory framework, if necessary with maximum extension and a strict precautionary criterion.

For example, the 'right to mental integrity' is already explicitly protected by Article 3 CFR as the 'right to physical and mental integrity'. Changing this to a separate 'right to mental integrity' would require differentiation, assuming that the legislature did not introduce this right frivolously; it must mean something different from the right already enshrined in Article 3. However, this raises new questions: is the understanding developed under Article 3 transferable to the new right? Where are the limits? Would other aspects of integrity also need explicit regulation? What is new?

The EU body of regulation, with strong consumer protection, fair competition, high product safety standards and comprehensive digital integration, is well prepared to address the recognised problems associated with NT. For example, medical devices and some NT devices are already heavily regulated by the MDR. Other NT devices not covered by the MDR have to meet the general high level of protection. However, adaptations could be considered, such as the explicit inclusion of neurological data in Article 9 GDPR or in an NT law, comparable to the AI law. In both cases, the focus is exclusively on the regulation of high-impact technologies.

The next logical step is to intensify law enforcement efforts.

To this end, the EU should actively participate in telling the story of NTs, which implies the encouragement of science and education, as well as strict control of their commercial communication. This comprehensive approach ensures that the public receives accurate and balanced information, which is crucial for the effective regulation and responsible development of NTs.

One of the main problems identified with NTs is our insufficient knowledge, which predominantly promotes commercially used success stories for advertising, leading to 'neuro-enchantment' and 'neuromyth'.

Consumer law, competition law and product safety law are well suited to counter false or exaggerated claims; they just have to be used. There is a social need to tell people the real story of NTs, clarifying what we know and do not know, where the opportunities, dangers and risks lie.

This means actively promoting NT research, publishing failures as well as successes, communicating results in a comprehensible form not only through science but also through public administration, integrating it into education and strictly controlling commercial representation.

Regulation

Directive (EU) 2019/1024 of the European Parliament and of the Council of 20 June 2019 on open data and the re-use of public sector information.

Directive (EU) 2019/2161 of the European Parliament and of the Council of 27 November 2019 amending Council Directive 93/13/EEC and Directives 98/6/EC, 2005/29/EC and 2011/83/EU of the European Parliament and of the Council as regards the better enforcement and modernisation of Union consumer protection rules.

Directive (EU) 2019/771 of the European Parliament and of the Council 20 May 2019 on certain aspects concerning contracts for the sale of goods, amending Regulation (EU) 2017/2394 and Directive 2009/22/EC, and repealing Directive 1999/44/EC.

Directive (EU) 2024/825 of the European Parliament and of the Council of 28 February 2024 amending Directives 2005/29/EC and 2011/83/EU as regards empowering consumers for the green transition through better protection against unfair practices and through better information.

Directive 2005/29/EC of the European Parliament and of the Council of 11 May 2005 concerning unfair business-to-consumer commercial practices in the internal market and amending Council Directive 84/450/EEC, Directives 97/7/EC, 98/27/EC and 2002/65/EC of the European Parliament and of the Council and Regulation (EC) No 2006/2004 of the European Parliament and of the Council ('Unfair Commercial Practices Directive').

Directive 2006/114/EC of the European Parliament and of the Council of 12 December 2006 concerning misleading and comparative advertising.

Directive 2011/24/EU of the European Parliament and of the Council of 9 March 2011 on the application of patients' rights in cross-border healthcare.

Directive 2011/83/EU of the European Parliament and of the Council of 25 October 2011 on consumer rights, amending Council Directive 93/13/EEC and Directive 1999/44/EC of the European Parliament and of the Council and repealing Council Directive 85/577/EEC and Directive 97/7/EC of the European Parliament and of the Council Text with EEA relevance.

European Convention on Human Rights.

European Parliament. (2022). *European Parliament resolution of 3 May 2022 on artificial intelligence in a digital age (2020/2266(INI)).* https://www.europarl.europa.eu/doceo/document/TA-9-2022-0140_EN.html

OECD. (2019). *Responsible innovation in neurotechnology enterprises.* https://www.oecd-ilibrary.org/science-and-technology/responsible-innovation-in-neurotechnology-enterprises_9685e4fd-en

Office of the High Commissioner for Human Rights (Ed.). *CCPR General Comment No. 16: Article 17 (Right to Privacy) The Right to Respect of Privacy, Family, Home and Correspondence, and Protection of Honour and Reputation: Adopted at the Thirty-second Session of the Human Rights Committee, on 8 April 1988.*

Proposal for a Regulation of the European Parliament and of the Council laying down harmonised rules on artificial intelligence (Artificial Intelligence Act) and amending certain union legislative acts, https://eur-lex.europa.eu/legal-content/EN/TXT/PDF/?uri=CONSIL:ST_7536_2024_INIT COM/2021/206). https://eur-lex.europa.eu/legal-content/EN/TXT/PDF/?uri=CONSIL:ST_7536_2024_INIT

Proposal for a Regulation of the European Parliament and of the Council laying down harmonised rules on artificial intelligence (Artificial Intelligence Act) and amending certain union legislative acts/ P9_TA(2024)0138, https://www.europarl.europa.eu/RegData/seance_pleniere/textes_adoptes/definitif/2024/03-13/0138/P9_TA(2024)0138_EN.pdf. https://www.europarl.europa.eu/RegData/seance_pleniere/textes_adoptes/definitif/2024/03-13/0138/P9_TA(2024)0138_EN.pdf

Regulation (EU) 2016/679 of the European Parliament and of the Council of 27 April 2016 on the protection of natural persons with regard to the processing of personal data and on the free movement of such data, and repealing Directive 95/46/EC (General Data Protection Regulation).

Regulation (EU) 2017/745 of the European Parliament and of the Council of 5 April 2017 on medical devices, amending Directive 2001/83/EC, Regulation (EC) No 178/2002 and Regulation (EC) No 1223/2009 and repealing Council Directives 90/385/EEC and 93/42/EEC.

Regulation (EU) 2019/1020 of the European Parliament and of the Council of 20 June 2019 on market surveillance and compliance of products and amending Directive 2004/42/EC and Regulations (EC) No 765/2008 and (EU) No 305/2011.

Regulation (EU) 2019/881 of the European Parliament and of the Council of 17 April 2019 on ENISA (the European Union Agency for Cybersecurity) and on information and communications technology cybersecurity certification and repealing Regulation (EU) No 526/2013 (Cybersecurity Act) (Text with EEA relevance).

Regulation (EU) 2021/2282 of the European Parliament and of the Council of 15 December 2021 on health technology assessment and amending Directive 2011/24/EU.

Regulation (EU) 2023/988 of the European Parliament and of the Council of 10 May 2023 on general product safety, amending Regulation (EU) No 1025/2012 of the European Parliament and of the Council and Directive (EU) 2020/1828 of the European Parliament and the Council, and repealing Directive 2001/95/EC of the European Parliament and of the Council and Council Directive 87/357/EEC.

Regulation (EU) No 1025/2012 of the European Parliament and of the Council of 25 October 2012 on European standardisation, amending Council Directives 89/686/EEC and 93/15/EEC and Directives 94/9/EC, 94/25/EC, 95/16/EC, 97/23/EC, 98/34/EC, 2004/22/EC, 2007/23/EC, 2009/23/EC and 2009/105/EC of the European Parliament and of the Council and repealing Council Decision 87/95/EEC and Decision No 1673/2006/EC of the European Parliament and of the Council Text with EEA relevance.

Regulation (EU) No 910/2014 of the European Parliament and of the Council of 23 July 2014 on electronic identification and trust services for electronic transactions in the internal market and repealing Directive 1999/93/EC.

Treaty of Lisabon Amending the treaty on European Union and the treaty establishing the European community.

Treaty on European Union.

Treaty on the Functioning of the European Union.

UNESCO. (2023). *The Risks and Challenges of Neurotechnologies for Human Rights*. https://unesdoc.unesco.org/ark:/48223/pf0000384185.locale=en

Constitution of the United Nations Educational, Scientific and Cultural Organization.

References

Abdulkader, S. N., Atia, A., and Mostafa, M.S. M. (2015). Brain computer interfacing: Applications and challenges. Egyptian Informatics Journal, 16(2): 213–230. https://doi.org/10.1016/j.eij.2015.06.002.

Adams, V., Murphy, M., and Clarke, A. E. (2009). Anticipation: Technoscience, life, affect, temporality. Subjectivity, 28(1): 246–265. https://doi.org/10.1057/sub.2009.18.

Ajunwa, I., Crawford, K., and Schultz, J. (2017). Limitless Worker Surveillance. California Law Review, 105(3): 735–776. https://doi.org/10.15779/Z38BR8MF94.

Alferova, E. V. (2023) Neurobiotechnology, Criminal Law And Process: A View Of Russian Scientists. Russian and foreign literature. Sir. 4, State and Law: Abstract Journal. 2023. https://cyberleninka.ru/article/n/neyrobiotehnologii-ugolovnoe-pravo-i-protsess-vzglyad-rossiyskih-uchenyh.

Ali, S. S., Lifshitz, M., and Raz, A. (2014). Empirical neuroenchantment: From reading minds to thinking critically. Frontiers in Human Neuroscience, 8. https://doi.org/10.3389/fnhum.2014.00357.

Almeida, M., and Diogo, R. (2019). Human enhancement: Genetic engineering and evolution. Evolution, Medicine, and Public Health, 2019(1): 183–189. https://doi.org/10.1093/emph/eoz026.

Alomar, S., King, N. K. K., Tam, J., Bari, A. A., Hamani, C., and Lozano, A. M. (2017). Speech and language adverse effects after thalamotomy and deep brain stimulation in patients with movement disorders: A meta-analysis. Movement Disorders : Official Journal of the Movement Disorder Society, 32(1): 53–63. https://doi.org/10.1002/mds.26924.

Angrisani, L., Arpaia, P., and Casinelli, D. (2017). Instrumentation and measurements for non-invasive EEG-based brain-computer interface. In 2017 IEEE International Workshop on Measurement and Networking (M&N) (pp. 1–5). IEEE. https://doi.org/10.1109/IWMN.2017.8078383.

Antal, A., Luber, B., Brem, A. K., Bikson, M., Brunoni, A. R., Cohen Kadosh, R. et al. (2022). Non-invasive brain stimulation and neuroenhancement. Clinical Neurophysiology Practice, 7: 146–165. https://doi.org/10.1016/j.cnp.2022.05.002.

Bakhteev, D. V. (2023) Ethical-Legal Models of the Society Interactions with the Artificial Intelligence Technology. Journal of Digital Technologies and Law. 2023; 1(2): 520–539. https://doi.org/10.21202/jdtl.2023.22.

Bareis, J., and Katzenbach, C. (2022). Talking AI into Being: The Narratives and Imaginaries of National AI Strategies and Their Performative Politics. Science, Technology, & Human Values, 47(5): 855–881. https://doi.org/10.1177/01622439211030007.

Baylis, F. (2013). "I Am Who I Am": On the Perceived Threats to Personal Identity from Deep Brain Stimulation. Neuroethics, 6(3): 513–526. https://doi.org/10.1007/s12152-011-9137-1.

Beauchamp, T. L., and Childress, J. F. (2019). Principles of biomedical ethics (8th ed.). Oxford University Press.

Beckett, A. E., and Campbell, T. (2015). The social model of disability as an oppositional device. Disability & Society, 30(2): 270–283. https://doi.org/10.1080/09687599.2014.999912.

Bernal, S. L., Celdrán, A. H., Pérez, G. M., Barros, M. T., and Balasubramaniam, S. (2022). Security in Brain-Computer Interfaces: State-of-the-art, opportunities, and future challenges. ACM Computing Surveys, 54(1): 1–35. https://doi.org/10.1145/3427376.

Bielefeldt, H. (2023). Freiheit als Anspruch: Eine menschenrechtliche Perspektive. pp. 187–196. *In*: Saam, N. J., and H. Bielefeldt (Eds.). Sozialtheorie. Die Idee der Freiheit und ihre Semantiken: Zum Spannungsverhältnis von Freiheit und Sicherheit.

Cagnan, H., Denison, T., McIntyre, C., and Brown, P. (2019). Emerging technologies for improved deep brain stimulation. Nature Biotechnology, 37(9): 1024–1033. https://doi.org/10.1038/s41587-019-0244-6.

Cinel, C., Valeriani, D., and Poli, R. (2019). Neurotechnologies for Human Cognitive Augmentation: Current State of the Art and Future Prospects. Frontiers in Human Neuroscience, 13, 13. https://doi.org/10.3389/fnhum.2019.00013.

Conitzer, V., Hadfield, G., and Vallor, S. (Eds.) (2019). Proceedings of the 2019 AAAI/ACM Conference on AI, Ethics, and Society. ACM.

Craig, J. N. (2016). Incarceration, Direct Brain Intervention, and the Right to Mental Integrity – a Reply to Thomas Douglas. Neuroethics, 9(2): 107–118. https://doi.org/10.1007/s12152-016-9255-x.

Di Salvo, M. (2024). Why AI is not intelligence and man's struggle to survive himself. Russian Journal of Economics and Law, no. 1, 2024, https://doi.org/10.21202/2782-2923.2024.1.264-279.

Drew, L. (2024). Elon Musk's Neuralink brain chip: What scientists think of first human trial. Nature. Advance online publication. https://doi.org/10.1038/d41586-024-00304-4.

Ehlen, F., Schoenecker, T., Kühn, A. A., and Klostermann, F. (2014). Differential effects of deep brain stimulation on verbal fluency. Brain and Language, 134: 23–33. https://doi.org/10.1016/j.bandl.2014.04.002.

Eubanks, V. (2018). Automating inequality: How high-tech tools profile, police, and punish the poor (First edition). St. Martin's Press.

Fenner, D. (2019). Selbstoptimierung und Enhancement: Ein ethischer Grundriss. UTB Philosophie: Vol. 5127. Narr Francke Attempto Verlag.
Floridi, L. (2023). The ethics of artificial intelligence: Principles, challenges, and opportunities. Oxford University Press.
Funke, A. (2023). Freiheit als konstitutives Prinzip der Rechtsordnung. pp. 169–176. *In*: Saam, N. J., and Bielefeldt, H. (Eds.), Sozialtheorie. Die Idee der Freiheit und ihre Semantiken: Zum Spannungsverhältnis von Freiheit und Sicherheit.
Ganzer, P. D., Colachis, S. C., Schwemmer, M. A., Friedenberg, D. A., Dunlap, C. F., Swiftney, C. E. et al. (2020). Restoring the Sense of Touch Using a Sensorimotor Demultiplexing Neural Interface. Cell, 181(4): 763–773.e12. https://doi.org/10.1016/j.cell.2020.03.054.
Gardner, H. (1987). The Mind's New Science. New York: Basic Books.
Giattino, C. M., Kwong, L., Rafetto, C., and Farahany, N. A. (2019). The Seductive Allure of Artificial Intelligence-Powered Neurotechnology. pp. 397–402. *In*: Conitzer, V., Hadfield, G., and Vallor S. (Eds.). Proceedings of the 2019 AAAI/ACM Conference on AI, Ethics, and Society. ACM. https://doi.org/10.1145/3306618.3314269.
Genser, J., Damianos, S., and Yuste, R. (2024). Safeguarding Brain Data: Assessing the Privacy Practices of Consumer Neurotechnology Companies.
Gilbert, F., Goddard, E., Viaña, J. N. M., Carter, A., and Horne, M. (2017). I Miss Being Me: Phenomenological Effects of Deep Brain Stimulation. AJOB Neuroscience, 8(2): 96–109. https://doi.org/10.1080/21507740.2017.1320319.
Gilbert, F., Cook, M., O'Brien, T., and Illes, J. (2019). Embodiment and Estrangement: Results from a First-in- Human "Intelligent BCI" Trial. Science and Engineering Ethics, 25(1): 83–96. https://doi.org/10.1007/s11948-017-0001-5.
Goering, S. (2015). Rethinking disability: The social model of disability and chronic disease. Current Reviews in Musculoskeletal Medicine, 8(2): 134–138. https://doi.org/10.1007/s12178-015-9273-z.
Goering, S., Klein, E., Specker Sullivan, L., Wexler, A., Agüera Y., Arcas, B. et al. (2021). Recommendations for Responsible Development and Application of Neurotechnologies. Neuroethics, 14(3): 365–386. https://doi.org/10.1007/s12152-021-09468-6.
Grunwald, A. (2019a). Digitalisierung als Prozess. Ethische Herausforderungen inmitten allmählicher Verschiebungen zwischen Mensch, Technik und Gesellschaft. Zeitschrift Für Wirtschafts- Und Unternehmensethik, 20(2): 121–145. https://doi.org/10.5771/1439-880X-2019-2-121.
Grunwald, A. (2019b). Der unterlegene Mensch: Die Zukunft der Menschheit im Angesicht von Algorithmen, künstlicher Intelligenz und Robotern (Originalausgabe, 1. Auflage).
Grunwald, A. (Ed.). (2021). Wer bist du, Mensch? Transformationen menschlicher Selbstverständnisse im wissenschaftlich-technischen Fortschritt. Herder.
Gulyaeva P.S. (2023) Medical nanorobots in the focus of law. Journal of Digital Technologies and Law. 2023; 1(1): 89–122. https://doi.org/10.21202/jdtl.2023.4.
Guy, V., Soriani, M. H., Bruno, M., Papadopoulo, T., Desnuelle, C., and Clerc, M. (2018). Brain computer interface with the P300 speller: Usability for disabled people with amyotrophic lateral sclerosis. Annals of Physical and Rehabilitation Medicine, 61(1): 5–11. https://doi.org/10.1016/j.rehab.2017.09.004.
Hallur, G. G., Prabhu, S., and Aslekar, A. (2021). Entertainment in Era of AI, Big Data & IoT. pp. 87–109. *In*: Das, S., and Gochhait, S. (Eds.). Digital Entertainment: The Next Evolution in Service Sector. Springer Nature. https://doi.org/10.1007/978-981-15-9724-4_5.
Heimbach-Steins, M. (2022). Sozialprinzipien. pp. 170–186. *In*: Heimbach-Steins, M., Becka, M., Frühbauer, J. J., and Kruip, G. (Eds.). Christliche Sozialethik: Grundlagen, Kontexte, Themen: ein Lehr- und Studienbuch. Verlag Friedrich Pustet.
Hull, G., and Pasquale, F. (2018). Toward a critical theory of corporate wellness. BioSocieties, 13(1): 190–212. https://doi.org/10.1057/s41292-017-0064-1.
Iamsakul, K., Pavlovcik, A. V., Calderon, J. I., and Sanderson, L. M. (2017). Project HEAVEN: Preoperative Training in Virtual Reality. Surgical Neurology International, 8: 59. https://doi.org/10.4103/sni.sni_371_16.
Ienca, M. (2021a). Common Human Rights Challenges raised by different Applications of Neurotechnologies in the Biomedical Field. Commitee on Bioethics of the Council of Europe. https://rm.coe.int/report-final-en/1680a429f3.

Ienca, M., and Andorno, R. (2017). Towards new human rights in the age of neuroscience and neurotechnology. Life Sciences, Society and Policy, 13(1): 5. https://doi.org/10.1186/s40504-017-0050-1.

Ienca, M., Fins, J. J., Jox, R. J., Jotterand, F., Voeneky, S., Andorno, R. et al. (2022). Towards a Governance Framework for Brain Data. Neuroethics, 15(2). https://doi.org/10.1007/s12152-022-09498-8.

Iuculano, T., and Cohen Kadosh, R. (2013). The mental cost of cognitive enhancement. The Journal of Neuroscience : The Official Journal of the Society for Neuroscience, 33(10): 4482–4486. https://doi.org/10.1523/JNEUROSCI.4927-12.2013.

Jarke, J., and Breiter, A. (2019). Editorial: the datafication of education. 1743–9884, 44(1): 1–6. https://doi.org/10.1080/17439884.2019.1573833.

Jasanoff, S., Kim, S., and University of Chicago Press. (2015). Dreamscapes of modernity: Sociotechnical imaginaries and the fabrication of power. London. http://www.degruyter.com/isbn/9780226276663.

Jiang, L., Stocco, A., Losey, D. M., Abernethy, J. A., Prat, C. S., and Rao, R. P. N. (2019). Brainnet: A Multi-Person Brain-to-Brain Interface for Direct Collaboration Between Brains. Scientific Reports, 9(1): 6115. https://doi.org/10.1038/s41598-019-41895-7.

Kirchschläger, P. G. (2019). Menschenrechte, Demokratie und Religionen. LIMINA - Grazer Theologische Perspektiven, 2(1): 17–39. https://doi.org/10.25364/17.2:2019.1.2.

Kirchschläger, P. G. (2022). Ethische KI? Datenbasierte Systeme (DS) mit Ethik. HMD Praxis Der Wirtschaftsinformatik, 59(2): 482–494. https://doi.org/10.1365/s40702-022-00843-2.

Kober, S. E., Schweiger, D., Witte, M., Reichert, J. L., Grieshofer, P., Neuper, C. et al. (2015). Specific effects of EEG based neurofeedback training on memory functions in post-stroke victims. Journal of Neuroengineering and Rehabilitation, 12: 107. https://doi.org/10.1186/s12984-015-0105-6.

Koska, C., and Filipović, A. (2017). Gestaltungsfragen der Digitalität: Zu den sozialethischen Herausforderungen von künstlicher Intelligenz, Big Data und Virtualität. pp. 173–191. *In*: Bergold, R., Sautermeister, J., and Schröder, A. (Eds.). Dem Wandel eine menschliche Gestalt geben: Sozialethische Perspektiven für die Gesellschaft von morgen : Festschrift zur Neueröffnung und zum 70-jährigen Bestehen des Katholisch-Sozialen Instituts. Verlag Herder.

Lavazza, A., and Giorgi, R. (2023). Philosophical foundation of the right to mental integrity in the age of neurotechnologies. Neuroethics, 16(1): 10. https://doi.org/10.1007/s12152-023-09517-2.

Legaspi, R., Xu, W., Konishi, T., Wada, S., Kobayashi, N., Naruse, Y. et al. (2024). The sense of agency in human–AI interactions. Knowledge-Based Systems, 286: 111298. https://doi.org/10.1016/j.knosys.2023.111298.

Li, Q., Ding, D., and Conti, M. (2015). Brain-Computer Interface applications: Security and privacy challenges. In 2015 IEEE Conference on Communications and Network Security (CNS) (pp. 663–666). IEEE. https://doi.org/10.1109/CNS.2015.7346884.

Ligthart, S., Bublitz, C., Douglas, T., Forsberg, L., and Meynen, G. (2022). Rethinking the Right to Freedom of Thought: A Multidisciplinary Analysis. Human Rights Law Review, 22(4), Article ngac028, 1–14. https://doi.org/10.1093/hrlr/ngac028.

Littlefield, M. M. (2018). Instrumental Intimacy: EEG Wearables and Neuroscientific Control. John Hopkins University Press.

Lozano, A. M., Lipsman, N., Bergman, H., Brown, P., Chabardes, S., Chang, J. W. et al. (2019). Deep brain stimulation: Current challenges and future directions. Nature Reviews. Neurology, 15(3): 148–160. https://doi.org/10.1038/s41582-018-0128-2.

Macgilchrist, F., Allert, H., Cerratto Pargman, T., and Jarke, J. (2024). Designing Postdigital Futures: Which Designs? Whose Futures? Postdigital Science and Education, 6(1): 13–24. https://doi.org/10.1007/s42438-022-00389-y.

Manahan-Vaughan, D. (Ed.). (2018). Handbook of Behavioral Neuroscience: Volume 28. Handbook of *In Vivo* Neural Plasticity Techniques: A Sytstems Neuroscience Approach to the Neural Basis of Memory and Cognition. Academic Press an imprint of Elsevier.

Markosian, C., Taruvai, V. S., and Mammis, A. (2020). Neuromodulatory hacking: A review of the technology and security risks of spinal cord stimulation. Acta Neurochirurgica, 162(12): 3213–3219. https://doi.org/10.1007/s00701-020-04592-3.

Martínez-Martínez, A. M., Aguilar, O. M., and Acevedo-Triana, C. A. (2017). Meta-Analysis of the Relationship between Deep Brain Stimulation in Patients with Parkinson's Disease and Performance in Evaluation Tests for Executive Brain Functions. Parkinson's Disease, 2017, 9641392. https://doi.org/10.1155/2017/9641392.

Martinovic, I., Davies, D., Frank, M., Perito, D., Ros, T., and Song, D. (2012). On the feasibility of side-channel attacks with brain-computer interfaces. In 21st USENIX Security Symposium (USENIX Security 12) (pp. 143–158). USENIX Association.

Marzbani, H., Marateb, H. R., and Mansourian, M. (2016). Neurofeedback: A Comprehensive Review on System Design, Methodology and Clinical Applications. Basic and Clinical Neuroscience, 7(2): 143–158. https://doi.org/10.15412/J.BCN.03070208.

Mathewson, K. E., Harrison, T. J. L., and Kizuk, S. A. D. (2017). High and dry? Comparing active dry EEG electrodes to active and passive wet electrodes. Psychophysiology, 54(1): 74–82. https://doi.org/10.1111/psyp.12536.

Mihara, M., and Miyai, I. (2016). Review of functional near-infrared spectroscopy in neurorehabilitation. Neurophotonics, https://doi.org/10.1117/1.NPh.3.3.031414.

Moradi, P., and Levy, K. (2020). The Future of Work in the Age of AI. *In*: Dubber, M. D., Pasquale, F., Das, S., Moradi, P., and Levy, K. (Eds.). The Oxford Handbook of Ethics of AI Oxford University Press. https://doi.org/10.1093/oxfordhb/9780190067397.013.17.

Nagl-Docekal, H., and Zacharasiewicz, W. (2022). Artificial Intelligence and Human Enhancement. De Gruyter. https://doi.org/10.1515/9783110770216.

Nam, C. S., Traylor, Z., Chen, M., Jiang, X., Feng, W., and Chhatbar, P. Y. (2021). Direct Communication Between Brains: A Systematic PRISMA Review of Brain-To-Brain Interface. Frontiers in Neurorobotics, https://doi.org/10.3389/fnbot.2021.656943.

Nickel, J. (2019). Stanford Encyclopedia of Philosophy: Human Rights. https://plato.stanford.edu/entries/rights-human/.

Olson, J. A., Cyr, M., Artenie, D. Z., Strandberg, T., Hall, L., Tompkins, M. L. et al. (2023). Emulating future neurotechnology using magic. Consciousness and Cognition, 107: 103450. https://doi.org/10.1016/j.concog.2022.103450.

Pycroft, L., Boccard, S. G., Owen, S. L. F., Stein, J. F., Fitzgerald, J. J., Green, A. L. et al. (2016). Brainjacking: Implant Security Issues in Invasive Neuromodulation. World Neurosurgery, 92: 454–462. https://doi.org/10.1016/j.wneu.2016.05.010.

Rahm, L. (2023a). Education, automation and AI: a genealogy of alternative futures. Learning, Media and Technology, 48(1): 6–24. https://doi.org/10.1080/17439884.2021.1977948.

Rahm, L. (2023b). Educational imaginaries: governance at the intersection of technology and education. Journal of Education Policy, 38(1): 46–68. https://doi.org/10.1080/02680939.2021.1970233.

Rao, R. P. N., Stocco, A., Bryan, M., Sarma, D., Youngquist, T. M., Wu, J. et al. (2014). A direct brain-to-brain interface in humans. PloS One, 9(11): e111332. https://doi.org/10.1371/journal.pone.0111332.

Raspopovic, S. (2020). Advancing limb neural prostheses. Science (New York, N.Y.), 370(6514): 290–291. https://doi.org/10.1126/science.abb1073.

Ros, T., Enriquez-Geppert, S., Zotev, V., Young, K. D., Wood, G., Whitfield-Gabrieli, S. et al. (2020). Consensus on the reporting and experimental design of clinical and cognitive-behavioural neurofeedback studies. Brain: A Journal of Neurology, 143(6): 1674–1685. https://doi.org/10.1093/brain/awaa009.

Rose, D., Buckwalter, W., and Nichols, S. (2017). Neuroscientific Prediction and the Intrusion of Intuitive Metaphysics. Cognitive Science, 41(2): 482–502. https://doi.org/10.1111/cogs.12310.

Schauer, F. (2020). Freedom of Thought? Social Philosophy and Policy, 37(2): 72–89. https://doi.org/10.1017/S0265052521000054.

Schlosser, M. (2024). Agency. *In*: Zalta, E. N., Nodelman, U., Allen, C., Kim Hannah, and Oppenheimer, P. (Eds.). The Stanford Encyclopedia of Philosophy (Winter 2019). https://plato.stanford.edu/archives/win2019/entries/agency/.

Schöne-Seifert, B. (2007). Grundlagen der Medizinethik. Alfred Kroner Verlag. http://gbv.eblib.com/patron/FullRecord.aspx?p=4341681.

Selwyn, N. (2022). The future of AI and education: Some cautionary notes. European Journal of Education, 57(4): 620–631. https://doi.org/10.1111/ejed.12532.

Shaheed, A. (2021, October 5). Freedom of thought: Interim report of the Special Rapporteur on freedom of religion or belief (A/76/380).

Sharon, T., and Gellert, R. (2023). Regulating Big Tech expansionism? Sphere transgressions and the limits of Europe's digital regulatory strategy. Information, Communication & Society, 1–18. https://doi.org/10.1080/1369118X.2023.2246526.

Shew, A. (2020). Ableism, Technoableism, and Future AI. IEEE Technology and Society Magazine, 39(1), 40–85. https://doi.org/10.1109/MTS.2020.2967492.

Shutova, A. A. (2023) Criminal risks of medical robots turnover. Russian Journal of Economics and Law. 2023; 17(3): 571–585. (In Russ.) https://doi.org/10.21202/2782-2923.2023.3.571-585.

Shutova, A. A. and Begishev, I. R. (2023). Draft of an ethical code of subjects implementing activity of creating, applying and utilizing medical products based on artificial intelligence technologies. Russian Journal of Economics and Law. 2023; 17(4): 873–881. https://doi.org/10.21202/2782-2923.2023.3.873-881.

Sturm, W., Willmes, K., Orgass, B., and Hartje, W. (1997). Do Specific Attention Deficits Need Specific Training? Neuropsychological Rehabilitation, 7(2): 81–103. https://doi.org/10.1080/713755526.

Suchman, L. (2023). The uncontroversial 'thingness' of AI. Big Data & Society, 10(2): 1–5. https://doi.org/10.1177/20539517231206794.

Suthana, N., and Fried, I. (2014). Deep brain stimulation for enhancement of learning and memory. NeuroImage, 85 Pt 3(0 3): 996–1002. https://doi.org/10.1016/j.neuroimage.2013.07.066.

Taylor, L., Martin, A., Souza, S. P. de, and Lopez-Solano, J. (2023). Why are sector transgressions so hard to govern? Reflections from Europe's pandemic experience. Information, Communication & Society, 1–5. https://doi.org/10.1080/1369118X.2023.2264919.

Tesink, V., Douglas, T., Forsberg, L., Ligthart, S., and Meynen, G. (2024). Right to mental integrity and neurotechnologies: Implications of the extended mind thesis. Journal of Medical Ethics, 1–8. https://doi.org/10.1136/jme-2023-109645.

Thibault, R. T., and Raz, A. (2017). The psychology of neurofeedback: Clinical intervention even if applied placebo. The American Psychologist, 72(7): 679–688. https://doi.org/10.1037/amp0000118.

Tirabeni, L. (2023). Bounded Well-Being: Designing Technologies for Workers' Well-Being in Corporate Programmes. Work, Employment and Society, Advance online publication. https://doi.org/10.1177/09500170231203113.

Yadav, D., Yadav, S., and Veer, K. (2020). A comprehensive assessment of Brain Computer Interfaces: Recent trends and challenges. Journal of Neuroscience Methods, 346: 108918. https://doi.org/10.1016/j.jneumeth.2020.108918.

van Elk, M. (2019). Socio-cognitive biases are associated to belief in neuromyths and cognitive enhancement: A pre-registered study. Personality and Individual Differences, 147: 28–32. https://doi.org/10.1016/j.paid.2019.04.014.

Vester, H.G. (2009). Kompendium der Soziologie (1. Aufl.). Lehrbuch. VS Verl. für Sozialwiss. https://doi.org/10.1007/978-3-531-91345-2.

Vogt, M. (2009). Prinzip Nachhaltigkeit: Ein Entwurf aus theologisch-ethischer Perspektive. Zugl.: Luzern, Univ., Habil.-Schr. Hochschulschriften zur Nachhaltigkeit: Vol. 39.

Warren, S., and Brandeis, L. (1890). The Right to Privacy. Harvard Law Review, 4(5): 193–220.

Wexler, A., and Thibault, R. (2019). Mind-Reading or Misleading? Assessing Direct-to-Consumer Electroencephalography (EEG) Devices Marketed for Wellness and Their Ethical and Regulatory Implications. Journal of Cognitive Enhancement, 3(1): 131–137. https://doi.org/10.1007/s41465-018-0091-2.

Whitham, E. M., Pope, K. J., Fitzgibbon, S. P., Lewis, T., Clark, C. R., Loveless, S. et al. (2007). Scalp electrical recording during paralysis: Quantitative evidence that EEG frequencies above 20 Hz are contaminated by EMG. Clinical Neurophysiology: Official Journal of the International Federation of Clinical Neurophysiology, 118(8): 1877–1888. https://doi.org/10.1016/j.clinph.2007.04.027.

Willoweit, D. (2023). Die vielen Freiheiten, die eine Freiheit und das Recht. pp. 161–167. *In*: Saam, N. J., and Bielefeldt, H. (Eds.). Sozialtheorie. Die Idee der Freiheit und ihre Semantiken: Zum Spannungsverhältnis von Freiheit und Sicherheit.

Wong, J. K., Mayberg, H. S., Wang, D. D., Richardson, R. M., Halpern, C. H., Krinke, L. et al. (2022). Proceedings of the 10th annual deep brain stimulation think tank: Advances in cutting edge technologies, artificial intelligence, neuromodulation, neuroethics, interventional psychiatry, and women in neuromodulation. Frontiers in Human Neuroscience, 16, 1084782. https://doi.org/10.3389/fnhum.2022.1084782.

Wood, G., Willmes, K., Koten, J. W., N. J. Kober, S. E. (2024). Fat tails and the need to disclose distribution parameters of qEEG databases. PloS One, 19(1): e0295411. https://doi.org/10.1371/journal.pone.0295411.

Yuste, R. (2023). Advocating for neurodata privacy and neurotechnology regulation. Nature Protocols, 18(10): 2869–2875. https://doi.org/10.1038/s41596-023-00873-0.

Zarzycki, M. Z., and Domitrz, I. (2020). Stimulation-induced side effects after deep brain stimulation – a systematic review. Acta Neuropsychiatrica, 32(2): 57–64. https://doi.org/10.1017/neu.2019.35.

PART II

AI in Court

1

AI in Administrative Justice in Italy

First Projects and Notes

The General Secretariat of Administrative Justice published a document in October 2024 on the ongoing activities related to the introduction of artificial intelligence technologies in administrative justice [1].

The aim is to provide initial information on the developments initiated by the General Secretariat of Administrative Justice, at a time when interest in the use of these technologies has reached a particularly high level, both because of the level of dissemination and technological development and as a result of regulatory initiatives in the EU and national spheres.

The paper describes strategies, methodologies and use cases of AI. AI implementation projects in administrative justice concern:

(a) the anonymisation of measures;

(b) supporting the judge's work by searching and displaying content;

(c) cyber resilience.

On the first aspect, that of anonymisation (a), the paper dwells on the explanation of the rationale followed, careful to reconcile two values: the confidentiality of the persons concerned and the intelligibility of the measure, which could be compromised, also with regard to the motivation, by unsupervised anonymisation.

"*Achieving a balance between the two aspects (protection of confidentiality and comprehensibility of the text) in fact presupposes an interpretative activity that can only be carried out by judges, who, at that stage, help to define the intrinsic value to be assigned to each piece of information, also considering its relationship with the context, distinguishing the nature and characteristics of the disputes. Artificial intelligence is thus modelled to suit the variability of the context, to then verify in the course of concrete use, thanks to the feedback received from users (feedback duly verified and administered to the AI itself), the correctness of the results obtained still under the control of judges, who, in this executive phase, monitor the development*

DOI: 10.1201/9781003731290-5

of the system, i.e., the way it responds to the feedback offered by users, supervising its evolutionary path'.

With regard to the judge's support activities (b), those activities considered high-risk by the AI act are excluded from the AI applications and instead included are those functional to facilitate various activities of the judge, in the different roles, and which, as structured, 'do not involve "creative" activity'.

These are, in particular:

- identification of related or similar appeals pending in the individual Sections and to be set for decision. Identification makes it possible to achieve, the Report specifies, several objectives, such as optimisation of study and analysis; evaluation for the purpose of discussion in the same hearing or in 'thematic' hearings; avoidance of conflicting decisions in individual court sections; better distribution of workloads; and faster decisions;
- search for case law precedents with a tool based not only, as now, on keywords, but on the detection of semantic connections, thus ensuring a higher degree of relevance of the search results;
- detection and possibility of immediate visualisation of the rules or case-law pronouncements indicated, explicitly or implicitly, in a defence document, thus preventing the judge from having to interrupt the analysis of the document to search external databases, thus ensuring time savings and also preventing his concentration from being diverted.

As for cyber resilience (c), specific defence strategies have been implemented against internationally identified adversarial machine learning techniques.
According to the intentions expressed in the document

"The guideline followed is that of valorising the positive impacts that can be derived from technological developments on the organisation of work, but with clear attribution to this technology of an instrumental role, of support to the judge in the phase of study, updating and analysis. The processing activity remains exclusively entrusted to the judge. On a conceptual level, it is more appropriate to speak of 'accelerated intelligence' instead of 'artificial intelligence'.

Machine learning models - especially deep learning models (i.e., machine learning systems that simulate, by means of multilayer artificial neural networks, the action of the human brain, such as, for instance, LLM - large language models that use systems of this type for linguistic purposes) are difficult to govern and can lead to so-called hallucination phenomena or even overfitting phenomena, when the model fits too closely to specific training data, or overgeneralisation, when the model, on the contrary, generalises too much.

Research in the field (notably at Stanford) has highlighted the difficulty of these AI models in performing the type of legal reasoning, identifying various negative impact factors, including the lack of uniformity and the length of sentences in legal documents. The approach can only be cautious, aware of the risks and at the same time free of bias but characterised by a critical spirit and constant supervision.

In the Italian legal system in particular, the centrality of the 'human' judge is constitutionally imposed: jurisdictional functions are by the Constitution entrusted to the judge who is a natural person, natural and pre-established by law, third and impartial, subject only to the laws; ethical values and the protection of rights cannot be delegated to technology; leadership cannot be automated. Considerations also reflected in the same document.

However, the risk remains high through the combination of uniform formats and AI applications, all integrated in the SIGA.

The use of formats in itself would conflict with the originality that is inherent in the intellectual profession of the lawyer; with decorum and, even before that, with the function of the legal profession, which requires that the lawyer's task not be restricted within rigid formalisms that would inevitably end up compromising the effectiveness of defences.

At a time when legal design is being discussed [2] what has already been said needs to be reinforced with regard to the format of judgements and acts.

A first step would be to guarantee all forms of cross-participation in the decision-making process in the introduction of AI systems in the administration of justice, not only therefore to ensure both the participation of lawyers in the process of regulating AI systems and that the latter are regulated at least by means of a delegated regulation, after agreement with the specialist legal associations, but also with the input of experts in the non-law specialist branches, which could detect and highlight heterogeneous weaknesses and frailties, even those not typified in the narrow procedural dynamics.

The use of artificial intelligence in administrative procedures should then be better regulated, in the sense of imposing on PAs the obligation to justify the use of AI as a function of real efficiency and improvement of the specific activity at the service of citizens and businesses, ensuring the interested parties the knowability of its operation and the traceability of its use and, more generally, the obligation of transparency; the reservation of autonomy and decision-making power of the person responsible for adopting the measure/activity and/or the person in charge of the procedure; the exclusion of the use of artificial intelligence for the generation of texts of any kind.

The topic is particularly delicate - especially in the context of the repeal of the offence of abuse of office and in the midst of the related events at the Constitutional Court - especially since there are essential declinations still to be clarified.

The justification of the procedure - an essential and central moment in Law 241/90 [3] - must be human, it must be specific, on the single/individual measure and not 'per tabulas or generalised', it must run through and be based on the entire procedural event, and be anchored to the specific subjective case. Intrinsic characteristics that ontologically exclude - today - the generic formula adopted with copy-paste, and - tomorrow - the mechanical delegation to digital automatism.

If in this sense motivation, even if discretionary, cannot turn into arbitrariness where motivation is absent or lacking or 'per tabulas', this applies even more so in the case of the use of a discriminating algorithm where the objective weight of each element and value to be weighed is not made public: in the absence therefore of absolute and verifiable ex ante transparency, a use of AI should be considered to be excluded a priori.

Even more so if we are talking about the motivation of a judgement. While on the one hand, the integration of AI forms in the search is certainly desirable - in any case, to our partial knowledge, this is already the case today in the daily use of classic search engines, which make wide and abundant and too indiscriminate use of them - on the other hand, the non-transparent and verifiable weighting of the 'weights' to be assigned to the results raises not a few perplexities in terms of risk: 5 judgments against 3, how much weight are they given, how much weight is to be given to chronological relevance or to the forum, what distinction is guaranteed with respect to the real traceability to the specific case dealt with, what guarantees of non-discrimination can be offered ex ante and in a transparent manner?

These are just a few of the prima facie findings that can be listed, each of which it would be desirable to dwell on in an analysis that is only incidentally legal in nature and that involves complexities that unequivocally call into question heterogeneous professionalism and research experience.

The judge in this sense, in his reasoning, must therefore make provision to clarify in a complete and transparent manner all these aspects of weighting, beyond any doubt and with the possibility of verification ... and in this sense it is not certain that the adoption of these systems can guarantee ex post effective economy and celerity to the proceedings. It is more immediate for the judge to clarify his own parameters than those adopted in the programming of a machine - which indeed are not necessarily his own nor that he must - rightly - share - triggering a new mechanism of counter-assessment.

[1] https://www.dirittobancario.it/wp-content/uploads/2024/10/Report-Segretariato-Generale-della-Giustizia-Amministrativa-ottobere-2024.pdf

[2] https://www.diritto.it/dalla-chiarezza-dell-atto-al-legal-design/

[3] http://www.salvisjuribus.it/lobbligo-di-motivazione-del-provvedimento-amministrativo-tra-rilevanza-costituzionale-e-concretizzazione-dei-principi-fondamentali-dellagire-della-pubblica-amministrazione-un-commen/

2

AI and Judicial Review of Technical Discretion

The Possible Procedural Fallout of a Massive Extension of Artificial Intelligence to Administrative Activities Connoted by Technical Discretion

In recent years, we are witnessing a progressive push towards the introduction of artificial intelligence in public administration. In this case, we are not talking about generative AI but about a set of processes performed by an algorithmic system, capable of going beyond the work of a 'traditional' algorithm.

The one based on A.I. is based on a machine learning system, which enables it to analyse data, make choices and take decisions independently, even without human intervention.

Over the years, the Council of State has broadened the range of hypotheses in which the P.A. In the course of the years, the Council of State has broadened the range of hypotheses in which the public administration may make use of automated decision-making procedures; in fact, while at first it was held that recourse to the algorithm was permitted only in the presence of binding activities, over time the judges have taken a more "open" attitude, arriving at the conclusion that: "if recourse to computer tools may appear easier to use in relation to so-called binding activities, there is nothing to prevent the [purposes established by law], pursued with recourse to the computer algorithm, from also being pursued in relation to activities characterised by areas of discretion. Rather, if in the case of the bound activity far more relevant, both in quantitative and qualitative terms, may be the use of tools for the automation of data collection and evaluation, even the exercise of discretionary activity, especially technical, may in abstract benefit from the efficiencies and, more generally, the advantages offered by the tools themselves" (Council of State, Sec.

DOI: 10.1201/9781003731290-6

VI, 13 December 2019, no. 84723) and that: "there are no reasons of principle, or rather concrete reasons, for limiting the use to binding rather than discretionary administrative activity, both of which are expressions of authoritative activity carried out in pursuit of the public interest" (Council of State, Sec. VI, 4 February 2020, no. 881).

It has been noted that the extension of the automated administrative decision to discretionary activities requires the judge to assess the correctness and transparency of the procedure in all its components, blurring the distinction between legitimacy - which can be reviewed - and merit - which cannot be questioned - of administrative action; in this way, the automated decision determines the reversal of relations between the administration and the judge - to the benefit of the latter - in the assessment of the correctness of the inter-subjective relations between the citizen and public power.

However, the Council of State clarified that, to be legitimate, the P.A.'s use of the algorithm must comply with three important principles:

1. **the principle of knowability - a strengthened declination of the principle of transparency** - by virtue of which, in order to prevent citizens from being excluded from decisions that affect them, the P.A. must prepare instruments capable of clearly illustrating the functioning and the impact of the algorithm on its decision-making process; if this were not the case, in fact, the correctness of the decision would be knowable only by those few extremely qualified subjects, and, consequently, democracy would give way to technocracy;
2. **principle of algorithmic non-discrimination**, by virtue of which it is necessary for the administrative officer called upon to instruct the machine to carry out a check on the input data aimed at preventing the output data from being discriminatory. It is undeniable, in fact, that the A.I., thanks to its capacity to process large volumes of data, to automate complex and repetitive processes - thus reducing waiting times for citizens - and to provide predictive analyses capable of satisfying citizens' needs in advance, is capable of improving the efficiency of the methods of management and delivery of public services, making them increasingly interactive and personalised; however, these benefits are counterbalanced by many pitfalls, since the use of I. A. projects the decision-making process into a more complex and more complex process, which is more and more complex, more and more complex, more and more personalised, and more and more complex.A. projects the decision into a sort of black box, an inextricable and indecipherable dimension in which man finds it difficult to orient himself;
3. **principle of non-exclusivity of the algorithmic decision:** that is, a mediation and interest-settlement role played by the administrative officer is always necessary upstream, the algorithm being a procedural and investigative tool, which, as such, does not escape the verifications typical of any administrative procedure. Therefore, far from becoming a substitute instrument for the indispensable human activity and de-empowering of administrative officials, the algorithm must limit itself to acting as a mere modus operandi; in other words, it is the algorithm that must place itself in a servant position with respect to man, and not the other way around.

In recent years, the doctrine has tackled the thorny problem of the imputability of the algorithmic decision in cases where the machine generates outputs that cannot be attributed either to the will of the public authority or to the programmer. In particular, a first thesis according to which the use of automated procedures would not affect the liability regime - with the consequent imputability of the decision to the holder of the public office - is countered by a second thesis that, by separating the moment prior to the compilation of the software - in which the rules for programming are established - from the actual computer programme for issuing the act, proposes a dualistic approach according to which the official would be liable for the pre-software errors and the programmer for the damages produced by the software.

Starting from the assumption that, as of today, recourse to the A.I. is deemed to be precluded in the presence of highly debatable or non-standardisable assessment criteria, and, therefore, in all the hypotheses in which a concrete assessment by the official is required, it appears extremely interesting to imagine the possible procedural consequences that would arise from a massive extension of the use of the A.I. to administrative activities connoted by technical discretion; think, for example, of the preparation of competition questions and the identification of correct answers, which, as the case law has often clarified, are not subject to any specific assessment by the official. to administrative activities characterised by technical discretion; one thinks, for example, of the preparation of competition questions and the identification of the correct answers, which, as case law has repeatedly clarified, are an expression of technical discretion and are beyond judicial review, in the sense that the judge cannot challenge the accuracy of the answers deemed correct by the commission of experts but must limit himself to detecting flaws of legitimacy in the presence of actual errors (TAR Lazio, sez. Quarta Ter, Order no. 4567 of 27 July 2023).

The real crux of the matter is precisely the reviewability of the decision, since there are several levels: a reviewability of the decision, one of the 'motivation', and above all one of the algorithm.

This would imply the recognition of a substitutive jurisdictional review in all cases in which the technical evaluation carried out by the I.A. proves to be inadequate/unattainable or incorrectly applied: the judge - availing himself of the technical advice - could in such cases (and only in such cases, in order to avoid serious distortions of the constitutional framework) replace the technical evaluation carried out by the I.A. with his own.

This path would appear to be the most rational and coherent with the system; in fact, in the absence of an ex ante control by the administrative authority, an intense ex post control by the judicial authority would be absolutely necessary to correct the technical appreciation made by the I.A.

Such reflection undermines those theoretical doctrinal reconstructions according to which the activity of technical evaluation is reserved to the P.A. (it *being understood that their reliability would already be indirectly denied by the recognition of the power of technical evaluation at the head of the* P.A.), among which stands out the one that derives the existence of a reserve of technical evaluation at the head of the P.A. from the principle of good performance enshrined in Article 97 of the Constitution.

Establishing that the P.A. must efficiently satisfy the needs of the community is not the same as excluding that there are other entities capable of making technical assessments in a more efficient manner. On the contrary, it seems probable that the Constituent Assembly had decided to introduce this rule precisely because of the fact that, often and often, the P.A. struggled - as, moreover, still happens today - to guarantee an adequate standard of efficiency.

It follows that it would be absolutely unreasonable to assume the existence of a reservation of administration (also) in respect of non-discretionary assessments. Even if, on balance, since the IA system adopted is in fact part of the P.A. itself, such reservation would in any case - in a different form - be guaranteed.

The principle of fullness and effectiveness of judicial protection - which can be derived from a joint reading of Articles 24 and 113 of the Italian Constitution - and the principle of equality of the parties to proceedings under Article 111(2) of the Italian Constitution, a corollary of the principle of due process and a specification of the broader principle of equality enshrined in Article 3, require that the parties to proceedings must be given the same rights and obligations as the parties to the proceedings. - and that of parity between the parties to the proceedings pursuant to Article 111, paragraph 2, of the Italian Constitution, a corollary of the principle of due process as well as a specification of the broader principle of equality enshrined in Article 3, require that "*all those judgments that do not impose the only choice reserved to the administration, which is that of opportunity/untimeliness, cannot be considered excluded from judicial review*".

This approach was also confirmed by the Strasbourg Court, which clarified that:

"*in a given case where full jurisdiction is contested, the proceedings could still satisfy the requirements of Article 6 § 1 of the Convention if the court deciding the matter would examine all of the plaintiff's claims on the merits, point by point, without ever having to decline jurisdiction in answering the questions or establishing the facts. By contrast, the Court found violations of Article 6 § 1 of the Convention in other cases where national courts had considered themselves bound by the previous findings of administrative bodies, which were decisive for the outcome of the cases before them, without independently examining the relevant issues.*"

(Judgment of 31 July 2008, Case 72034/01, Družstevní záložna Pria and Others v. the Czech Republic)

The judge could repeat in its entirety the technical assessment carried out by the I.A. - even if complex - and would not be bound by it in any way; in fact, a judicial review limited to the verification of the legitimacy and manifest unreasonableness of the robotized decision would be contrary to constitutional and European principles, as well as the rulings of the European Court of Human Rights.

Recognition of the power of technical assessment in the hands of the public authority would require overcoming the traditional orientation of the so-called weak intrinsic review, inaugurated in 2001 by the Council of State - according to which, under the general jurisdiction of legitimacy, the judge could verify the suitability/adequacy of the technical criterion used by the public authority and the correctness of its application procedure, but not, by applying the principle of separation of powers, replace the public authority. and the correctness of its application procedure, but not, in application of the principle of separation of powers, to substitute itself for the public authority to the advantage of the so-called strong intrinsic - hence substitutive - review, which to date is commonly held to be exercisable only in the matter of sanctions imposed by the Competition and Market Authority (Council of State, Sec. VI, judgment no. 4990/2019).

3

Substitutions and Algorithms

A Commentary on the Judgment of the Court of Turin

The judgment of the Court of Turin, Employment Section, 19 September 2024, which declared the algorithm for assigning substitutions to be non-functional, provides an opportunity to reflect on the regulation of automated systems, highlighting the need to reconcile the protection of personal data with the correct use of artificial intelligence to ensure a responsible and fair use of technology.

This judgment highlighted the risks associated with the use of algorithms in automated decision-making processes. In this specific case, an algorithm used by the Ministry of Education and Merit (MIM) for the assignment of substitutes unfairly disadvantaged a teacher, demonstrating how even apparently neutral systems can hide implicit biases and produce discriminatory effects.

The algorithm, based on an analysis of the scores and preferences expressed by the teachers, assigned the applicant a partial contract, denying her the possibility of obtaining a full-time position: instead of ensuring fairness in the allocation of school assignments, it ended up penalising the teacher, assigning the remaining hours to less deserving colleagues and causing a clear violation of the principles of impartiality.

The case raises crucial questions about the transparency and reliability of automated decision-making processes and, in any case, of artificial intelligence systems that significantly impact the legal sphere of data subjects. While these systems offer the possibility to analyse large amounts of data quickly and efficiently, they also pose serious risks to privacy and fairness, especially when the decisions taken have a significant direct impact on people's lives.

The EU Data Protection Regulation No. 679 of 2016 ('GDPR') and the recently enacted Artificial Intelligence Regulation No. 1689 of 2024 ('AI Act') set out a number of requirements that automated decision-making processes must comply with in order to ensure that individuals' rights are protected. Among these, transparency, accountability and human oversight are key elements.

Although the Court merely declares the malfunctioning of the algorithm without elaborating on its privacy implications, the ascertained assignment error could be a symptom of a possible lack of adaptation of the algorithm to the fundamental

DOI: 10.1201/9781003731290-7

principles of data minimisation, accuracy and security, which must be respected in any processing of personal data, including those relating to automated decision-making processes (as required by Articles 5 and 32 GDPR).

On the other hand, automated decision-making should respect high standards of protection and that adequate control mechanisms are in place to ensure data integrity and prevent breaches that could jeopardise regulatory compliance or expose personal information to unlawful processing. Data protection, in the context of automated selections such as the one under consideration, is not limited to compliance with sector-specific rules, but is an essential prerequisite for consolidating the trust of data subjects and ensuring the proper functioning of public systems.

The case raises questions, therefore, not only in terms of privacy but also and especially in terms of the potential bias of the automated process against the data subjects. Automated decision-making' is to be understood as a decision - with binding legal effects on a natural person - taken by an algorithm, often based on artificial intelligence, without human intervention, by processing specific data.

These systems are progressively influencing crucial areas of everyday life, such as the selection of candidates for job positions or the granting of loans ('credit scoring' [1]). By replacing human decisions, algorithmic evaluations require rigorous control, especially when they involve sensitive areas such as education, careers and professional advancement. Algorithmic assessments creep into the lives of individuals, eventually replacing human decisions.

The GDPR places strict limits on the use of these processes that in fact allow decisions to be made using technological means without the intervention of a human being. Pursuant to Article 22, the provision also establishes a general prohibition on the use of automated decision-making processes under three cumulative conditions: (1) that the decision is based solely on automated processing, including profiling; (2) that the decision produces legal effects; (3) that the decision significantly affects the natural person (CJEU 7/12/2023, C-634/2021).

Data subjects whose data are subjected to an automated decision-making process should have the right to access clear and understandable explanations about the functioning of the algorithm and the logic behind the decisions taken by the algorithm. This principle of transparency is essential to ensure that data subjects can understand how their data are processed and how decisions affecting them are made.

The GDPR provides for real safeguards to protect individuals, to prevent automated decision-making from adversely affecting their rights: the party carrying out the automated decision-making process should implement appropriate measures to guarantee the data subject at least the right to obtain human intervention in the automated decision-making process, as well as to express his or her opinion and challenge the decision.

Human intervention is a key aspect. Any review should be conducted by a person with the appropriate authority and competence to modify the decision. The person responsible for such a review should make a thorough assessment of all relevant data, including any additional information provided by the person concerned.

Recital 71 of the GDPR emphasises that: "In any event, such processing should be subject to adequate safeguards, which should include specific information to the data subject and the right to obtain human intervention, to express one's opinion, to obtain an explanation of the decision reached after such assessment and to contest the decision."

Transparency of the process therefore becomes indispensable since the person concerned will only be able to challenge a decision or express his or her opinion if he or she is put in a position to fully understand how the decision was made.

In the case of the Court of Turin, it is possible to assume that the malfunctioning of the algorithm has compromised not only the right to the correct allocation of school assignments, but also the right to transparency and comprehensibility of the decision-making process affecting them. These principles are crucial to ensure that automated processing not only complies with the law, but is also perceived as fair and legitimate by the data subjects, preventing any abuse or error that could damage their rights.

In view of the principle of accountability, when implementing automated decision-making processes, one should in fact ensure:

- Transparency: data subjects should be informed in a clear and comprehensible manner about how the processing works, including the logic behind the algorithm;
- accuracy and minimisation: processing should be accurate and limited to data that are strictly necessary. The attribution errors highlighted by the judgment suggest possible shortcomings in compliance with these principles, with a direct impact on the rights of data subjects;
- Security: according to Article 32, the system should be designed to ensure the integrity and protection of personal data, preventing breaches and misuse.

Finally, the affair also gives rise to important points for reflection with reference to the broader context of European artificial intelligence legislation. The algorithm used by MIM undoubtedly falls within the application space of the AI Act:

- reliability and accuracy: testing the system to ensure correct performance free of systematic errors, such as those found in this case;
- Transparency and intelligibility: it is mandatory that algorithms are documented and that their decisions are comprehensible, both to citizens and public operators;
- Human supervision: the algorithm's decisions should be monitored and validated by a human subject, especially when they may affect the fundamental rights of the people involved.

In other words, a system that fully complies with the applicable regulations on the subject should have ensured accuracy, consistency and non-discrimination in its decisions arising from and affecting the legal sphere of the person concerned.

The system used by MIM, on the other hand, likely failed these basic requirements. The error in the allocation of assignments may have resulted from inadequate decision-making logic, as well as a lack of prior verification and testing, and ended up undermining the lecturers' right to fair and transparent management of job opportunities, with significant effects on their professional standing.

It is necessary, therefore, that any AI-based system be designed and implemented following an approach that combines transparency, accountability and protection of individual rights, making technology a means to promote equity and justice, and not a source of new inequalities or inefficiencies.

In this specific case, the judgment under comment belongs to the wide-ranging litigation concerning precarious personnel in public schools of all levels. Some preliminary remarks on the jurisdiction of disputes are also useful for cases, such as this one, in which administrative acts with a general content are at issue.

Alongside the posts available for tenure, the school, as is well known, also hires teachers with fixed-term employment contracts, corresponding to the so-called substitutions, and this type of recruitment also takes place through rankings. This being the case, with specific reference, at first, to the "graduatorie ad esaurimento" (so-called GAE), an institution analogous to the provincial lists for substitutions (so-called GPS), and, subsequently, with reference to the latter, administrative jurisprudence has upheld:

- first, that the procedure for the formation and amendment of the exhaustive lists is not competitive in nature, with the result that the jurisdiction of the administrative court cannot be established;
- moreover, that the acts of management of the rankings themselves are taken with the powers of the employer, so that, in order to identify which court has jurisdiction, it is necessary to verify whether the appeal concerns a particular act of management of the rankings or a general administrative act, and, therefore, whether it concerns subjective rights or legitimate interests (Cons. Stato, Ad. plen, 12/7/2011, no. 11; T.A.R. Campania Salerno, Sec. I, 11/10/2019, no. 1732; T.A.R. Lazio Roma, Sez. III-bis, 30/10/2017 no. 10803; T.A.R. Piemonte, Sez. I, 8/9/2017, no. 1055; T.A.R. Calabria Reggio Calabria, Sez. I, 15/3/2017, no. 210; T.A.R. Lombardy, Milan, Sec. IV, 13/6/2014, no. 1564);
- that, in addition, the phase subsequent to the conclusion of the competition procedure is outside the jurisdiction of the administrative judge, so that the position of the person who has been successfully placed in the ranking list and who claims the right to be hired falls within the jurisdiction of the ordinary courts, unless the dispute concerns the alternative between the selection process and the call for a new competition, which falls within the jurisdiction of the administrative judge (T.A.R. Lazio, Rome, Sec. III-bis, sentence no. 12631 of 7/12/2021 and T.A.R. Campania, Naples, Sec. IV, sentence no. 7763 of 13/12/2022).

The institution of the so-called teacher's charter should be placed in the context of the school teacher training system. Article 282 of Legislative Decree no. 297/1994 establishes, in paragraph 1, that "*refresher training is a fundamental right and duty of inspection, management and teaching staff (...) understood as the adaptation of knowledge to the development of science for individual disciplines and in interdisciplinary connections; as the deepening of teaching preparation; as participation in research and teaching-pedagogical innovation*".

Consistently, according to Article 63 of the Education and Research CCNL 2016–2018, "training constitutes a fundamental strategic lever for the professional development of staff, for the necessary support to the objectives of change, for an effective human resources development policy". Article 64 of the same CCNL then states that "participation in training and refresher courses is a right for staff as it is functional to the full realisation and development of their professionalism".

There is no doubt that the training right-duty proclaimed and reaffirmed by the aforementioned regulations concerns not only tenured staff, but also so-called substitute or precarious staff, since there is no distinction in this sense in the aforementioned regulations. The Council of State, Sez. VII, 16/3/2022, no. 1842 was very clear in this sense, highlighting the need for training of the entire teaching staff, tenured and non-tenured, necessary for the provision of school services.

The so-called teacher's charter was introduced by Article 1, paragraph 121 of Law No. 107/2015 and is to be referred primarily to the training and refresher plan and not to that of individual job endowments in the strict sense. According to the textual data, on the one hand, it is intended only for tenured teachers, manifesting a legislative direction rooted in the decision to take care, through that instrument, of the training and refresher courses for staff who represent, precisely because they are permanent employees, the underlying structure through which the educational service is provided.

On the other hand, the calibration of that amount of EUR 500 in an 'annual' measure and per 'school year' emphasises the temporal connection between that support for training and teaching, calibrating it by reason of the latter's duration.

The allocation of the teaching card only to tenured teachers intersects, in terms of labour law, with the issue of the prohibition of discrimination against fixed-term workers. The Court of Justice of 18 May 2022, on the premise that the benefit of the teacher's card relates to the sphere of "conditions of employment" (paras. 35–38) and excluding that the mere fact of the duration of the relationship can constitute an objective reason (para. 46), held that in the presence of 'the same or similar work' and therefore of comparability (paras. 41–43), clause 4(1) of the framework agreement annexed to Directive 1999/70/EC and the principle of non-discrimination enshrined therein preclude national legislation reserving that benefit only to teachers on permanent contracts. Thus, it is precisely the objective reasons pursued by the legislature, from the standpoint of supporting annual teaching, that prevent the educational benefit from being taken away from precarious teachers when the same timeframe arises. "They, in fact, when they perform a fully comparable work service, must consequently receive similar treatment" (Cass. civ., Sez. lav, sent. 27/10/2023; no. 29961).

The Court of Turin, with the judgment under comment, extends the principle also to the case of annual assignments with non-full time; after all, the Court of Cassation had also recognised the benefit to tenured teachers with weekly part-time hours, which in its horizontal variants (fewer hours every day) and vertical variants (work only on certain days) is tared over the entire school year and therefore falls within the concept of 'annual' teaching.

[1] http://www.salvisjuribus.it/i-criteri-del-credit-scoring-e-i-diritti-degli-interessati/

4

From the Judgment of the European Court of Justice of 4 July 2023 (Case C-252/21) to Paid Social Profiles

The Intervention of Ex-Post Justice That Doesn't Solve the Problem of Citizens' Data Management

The issue of the relationship between the processing of personal data by social networks, and in general by web companies, and national and European regulations is as topical as ever, especially in the broader context in which IAs become protagonists in the management and processing of personal data.

The issue is made even more complex by the fact that there has been no 'ex ante' regulation of the phenomenon, but general regulatory interventions have occurred ex post. This has meant that the regulatory process has not been free, but always conditioned by the need to balance the interests of citizens and the somewhat 'de facto acquired' rights of companies, in a context of rapid technological and process progress and a context of substantial regulatory vacuum.

The picture has not been simplified by the transnationality and transcontinentality of the phenomenon - the first truly global soft economy - which has highlighted inconsistencies and incompatibilities of regulations.

The case under comment is illustrative of the situation 'to date' and how it is destined to be only one of the first steps in a chasing process in which public slowness cannot keep pace with the technological and managerial and decision-making speed of private actors.

Hence the need to rethink, well in advance, a general framework of regulatory principles within which to act.

DOI: 10.1201/9781003731290-8

User payment plans

The decision by Meta - the social networking conglomerate of Facebook, Instagram, and WhatsApp - to introduce 'paid user plans' unveils and clarifies once and for all a misunderstanding long knowingly concealed, and when impossible to conceal, instrumentally underestimated and undersized, by the cyber-utopianism (the Silicon Valley propaganda office).

The fairy tale whereby '*we create applications that improve your life*' basically for free, and in exchange for a few 'advertising messages' from advertisers who act like 'any' other TV inertia.

And as is often the case, the price of compliance with a regulation - which always comes after the damage has been done - is passed on to the users.

But if we dig into Meta's proposal, we discover that even this formula is elusive of the meaning of the rule.

Meta has decided that there is a price to pay 'to protect one's data' on social.

From November 2023, a paid version of Facebook and Instagram will be launched for all those users who do not want to see their data used to create customised advertisements. Those who do not want to take out a monthly subscription will still be able to continue using Meta's services for free, but displaying advertisements sent based on the data collected.

"We firmly believe in an ad-supported free internet and will continue to offer free access to our products and services regardless of different budgets. We are committed to keeping people's information private and secure, in accordance with our regulations and the EU Data Protection Regulation," reads a note from the company founded by Mark Zuckerberg.

"In order to comply with changing European regulations, we are introducing a subscription option in the EU, SEA and Switzerland. In November, we will offer people using Facebook or Instagram who reside in these regions the option to continue using these personalised services free of charge with advertising, or to subscribe to stop viewing ads. The information of people who decide to subscribe will not be used for advertisements.

The decision of the European Court of Justice

The announcement comes after last July's decision of the Court of Justice of the European Union [Case C-252/21 - *Meta Platforms Inc., formerly Facebook Inc., Meta Platforms Ireland Ltd, formerly Facebook Ireland Ltd, and Facebook Deutschland GmbH* v. *Bundeskartellamt* (the equivalent of the German antitrust authority) on a reference for a preliminary ruling from the Oberlandesgericht Düsseldorf (the Dusseldorf Higher Regional Court) [1]]

The court had ruled that companies should consider [not an obligation, but an option] to offer an alternative paid service for customers who do not want their data collected.

The Court's 4 July ruling had confirmed the German government's 2019 antitrust authority ruling, which ordered Facebook to change the way it tracks users' web surfing behaviour and use of browser applications. This hindered Facebook's way of collecting data for the purpose of personalising advertising.

According to the Court, social network users must have the freedom to refuse to give their consent to particular data processing operations when these are not necessary for the performance of the contract.

"This implies that those users should be offered, where appropriate in return for appropriate remuneration, an equivalent alternative not accompanied by similar data processing operations," the judgment states.

Tariff plans

The cost of the monthly subscription will be EUR 9.99 on the web or EUR 12.99 on iOS and Android mobile devices, respectively. "Until 1 March 2024, the initial subscription will be valid for all accounts linked to the User Account Management Centre. From 1 March 2024 onwards, for each additional account entered into the User Account Management Centre, an additional charge of €6 per month will apply for subscriptions subscribed on the web, and €8 per month for those activated on iOS and Android," Meta's note reads.

It is not clear whether the user has to pay 12.99 for the account on a mobile device and also 9.99 for access from a desktop, nor whether having access from three devices to the same account (ios, android and desktop) means paying three times or the most onerous prevails, but this will be an element of ex post commercial evaluation. And we are certain that the evident excessive onerousness will be a harbinger of further action.

The economic calculation is obvious: given that the decision was arrived at in 2023 from 2019, the asymmetry of the decision-making timeframe is all in favour of private companies, which will benefit from no less than a further five years to possibly revise their pricing policies in a few days (and then start again).

The critical aspects of the ruling

While the debate has shifted to the distracting level of the appropriateness of the service subscription tariff proposal, the technical breach - which is more complex to implement and to explain and to verify - has been lost sight of in relation to the data to which Meta does not actually respond.

In fact, the ruling establishes two essential points:

- offer an alternative paid service for customers who do not want their data collected
- such users are offered, where appropriate in return for adequate compensation, an equivalent alternative not accompanied by similar data processing operations
- Meta's unspoken vulnus fails to clarify the essential point, which is that Meta implicitly on the one hand commits itself not to use that data for profiled advertising to be administered to these paying users, but does not say how it will process this data.
- Meta does not say

- who will not pick them up
- which will not use them for aggregates in the form of meta-data useful for profiling the user ecosystem
- it does not clarify or state one fact: that it involves the collection, profiling and segmentation and aggregation into forms of meta-data useful for generating advertising revenue (towards the broader set of non-paying customers)
- does not clarify how it will use this data
- does not clarify whether by advertising he means only direct advertising (sponsored content) or also indirect advertising (i.e., all forms of signalling and highlighting of content 'of interest' to the user)
- does not clarify how this user distinction will affect the internal Page and Content Rank for the selection criteria for content visible in the feeds

The Vulnerability of the Judgment

The door to continued processing of users' data is offered by the general and atechnical wording of the judgment in the passage according to which '<u>users of the social network must have the freedom to refuse to give their consent to particular data processing operations when these are not necessary for the performance of the contract</u>'.

In the interpretation 'according to Facebook' of this expression, in essence and in practice, social networks will be able to continue to process data under the interpretative shield of their 'necessity for the performance of the contract'.

The real risk, therefore, is that user data will continue - in other forms, increasingly hidden and complex and therefore difficult to identify and clarify - to be used as and more than before for profiling and aggregation, to generate revenue, with the added mockery of having opened the door to 'paid' subscription formulas.

It is not Facebook that has broken its promise to be 'free forever' but a ruling that has imposed this form of additional income on it.

And this without actually affecting the ability to collect and process users' personal information.

The ruling is important in terms of both legal principles and the position of governments in relation to the handling of their citizens' private data.

However, it risks remaining a statement of principle insofar as it does not provide for a concrete restriction on the use of 'individual data' as a component of the 'aggregate meta-data' that constitutes the true wealth (not only financial but also patrimonial) of the social networks' operating system.

It is entering technically into this logic that will be able to concretely determine the limits to an increasingly elusive and viscous management of data.

This is in order not to end up in the 'Google paradox' that states the truth when it replies that it 'cannot give access to the data held on the individual user... because it does not know them'.

Inserted in a macro-aggregate of algorithms that grind up information and re-aggregate it according to non-compartmentalised needs, in Google's meta-sphere it is technically impossible to trace back 'the user's data', and even if Google wants to, it is not able to tell and return the data to its 'owner', also because the data is now technically disjointed and has become 'something else' that can no longer even be traced back to 'the original owner's property'.

A bit like the Brazilian coffee bean ground with thousands of others and turned into coffee in any cup in Berlin: it's not just one part, or discoloured elsewhere, it's something else!

An 'old economy' approach to these dynamics is a loser in itself, not so much and not only for reasons of chronology or temporal asymmetries between the decision of the private company and those of public regulatory determination.

It is the lexical clarification of the concept of data and information that needs to be reformulated in order to be concretely adherent to its use, which is evidently different between the regulatory, judicial and social network venues.

The process of selling the meta-processed data, which is a hugely valuable asset for web companies, also remains unaffected.

Composed of aggregates of disaggregated user data (indistinct between payers and non-payers), the meta-processed data is atechnically describable in statistical terms, but on closer inspection it is much deeper than an apparently horizontal statistical description of societies and ends up becoming a truly powerful stochastic indicator of decision-making processes (as much of purchasing propensity as of political and social choice).

This datum, its elaboration, its management and its commercialisation, is not addressed in the slightest either in this judgment or in the regulatory decision-making process, which in truth should act according to the principle of greater (preventive) protection and not ex post, as a regulatory moment damning the fact already accomplished (which as the environmental impact issues demonstrate is difficult to remedy).

The vulnus in this case lies in the continuous revolving door between public and private, where private companies - which can pay much higher salaries - have a greater capacity to absorb 'the best minds' for the definition of their processes, and also have the fullest purses to finance the places of scientific research, where these processes are studied, imagined and designed, and from where the remedies and solutions to the degeneration of their uses should come.

But this is an endemic evil, which first affected the defence sector and then the health sector, and from which the silicon-valley-philosophy has only taken the most recent discouragements and immediate remedies, other sectors having dealt with the belated antitrust and conflict-of-interest regulations before them.

[1] https://curia.europa.eu/juris/document/document.jsf?text=&docid=275126&pageIndex=0&doclang=IT

5

ChatGPT vs. Privacy Guarantor

The Garante per la Privacy has notified OpenAI (the company that owns ChatGPT) of objections for breach of privacy due to non-existent information, lack of legal basis for the collection and processing of personal data for algorithm training purposes, and lack of verification of users' age.

ChatGPT, the best known relational artificial intelligence software, has rapidly acquired millions of users, bringing the potential of artificial intelligence to the fore.

Following the dissemination of this product, the European Supervisory Authorities put the numerous processing operations of personal data carried out by ChatGPT under the magnifying glass, and the Italian Garante, first of all, on 30 March 2023, imposed a restriction on processing, pursuant to Article 58(2)(f) of European Regulation 679/2016.

A first immediate finding was how, in just a few days, so many actors (content creators, web agencies, professional programmers) - who claimed to operate with 'human resources' - suffered a real blackout.

From an audit carried out on the operation of the platform, the Garante had found that no information was provided to the users, nor to the data subjects whose data were collected by OpenAI, L.L.C. and processed through the ChatGPT service, also pointing out the absence of an appropriate legal basis in relation to the collection of personal data and their processing for the purpose of training the algorithms underlying the operation of ChatGPT.

In addition, he had been able to verify that the processing of personal data of the persons concerned was inaccurate and that any verification of the age of the users was absent.

The absence of filters for minors under the age of 13 exposes them to responses that are totally unsuitable in relation to their level of development and self-awareness, which is why, pursuant to Article 58(2)(f) of the Regulation, it ordered, as a matter of urgency, the measure of provisional restriction of processing (in fact interrupting the service), considering that there was a breach of Articles 5, 6, 8, 13 and 25 of the Regulation.

In the absence of any verification mechanism, this provisional limitation was extended to all personal data of data subjects established on Italian territory.

Following the meeting between OpenAI's top management and the Guarantor's Board, which took place by videoconference, the day after the notification of the

DOI: 10.1201/9781003731290-9

measure, while reaffirming its conviction that it complies with the rules on the protection of personal data, the US company had confirmed its willingness to collaborate with the Italian Authority with the aim of reaching a positive solution to the critical issues identified by the Guarantor regarding ChatGpt.

An article on 5 April on the American company's website, for its part, reiterated its commitment to keeping artificial intelligence safe and profitable.

"Our users around the world have told us that ChatGPT helps increase their productivity, enhance their creativity and provide tailored learning experiences. The company also recognises that, like any technology, these tools carry real risks, so it works to ensure that security is built into the system at all levels. For example, after our latest model, GPT-4, finished training, we spent more than 6 months working across the organisation to make it more secure and aligned before releasing it publicly.

"We actively engage with governments on the best form such regulation could take. We work hard to prevent predictable risks before deployment, however, there is a limit to what we can learn in a lab. Despite extensive research and testing, we cannot predict all the beneficial ways people will use our technology, nor all the ways they will abuse it. That's why we believe that learning from real-world use is a key component in the creation and release of increasingly secure artificial intelligence systems over time'.

"One of the key objectives of our security efforts is the protection of children. We require people to be at least 18 years old or at least 13 years old with parental approval to use our artificial intelligence tools and are reviewing verification options. We do not allow our technology to be used to generate content that incites hatred, harassment, violence or for adults, among other categories. Our latest model, GPT-4, is 82 per cent less likely to respond to requests for disallowed content than GPT-3.5, and we have established a robust system to monitor for abuse. We have made significant efforts to minimise the potential for our models to generate content that harms children. For example, when users attempt to upload child pornography to our image tools, we block it and report it to the National Centre for Missing and Exploited Children."

Regarding privacy, in particular, OpenAI made it known that it did not use the data to sell services, advertisements or create user profiles, but to make the system more useful for people, that it took technical measures to remove personal information from the training dataset, to refine the templates in order to refuse requests for personal information from individuals, and to respond effectively to requests from individuals to remove their personal information from our systems.

So far, it is the standard response of companies loyal to cyber-utopianism: 'we do it for you, to improve your life... give us the data because we need it to improve a service that is essential to improving your lives'.

Forget OpenAI that their service is chargeable, that training AI machines costs money, and they need data: it is like us giving away petrol (our data) to walk the car (owned by them) that they then rent to us (for a fee).

Perhaps giving a correct metaphor helps to better understand a discourse that appears decidedly opaque, or at least unclear.

The consequence of the above-mentioned interlocutions is the notification on 29 January of the notice of objection for violating data protection regulations, which, although not a public act, will contain the arguments that have already been partly resolved following the reopening of ChatGPT for Italian users. The counter-deductions of the US company must be received by the independent Authority within 30 days. In the definition of the proceedings, the Garante will take into account the ongoing work of the special task force, set up by the Board that brings together the EU Data Protection Authorities (Edpb) and that will have the task of promoting cooperation and exchanging information on the possible control actions carried out by the European data protection authorities.

6

Liability for Chatbot Error

A Commentary on the Case Moffatt vs. Air Canada

The principle of the Canadian judgement is simple and clear: if a chatbot provides misleading information, the site operator is liable for it due to a duty of care.

The increasingly frequent use of chatbots, i.e., systems capable of autonomously providing answers to a user based on requests made, fuels the debate concerning legal liability in the event of error or inaccuracy in the answers provided by automated software.

In the measure under review, the Canadian British Columbia Civil Resolution Tribunal (BCCRT) analyses the issue in light of the legal principles of duty of care and legitimate expectations.

Fact

Following a family bereavement, Mr. Moffat booked a return ticket to Toronto on Air Canada's website. During the booking process, he used the online chatbot to find out whether the company offered discounts for travel caused by family bereavement. The chatbot then instructed the user about the discounted fares available and how to access them, adding that if the ticket was purchased at the full price, it would still be possible to take advantage of the reduction by proving the cause of bereavement and asking Air Canada, within 90 days of purchase, to refund the difference between what was paid and the reduced price. Mr. Moffat, given the urgency of the moment, therefore decided to purchase the tickets at full price, to then take advantage of the reimbursement once he returned, but Air Canada rejected his subsequent request on the grounds that the company's policy did not in fact foresee any reimbursement after the fact (as foreseen in the section of the website dedicated to the modalities of use of the reduced fares in the case of travel caused by bereavement). Mr. Moffat then showed the chatbot's reply to the company, which, while acknowledging the error, denied its responsibility for the incident on the ground that the automated software "reasoned" autonomously and could not be foreseen beforehand.

DOI: 10.1201/9781003731290-10

The position of the BCCRT

The court analysed the case from a purely civil law perspective.

Firstly, Mr. Moffat's claim was framed as a tort of negligence - a civil action analogous to negligent misrepresentation in civil law -, and in particular as an alleging negligent misrepresentation: this occurs when a seller, on whom there is a duty of care, causes damage to a customer due to inaccurate and misleading statements. To obtain compensation, the injured party must prove in court the inaccurate nature of the statement, the breach of the duty of care on the part of the seller, the causal link, and the amount of the damage. The Canadian court therefore agreed that, under the duty of care, Air Canada was liable for all information provided to the user through its website, regardless of the specifics.

The chatbot, although considerably more articulate than the static web page, is still a component of Air Canada's website, lacking an existence of its own and incapable of being legally accountable for its actions: hence the liability of Air Canada for damages caused by inaccurate information provided by its chatbot.

It is to be considered irrelevant that the user could have realised the inaccuracy of the chatbot's answer by carefully consulting the webpage: according to the Judge, he had no reason to doubt the accuracy of the chatbot's answer, nor possibly to consider it less reliable than what was written on Air Canada's website.

In conclusion, the court recognised the existence of a legitimate presumption of reliance on the plaintiff such as to exempt him from any involvement in the misrepresentation.

A general reflection

The Canadian court's reasoning aims to emphasise the duty of care in order to prevent the vendor from exonerating himself from liability arising from the use of automated software by invoking an alleged 'legal liability of the software'.

Despite the differences between common-law and civil-law systems, on closer inspection, even in a civil-law system the same conclusions could be reached as in the present case, due to the provision of a strict liability regime for those who make use of the aforementioned automated software.

The principle of liability must be more broadly traced back to the fact that the site owner cannot consider himself exonerated by claiming that the automated software 'reasons' autonomously and cannot be foreseen beforehand.

It is the programming and definition of the response criteria, the resources that the computer system accesses to retrieve the information to be processed, and the programming algorithm underlying the processing of the information returned in terms of response, which is the precise responsibility of the person who enters these systems.

The chatbot, although considerably more articulate than the static web page, is still a component of the website, lacking an existence of its own and incapable of being legally accountable for its actions:

In fact, one of the frontiers of the possible de-liability of companies could be precisely the 'creation of an environment' (chatbots, automated response systems, etc.) that is in fact capable of de-liabilising the entity with respect to the information returned, an environment that is in fact ontologically itself not responsible.

Hence the need for clear a priori principles that do not allow for loopholes.

7

Artificial Intelligence
The Proposed Directive on Non-Contractual Liability

The EU Commission has presented a proposal for a directive on the adaptation of tort law to artificial intelligence (accompanied by an impact assessment), an issue which, according to a survey carried out by the EU Commission in 2022, is one of the three barriers to the use of AI by European companies.

In view of the fact that national liability rules, in particular fault-based liability rules, are not suitable for dealing with liability actions for damage caused by AI-based products and services, this proposal - which is part of the broader framework of AI regulation in the EU, including the so-called AI Act and the review of product safety rules - aims to promote the deployment of reliable AI by ensuring that those who have suffered damage caused by AI enjoy equivalent protection to that enjoyed by those who have suffered damage caused by AI. IA Act and the revision of product safety regulations - aims to promote the spread of reliable AI by guaranteeing those who have suffered damage caused by AI protection equivalent to that enjoyed by those who suffer damage caused by other products.

The Proposal applies to non-contractual liability civil actions brought after the date of transposition of the Directive by parties directly harmed by the IA, parties subrogated/surrogated to the rights of the injured party by the IA (e.g., heirs; insurance company) and parties acting on behalf of one or more injured parties (representative actions), in order to obtain compensation for damage caused by the output of an IA system or the failure to produce an output (that should have been produced by that system) under fault-based liability regimes.

The new liability regime is thus intended to be applicable to products and services based on AI systems, with an impact on a very large (and today undetermined) number of industries.

The main objective of the directive is to introduce simplifications to the burden of proof for any party bringing an action for damages caused by AI systems in a Member State, in order to overcome the main problems encountered in the area of civil liability, namely:

DOI: 10.1201/9781003731290-11

- uneconomic: national liability rules are often difficult to apply to the subject of IA (in particular, in relation to the identification of the liable party);
- uncertainty: national rules may, moreover, be interpreted differently according to the appreciation of the national court;
- Fragmentation: an aspect resulting from specific adaptations to AI by national liability rules.

It introduces the right for the injured party to obtain in court evidence on the so-called 'high-risk' AI system, by means of a judicial order to disclose such evidence: this constitutes, in fact, an objective and effective means of identifying the persons responsible, and the relevant evidence, net, however, of any inherent limitations, such as, first and foremost, the protection of trade secrets and confidential information.

The directive aims to provide an effective basis for claims for damages in relation to fault consisting in non-compliance with a duty of care under Union or national law: on this point, therefore, in Article 4(1) of the directive, a targeted rebuttable presumption of causality has been provided for in relation, precisely, to the causal link between the non-compliance and the output produced by the IA system or the failure of the IA system to produce an output that caused damage.

Worthy of attention is the suggestion, included in the supplementary report to the directive, concerning the introduction of a so-called mixed regime, combining elements of fault-based liability and strict liability: specifically, the former would remain applicable in general, while the latter would be reserved for cases of damage caused by high-impact or so-called general-purpose AI systems (e.g., healthcare).

Certainly the purpose of this 'draft directive' is worthy of appreciation.

At least it is clear in the protection objectives it would like to pursue.

In this context, however, it is not clear how an action against a non-European company (like most of the better-performing ones in the field of AI) can really be exercised in a concrete manner, especially in the face of very extensive disclaimers signed by users before accepting the service. This already happens in a totally opaque manner with those extraordinary 'policy update' formulas with a kilometre-long text to be accepted per tabulas, and which no one really reads.

In addition, it has to be said that in general every form of liability recognised today benefits from insurance cover - certainly not compulsory, but - at least in theory - stipulated. In this case there are no policies on AI products.

Finally, it is good to remember that it is not possible to impose on a company a disclosure of its algorithms, the mere assumption of which jeopardises - at this time and in this context - its very ability to stay on the market and compete.

In the face of these perplexities, a contrast now emerges between the theoretical good intentions of regulation - or proposals for regulation - and the concrete reality of its applicability.

Finally, it is worth remembering that even in the presence of the obtaining "in court of evidence on the so-called 'high-risk' AI system, by means of a judicial order to disclose such evidence", it is not clear how this can be useful if "net of any inherent limitations, such as, first and foremost, the protection of trade secrets and information, the disclosure of the so-called 'high-risk' AI system is not possible". "high risk", by means of a judicial order to disclose such elements" it is not clear how this can be useful if "net of any intrinsic limits, such as, first and foremost, the protection of trade secrets and confidential information" hat falls under which anything in this field falls (e.g., during interrogation an engineer might unknowingly and involuntarily violate a trade secret), in addition to the technical fact that - if one is aiming at an 'affordable prosecution' - we do not understand how such information can be used as evidence without an adequate and costly technological infrastructure that - by 'putting the evidence to the test' i.e., by running the algorithm - confirms a finding of guilt.

8

The Use of AI in Parliamentary Processes

A First Critical Examination

Artificial Intelligence has now established itself in several areas of society and one of the main challenges for democratic institutions has been to ensure that emerging technologies, such as AI, are used ethically and effectively to improve decision-making and governance.

The latest frontier in the integration of AI with policy and regulatory processes emerges from its use in parliamentary legal activities, particularly as support for data and information analysis, language processing, decision assistance, communication and interaction between legislators and citizens.

The use and integration of Artificial Intelligence in the parliamentary field has been proposed as an opportunity to optimise decision-making processes.

But above all, due to the sensitive scope of use, it is important that the development and use of AI is accompanied by an appropriate legal and legislative framework that takes into account the challenges and risks involved.

In fact, when we speak of parliamentary activity, we are not limiting ourselves to those 'media-visible' activities, such as life in the chamber, but rather to the more technical ones, linked to the legislative and regulatory process, to the examination and interpretation of data in order to 'make a decision' that leads to the definition of a rule, which regulates human life and relations between citizens.

As AI progresses in parliamentary proceedings, the need emerges to outline precise ethical and operational guidelines aimed at ensuring accountability, transparency and the preservation of human autonomy.

This innovative process of its use should further the goals of sustainable development while preserving privacy, security and diversity.

It is becoming increasingly evident - especially on the American continent where these technologies have now pervasively entered legislative decision-making processes - that there is a need to discuss and establish ethical and operational guidelines for the introduction of AI in the parliamentary context, the balance between technological innovation and the protection of fundamental rights, and how

DOI: 10.1201/9781003731290-12

to ensure human responsibility and autonomy in the implementation of technological solutions.

In Brazil, the first 'LegisTech: the Americas' was held last year (April 2023), organised by Bússola Tech, a global Think Tank working on 'promoting institutional modernisation and digital transformation in Parliaments and Legislatures, through parliamentary diplomacy, cooperation and research'.

On their website is the portal 'LegisTech Library: archive of parliamentary modernisation', whose purpose is to monitor the evolution of modernisation and digital transformation within parliaments and legislatures, showcasing their experiences and efforts in embracing innovative solutions to improve their operations and activities.

Currently, AI can play a number of key roles in the parliamentary context, including data and information analysis (AI can be used to analyse large amounts of data and information from a variety of sources, enabling legislators to gain insight into complex issues) language processing and analysis (AI systems can be used to extract relevant information from legislative texts, politicians' statements and official documents, facilitating research and content analysis), decision-making assistance (e.g., providing predictive analysis, simulations and evaluations of legislative proposals).

In line with the process of full digitisation of the parliamentary scrutiny process of draft laws, the use of such algorithms allowed for the rapid and efficient creation and sorting of amendment files, freeing specialised operators from basic preparatory work. In this way, technology was adopted as a tool for optimising and enhancing human activity.

Awareness is a key element in ensuring that the adoption of AI, in the parliamentary context, promotes the common good and preserves democratic values and fundamental rights.

Generative Artificial Intelligence in general raises fundamental ethical and social questions, such as the possibility of algorithmic discrimination or the loss of human decision-making autonomy. Therefore, it is imperative to develop appropriate regulatory mechanisms that regulate the use of AI in law, ensuring that its benefits are fairly distributed and that the fundamental rights of citizens are preserved.

From an academic point of view, however, the exploration of GenAI requires a multidisciplinary approach, since only through a rigorous interdisciplinary analysis will it be possible to fully understand the long-term implications of the adoption of GenAI in the parliamentary context and to outline guidelines and best practices to ensure the proper use of this technology.

The key and critical issue therefore remains that of defining the working criteria of the algorithm used by the individual system, and at the same time what data the underlying machine learning engine has access to.

It is evident that the inclusion of even a potentially discriminating element, the elimination of a variable, the weight to be assigned to each criterion or variable, greatly affect the outcome of the final analysis. Worse when 'the machine' does not have access to 'all the information' but only to some (partial information) and/or the weight, relevance and reliability of the source is not even calibrated (e.g., assigning the same value to a Facebook post and a scientific article, or to a Treccani entry and the same one on Wikipedia).

Parliaments are collegial-collective bodies precisely for this reason: they constitute an assembly in which people with different sensitivities, cultural backgrounds, knowledge and sources meet and integrate, and which individually assign different weights to different information and sources. The legislative process, which is unique and synthesising, stems from this integration.

Entrusting a single entity (the AI) with these analyses and predictions means integrating the algorithm with these human differences, weighting and assigning the 'correct' weight to sources, data, information, an algorithm that - to be controllable and verifiable - should expose these criteria and weightings 'in the clear' so that both parliamentarians and citizens can intervene, verify and demand accountability for these discriminating factors.

A process that has so far never been initiated or defined in any forum.

Some examples

The use of Artificial Intelligence in the **US Parliament** represents a significant evolution in the way legislative and administrative processes are managed. AI platforms can be used to analyse large amounts of data from various sources, allowing legislators to quickly access relevant information to make informed decisions. In addition, the introduction and use of AI in the legislative processes of the US Congress and state legislatures is an area of increasing interest in contemporary governance and politics.

In 2023, some members of Congress drew attention for using ChatGPT and other LLMs to compose speeches, formulate questions and draft bills.

Massachusetts Democratic Representative Jake Auchincloss became the first member of Congress to deliver a written speech on Artificial Intelligence in the House of Representatives. The speech was delivered in support of a bill to create a joint AI research centre run by the US and Israel.

In April 2023, the Chief Administrative Officer (CAO) of the House promptly responded to the Committee on House Administration's (CHA) guidance by establishing a voluntary 'AI Working Group', formalising a structure through which Congressional staff could securely deploy new technological tools, including generative language models, and share their results anonymously. This initiative was accompanied by the CAO's issuance of a collection of best practices on safeguarding sensitive data, demonstrating a tangible commitment to AI privacy and data security.

A significant case comes from **Brazil**, where the President of the Senate has presented a bill to regulate AI, which not only defines citizens' rights in relation to its use, but also prohibits discrimination by systems based on this technology, while establishing institutional provisions for the inspection and supervision of AI systems. Just in Brazil, the Chamber of Deputies has adopted an advanced strategy in the use of Artificial Intelligence to improve the efficiency and accessibility of its legislative process through a platform called 'Ulysses', powered by Machine Learning (ML) technologies. This is characterised by its ability to analyse and categorise large amounts of documents and data, and to adapt content to the specific interests of users. It offers the public the possibility of expressing opinions, supporting or opposing bills and commenting on them. Ulysses also uses Natural Language Processing (NLP) to effectively analyse and interpret these comments. Brazilian legislators are experimenting with the use of AI-based chatbots to provide an intuitive conversational interface to citizens, allowing them to access information about: legislators, bills and budget data.

South Korea's National Assembly is also currently considering an 'AI Industry Promotion and Reliable AI Framework Act'. This is a legislative proposal that aims to consolidate seven previous AI laws into a unified regulatory framework, specifically identifying uses of AI that are considered high-risk and establishing ethical guidelines for its use. This initiative highlights the importance of a comprehensive approach to regulating AI that takes into account not only the technical and economic aspects, but also the ethical and social implications associated with this technology.

The case of **Ireland** is also particularly interesting. The adoption of guidelines on the use of Artificial Intelligence in the public sector by the Irish government (January 2024) was a notable step towards the responsible and effective implementation of this emerging technology. The guidelines are essential tools to guide the decisions and actions of government institutions in harnessing the potential of AI to improve public services while ensuring the protection of fundamental rights and transparency in decision-making.

9

Artificial Intelligence at the Service of Legal Systems

Saudi Arabia Introduces Enhanced 'Turjman' Translation Device

In an initiative to improve the efficiency and fairness of the judicial system, Saudi Arabia breaks down language barriers and introduces an AI-powered translation device called 'Turjman'.

The National Centre for Artificial Intelligence (NCAI) - SDAIA plays a key role in AI initiatives in Saudi Arabia, overseeing data management, policy-making, data platforms and the development and adoption of AI solutions. NCAI, as a division of SDAIA, focuses on research, development and implementation of AI solutions across the Kingdom.

The main objective is to take responsibility for innovation and adoption of AI in government services by developing locally sensitive solutions adapted to Saudi culture, customs and needs.

Advances in the field of Artificial Intelligence have made possible the development of increasingly sophisticated translation tools capable of understanding and translating both complex contexts and specific legal terminology.

Instruments that have the potential to significantly reduce language barriers in the justice system, allowing fairer access to justice regardless of their mother tongue.

The introduction of the advanced translation device, known as Turjman, is designed to provide instant and accurate translations in 142 languages, facilitating communication between lawyers, judges, witnesses and other parties.

These instruments can contribute to a swift resolution of disputes and greater transparency in the legal process. Of course, the use of such devices must be complemented with other measures to ensure the fair administration and enforcement of justice. For instance, it is essential to guarantee the quality and accuracy of the translations provided by the device and to ensure that all parties involved have access to adequate legal assistance in their mother tongue.

The legal system in Saudi Arabia is mainly based on Islamic or Sharia law.

DOI: 10.1201/9781003731290-13

Saudi courts deal with a wide range of legal issues, ranging from civil and commercial disputes to criminal offences.

In such a diverse context, effective communication between all parties involved is essential to ensure a fair process. It is therefore crucial to understand the role and importance of translation services, especially considering the linguistic and cultural diversity within the country.

Although Arabic is the official language of the country, there are several language communities within the Kingdom that may have difficulty understanding or communicating in Arabic. This can lead to misunderstandings, miscommunication and potential injustices in the legal process. Furthermore, with an increasing number of foreigners working and residing in Saudi Arabia, the need for effective translation services has become more and more apparent: a lack of language understanding can hinder access to justice for these communities, jeopardising their rights and procedural fairness. But it is also clear that this need has been made possible and prioritised by economic necessity, i.e., to make the country attractive to foreign investment, and to do so by offering more protective tools.

Turjman is not the first advanced translation tool to be used in the context of the Saudi legal system, nor was it the first of its kind to be implemented for this purpose.

The Saudi government's initiative to grant licences to three foreign law firms to operate in the Kingdom was a significant step towards the development of the justice sector and the anticipation of technology and Artificial Intelligence in the courts.

At the International Justice Conference in Riyadh (March 2023), the Saudi Minister of Justice, Dr. Walid Al-Samaani, highlighted the success of the Kingdom's digital legal experience, with millions of documented video sessions and verdicts issued by various courts, emphasising that the digital transformation is not only about upgrading infrastructure, but directly affects the procedures and transparency of the justice system.

The primary aim is not only to improve the efficiency of procedures, but also to increase their level of digitisation, so as to contribute, overall, to the creation of more judicial activity.

Turjman (from Arabic, 'translator' or 'interpreter') is a state-of-the-art translation device designed to overcome linguistic challenges in the Saudi legal environment.

Leveraging sophisticated Artificial Intelligence technologies, it provides instant and, basically, accurate translations in a wide range of languages.

One of its distinguishing features is the ability to translate statements and conversations in real time.

Through the use of sophisticated speech recognition and machine translation algorithms, the device is able to interpret and translate spoken language with an unprecedented level of accuracy.

This not only speeds up the legal process, but also helps to ensure a full understanding of the information conveyed during hearings or depositions by all parties involved.

Turjman is designed to be highly versatile and adaptable, capable of handling a wide range of legal contexts, from court hearings to legal negotiations. It provides reliable translations in any situation, allowing users to interact with the device easily, through an intuitive and user-friendly interface, even without advanced technical skills.

At the same conference, the Minister of Higher Education and Scientific Research, Al Mojeb, emphasised the importance of using advanced technologies and AI systems in the context of the Turjman device, with the main goal of facilitating the services offered - also and above all - to foreign pilgrims. He clarified that this project aims to ensure both the protection of their rights and the promotion of accelerated justice, i.e., it was emphasised that the handling of a case through this system should not take more than an hour.

The use of advanced technology in Turjman's device not only aims to simplify multilingual communication, but also to ensure the accuracy and reliability of translations in such a sensitive legal context.

The use of such a device entails - certainly - a number of significant benefits, such as fair access to justice, as mentioned above, a reduction in timeframes and an increase in efficiency, as it allows for faster handling of cases and a reduction in the administrative workload for courts and lawyers, and the promotion of linguistic diversity.

Moreover, it must be able to adapt to the different linguistic and cultural nuances within and outside the Saudi legal context.

Despite its many advantages, the use of Turjman, as the main resource, can also present some challenges and limitations that need to be considered.

As with any AI-based technology, its reliability depends on the accuracy and effectiveness of its translation algorithms.

It is essential to ensure that the device undergoes rigorous testing and review, as it can be used to translate sensitive and confidential information during legal proceedings. It is essential to ensure that data is protected.

The use of AI-enhanced translation devices is likely to become more and more widespread in the legal context, not only in Saudi Arabia, but worldwide.

With continued technological advances and an increased awareness of language challenges in the legal system, one can expect such devices to become an essential tool.

Therefore, it is essential to develop appropriate regulations and guidelines to ensure the effectiveness and reliability of these devices in the legal context, while continuing to invest in training legal personnel on the use of these technologies and the correct interpretation of the translations provided, in order to maximise the benefits of Turjman and other similar devices in the future.

10

Copyrights and Artificial Intelligence Systems

Legal Principles and Requirements Underlying Law in a Globalised World

The man-machine relationship has always been at the centre of copyright considerations, always shifting the boundary and periodically necessitating extensive interpretative revisions as technical innovations have enabled human 'new action'.

The essential point of innovations in the technical field, however, considered unchanged the fact that the agent-creator of the 'final product' and the 'creation process', was and always remained a human being.

For example, despite the express legislative provision on the authorship protection of a photographic work, no one doubts that a photograph constitutes an intellectual work deserving of protection. The first photographs became widespread in the mid-19th century, contributing to a heated debate not only among jurists. There were those who argued that a photograph could not be considered a creative work deserving of protection (first and foremost the publishers), insisting that the photograph was the result of a mechanical process of a camera reproducing reality without human intervention.

It was the US Supreme Court justices who settled the debate, recognising the authorial nature of the photograph entitled 'Oscar Wilde No. 18' taken by Napoleon Sarony of the writer Oscar Wilde, qualifying the photographer as the author of an original work of art.

In the words of the Court, Sarony '*did not merely use the camera placed in front of Oscar Wilde but arranged the subject in such a way as to present graceful ornamentation, managing light and shadow, suggesting and evoking the desired expression*'. Sarony was thus able to assert his copyright on the photograph against the Burrow-Giles Lithographic Company that had marketed lithographic reproductions of the work without the photographer's consent.

With this ruling, the US Supreme Court resolved the complex relationship on machine-mediated creativity.

DOI: 10.1201/9781003731290-14

Today, we have moved beyond 'machine-mediated creativity' and the debate centres on the question of the protectability of creations 'made with' artificial intelligence systems and the protectability of creations 'made by' artificial intelligence systems.

In the context of this technological revolution, more and more human authors (from the music sector, to the graphic, literary, design...) are using artificial intelligence systems to achieve a creative result with 'non-negligible' or marginal contributions from the machine or, often, see the use of data retrieved on-line to feed an A.I. system.

The traditional anthropocentric model of copyright was profoundly challenged first by the human-machine relationship, and then by the processes of 'duplication' in which the unique work became a potentially mass object. But these two phases have so far always involved an undisputed authorship: whoever was the full author of the creative work was always a human being.

In Italy, which has an avant-garde and particularly protective legislation, Law 633/1941 on copyright does not provide a definition of author nor of creativity and originality that can be useful today to understand the complexity of A.I. systems.

Both jurisprudence and doctrine have made a relevant (sometimes even supplanting and integrating) contribution to defining a creative work, i.e., a new and original work that is capable of revealing the author's personality, making a non-trivial creative contribution that differs from previous works.

In common-law systems, on the other hand, copyright depends on the threshold of originality, i.e., on three assumptions: skill (creative competence), labour (commitment, work) and judgement (ability to discern, distinguish and choose the distinctive elements of the work).

In extreme synthesis, we can say that using this threefold parameter (simultaneously subsisting and in which the elements must be at least equivalent, if not quantitatively equivalent) for Anglo-American jurisprudence, works produced with artificial intelligence systems present skills and labour. Lacking, however, is the judgement that belongs to the human being.

It is man who gives the input to the system and it is always man who decides whether the result, i.e., the output, corresponds to his taste and creative idea.

There are numerous cases in which an artificial intelligence system has written books, created paintings or musical melodies completely autonomously.

The question arose as to whether such works were protectable, and to whom such protection should go (who was the subject of the right to be protected).

Decisions denying copyright protection to works created with artificial intelligence systems include the recent order of 18 August 2023 by the Court of the District of Columbia upholding the 14 February 2022 decision by the Copyright Review Board of the U.S. Copyright Office.

This order again rejected the application for registration of the artwork entitled 'A Recent Entrance to Paradise' in the name of Steven Thaler's AI 'Creativity Machine'.

The Court denied Artificial Intelligence the possibility of being recognised as the author of a work of art because of the lack of intellectual creativity that the law reserves to humans.

To date, it is denied that an Artificial Intelligence ('AI') can be a creator of works of art (*although there are isolated cases such as the decision issued by the Chinese Court of Shenzen that granted copyright protection to an article written by an AI programme*).

In the past, works created by animals had already been denied authorial protection (*among the most emblematic cases, the mural painted by an elephant or the famous selfie, called Monkey Selfie, taken by a female macaque with a camera, deliberately left by photographer Slater*) but artificial intelligence systems force us to rethink the concept of creativity.

In addition to copyright, the question has also arisen as to whether an artificial intelligence can be considered the inventor of the system created and, therefore, the owner of the invention itself.

For example, in 2020 the EPO (European Patent Office) expressly ruled in the DABUS case that A.I. systems cannot be employees, hold inventions and transfer their rights (Article 81 and Rule 19 of the European Patent Convention).

IP offices in other jurisdictions, such as the UKIPO, USPTO and Australian Deputy Commissioner of Patents, have expressed a similar view.

The most recent regulatory interventions on the regulation of artificial intelligence with respect to IP rights are the European Parliament Resolution No. 2020/2015 on IP rights and AI-generated technologies; the establishment of an Ad Hoc Committee at the EU Council to study the AI legal framework; the 'Draft Regulation on a European Approach on AI' and the WIPO 'Open Processes' that open debates and discussions on the patentability of AI-generated intangibles.

Among the various legal issues, worthy of further study and interpretative effort, there is certainly the protection of copyright-protected works against generative A.I. platforms (exploded especially in 2022) that use already existing and copyright-protected intellectual works from which they draw 'inspiration' and input for new creative works.

Part of the doctrine has introduced a hypothetical solution in the possibility of requiring the machine, in its work of learning and creation, to use only legitimately acquired material (the so-called *'copyright by design'*).

On the other hand, artificial intelligence systems are spreading, which, through deep machine learning mechanisms called 'deep learning', generate melodies, texts and images using an enormous amount of on-line data. The A.I. system collects and extracts data from the Internet (including copyrighted content), through indistinct collection methods, so-called *web-scraping*.

The copyright holders of the content used (without consent) by A.I. tools have already taken legal action; for instance, Universal took legal action against the start-up Anthropic in connection with an A.I. model called Claude that was allegedly able to generate lyrics identical to the song *I Will Survive* by Gloria Gaynor.

Another lawsuit has been filed in San Francisco Federal Court against the companies GitHub, Microsoft and OpenAI. According to the proposed actions, their artificial intelligence software, GitHub Copilot and OpenAI Codex, have allegedly exploited a huge amount of other people's code, present in the GitHub open-source platform, to produce their own code in defiance of users' licence rights as governed by the terms and conditions of use of the platform itself.

Coinciding with Joe Biden's executive order on Artificial Intelligence, the Northern California District Court issued Order 23-cv-00201-WHO in connection with the class action brought by Sarah Andersen, Kelly McKernan and Karla Ortiz.

The artists challenged the legality of the image-generating software Stable Diffusion, Midjourney and DreamUp, owned by the companies Stability AI, Midjourney and DeviantArt respectively, complaining:

(i) copyright infringement both in the way the software used is trained (which draws on databases available online containing billions of images and photographs) and in the output generated by the artificial intelligence systems themselves due to the frequent similarity between the final product of the algorithm and the protected work of others;
(ii) infringement of the artists' image and name rights;
(iii) acts of unfair competition and breach of contract (the latter alleged by the artists only against DeviantArt).

The order is useful to understand the great evidentiary difficulties in enforcing protected content against A.I. systems.

As stated in the same decision, Stable Diffusion is a 'software library' that provides *image-generating services through a mathematical process 'Images are created through a mathematical process that is entirely based on and "derived" from the training images*'.

As explicitly recognised by Stability AI, the images released by the system are not perfectly the same as the original ones but '*in the style*' *of* the artists. The dissemination process would therefore not involve copying the images but applying mathematical equations and algorithms to capture concepts from the training images.

The artists claimed infringement of their works based on a mere search of their names at *www.ihavebeentrained.com* without being able to prove exactly which specific works, registered with the U.S. Copyright Office, had been used as images for the A.I. system training.

The Court upheld all of the defendants' *motions to dismiss* (with the exception of the claim of copyright infringement brought by Anderson v. Stability) and granted a 30-day period to amend and attempt to cure the evidentiary deficiencies in the artists' allegations so that:

(a) provide concrete evidence of works created by AI tools that are identical to their copyrighted material, expressly inviting artists to identify which works have been protected at the U.S. Copyright Office "*provided that none of the images generated by Stable Diffusion provided in response to a particular text command match a specific image in the training data.*
(b) proceed with "*a supplement to clarify their theory regarding compressed copies of training images and to set out facts to support how Stable Diffusion - a programme that is open source, at least in part - operates with respect to training images*".
(c) clarify the allegations made against Midjourney that it has apps and websites for use of Stable Diffusion, stating that "*It is unclear, for example, whether Stable Diffusion contains only algorithms and instructions that can be applied to the*

creation of images that include only certain elements of a copyrighted formation image, whether DeviantArt or Midjourney may be liable for direct infringement by offering its customers use of Stable Diffusion's 'library' through its apps and websites." In the Court's view, the reconstructions provided by the artists do not contain "*facts that support an inference that Stability is bound by the Terms of Service or that Plaintiff McKernan or others are third-party beneficiaries of specific provisions in the Terms of Service that they can sue to enforce the terms of the agreements between DeviantArt and Stability.*"

This first order is useful to understand the high difficulties of asserting, and especially proving, the infringement of rights against artificial intelligence systems.

At the same time, Stability AI was involved in another court case, filed in the Federal Court of Delaware and the High Court of Justice in London, by the Getty Images company, according to which Stability AI had copied - without the appropriate licence - numerous images, texts and metadata retrieved to train its Stable Diffusion.

Getty Images, one of the world's leading photo agencies, announced the launch of a generative AI platform capable of generating content with remuneration from the original works used to train the algorithms.

It would seem, pending details, to be a virtuous artificial intelligence system that does not merely aim to retrieve data from the Internet in a web-scrambling manner.

It is no coincidence that the majority of actions against alleged copyright infringements by A.I.'s have been brought in the US where courts apply the doctrine of '*fair use*' that allows judges to flexibly follow copyright rules and balance the needs at stake according to the specifics of the case.

In the UK, the 'fair dealing' exception has narrower limits than the US 'fair use' exception, allowing the use of someone else's work only for non-commercial purposes, e.g. for research, criticism, news reporting and personal use.

In the European Union there is the so-called Copyright Directive (no. 790/2019) which introduced an express regulation of exceptions to copyright for text and data mining operations transposed in Italy by Legislative Decree no. 177/2021 (*art. 3 Directive and art. 70-ter LDA and art. 4 Directive and 70-quater LDA*).

***

There can be many parameters to follow, and what must be sought is a useful and comprehensive approach that focuses on general considerations that are anything but merely theoretical.

First and foremost, in a globalised world, where the challenge is no longer only technical but above all technological, the timing of this development (and transformation) is exasperatingly accelerated compared to recent history, which poses quite a few difficulties for rigid ex ante regulatory systems to keep up with the times and phenomena in practice.

Globalisation itself poses serious problems for territorial management in the area of copyright protection, in a context strongly oriented in all sectors to 'forum shopping', i.e., to companies taking root in that territory that is normatively favourable, not only for tax purposes.

In this sense, the relative flexibility of common-law systems can effectively supplant and complement the traditional European positivist approach.

It is not secondary to consider that regulation 'applied in practice' is a far more powerful attractor in the AI sector than elements such as 'regulation in the abstract' or advantageous taxation: the interventions of greater corporate protection, and lesser author protection, by China, for example, should be read in this direction.

In such an articulated framework, some principles can be diriment pillars as well as other implications.

The first can focus on the precise and timely identification - also a political choice upstream - of who is ultimately worthy of protection.

Copyright stems from the need to protect - and thus stimulate - human creativity, ingenuity, and its capacity to generate widespread progress, in every field, from scientific research to the expressive arts.

In this frame of reference, the subject of protection remains man, and thus settling the question of proprietorship, it is clear that only if an IA considers itself to be creative, and at the same time self-conscious of its creative act, and if it considers the IA to have 'created something independently worthy of protection on account of originality', then the IA itself must also - on its own - be 'capable' with its 'legal personality' of taking legal action to enforce its rights.

Until this happens - and not partially, but by realising the elements mentioned in full - the IA cannot be a 'copyright holder'.

In fact, in concrete terms, it is the CEOs of IT companies who are acting, and the copyright that may be recognised goes to the company - understood as a subject and as an organisation of men - and not to the allegedly 'declared and asserted author', i.e., the IA.

Already this element, of who decides, of who is aware, of who acts in court, is diriment to affirm that the IA does not have a legal personality autonomously capable of creative action, and is not capable of enforcing the resulting right.

Certainly, the upstream copyright of those who programmed and implemented the functions and algorithms 'with which' the AI machine works is protectable - and indeed is protected as such.

Consequently, the 'fruits' of such an algorithm and of the fully understood functionality are derivative and consequential products of the same process already - and rightly - protected. But they are not 'something new', nor something different, nor something original.

Ultimately, we are now at the same manipulation of digits as a calculator, which returns a result given an input, following upstream programming.

As long as human mediation is required, and as long as there is no truly proven and independent self-awareness and self-consciousness of creation itself (for which one need only ask a human artist or inventor what it actually consists of), an equal right to an AI cannot be recognised.

In this sense, to the 'threshold of originality' given by the three presuppositions of skill (creative competence), labour (commitment, work) and judgement (ability to discern, distinguish and choose the distinctive elements of the work), another must be added - which we consider pleonastic to ask of the human being, but which we must include in the case of AI, namely the self-consciousness and self-awareness (not assisted or supplemented by man) of the creative act, and of the final creation, as an act independent of the processing programme received from the programmer and the algorithm.

11

Image Generated By AI

For a Chinese Court Can Be Protected By Copyright

A First Comparison with American Jurisprudence

Recently, a decision by a Chinese court (Beijing Internet Court), which addressed the issue of the relationship between generative artificial intelligence and copyright, regulated by "The right of authorship under Chinese Copyright Law [1].

The court in Beijing had to rule on the protectability of a work created with the help of generative artificial intelligence.

In the present case, the plaintiff (Li), after having created, by means of the artificial intelligence text-to-image conversion software Stable Diffusion (owned by the company StabilityAI), the image of a young Asian woman, published it on the Chinese social platform 'Xiaohongshu'.

Shortly afterwards, he realised that the image had been published, without authorisation or licence, by a blogger on another content sharing platform.

On this basis, Li brought the case before the Beijing Internet Court, which was faced with three main issues:

(a) whether the image in question may constitute a 'work of art' under Chinese copyright law,

(b) whether he can be qualified as the author of that work, and finally

(c) whether the other party, by republishing the image, has infringed the plaintiff's copyright.

In a decision that will have far-reaching implications for future litigation on the subject, the Chinese court answered these questions with the following reasons.

DOI: 10.1201/9781003731290-15

(a) Whether the image in question may constitute a 'work of art' under Chinese copyright law

The court applied a four element test to determine whether the challenged image constitutes a work under China's Copyright Law: (1) belonging to the fields of literature, art or science; (2) possessing originality; (3) having a form of expression; and (4) being the result of 'intellectual achievement'. He paid special attention to the elements of 'intellectual achievement' and 'originality'.

"Intellectual achievement" refers to the result of the intellectual activities of a human being. The intellectual activity of the plaintiff manifests itself from the conception to the final realisation of the contested image. Through stable dissemination, the plaintiff selected over 150 suggestions, organised their order and set specific parameters. He continued to adjust and modify those suggestions and parameters until the final image aligned with his conception. These steps sufficiently demonstrate that the disputed image was created as a result of the plaintiff's intellectual input.

Furthermore, 'originality' manifests itself in the customised choices and aesthetic judgement of the Applicant throughout the generation process. This involved not only the selection and arrangement of prompts and parameters, but also the refinement of the final output. Therefore, such 'intellectual achievements' transcended the merely 'mechanical' ones lacking originality.

(b) Whether he can be qualified as the author of that work

On the second question, the court first ruled out the possibility that the AI model could be an author because Article 11 of China's Copyright Law explicitly limits the definition of 'author' to natural or legal persons. Moreover, the designers of the AI model are not authors since their intellectual contribution lies in the creation of the AI tool rather than the generated image itself.

On the contrary, the plaintiff deliberately selected and organised multiple suggestions that led to the creation of the contested image. Acknowledging his direct intellectual contribution, the court attributed authorship to the plaintiff. However, the court emphasised the need to disclose the use of artificial intelligence as a matter of good faith and publicity.

In this sense, the Chinese court's decision is also interesting for European legal systems, in the sense that it adopts a parameter often used by the Court of Justice, recognising protection when the author has made a selection among several available technical possibilities (see, e.g., *Painer*, C-145/10, EU:C:2013:138, which, referring to Recital no. 17, stated that a "creation is the author's property if it reflects his personality" and that "the author has been able to express his creative capacities in the production of the work by making [...] a selection among several technical possibilities"). 17 of the Rental Directive, stated that a '*creation is the author's property if it reflects his personality*' and that '*the author has been able to express his creative abilities in the production of the work by making [...] free and creative choices in various ways and at various points in his production*').

Likewise, originality would manifest itself in the author's personalised choices (i.e., his ability to select between different options) and aesthetic judgement throughout the generation process. This would involve not only the selection and organisation of suggestions and parameters, but also the refinement of the final output. Therefore, such 'intellectual results' transcended mere 'mechanical' commands lacking in originality.

Historically, authorship protection is granted to human beings who are capable of expressing creativity and originality; the tools used are at most "extensions" that help the author express himself, i.e., they are objects in the hands of human beings, who use them to realise works of genius. In common law jurisdictions, the idea is widespread, typical of utilitarian doctrine, that *copyright* should aim at a social utility, increasing wealth [on this theory, for all see J.C. Fromer, *Expressive Incentives in Intellectual Property*, Virginia L. Rev. 1745 (2012) with the further references cited *therein*]: now, granting rights to automated creations, in which there is no intellectual effort and in which artificial intelligence technologies can easily and quickly generate text, drawings, sounds, and so on, creates an economic disincentive to create works.

If we start from the idea that copyright is an incentive, even an economic one, to creativity, then it should be agreed that the decision to deny authorial protection to the creation of works generated autonomously by a machine is justified by the need not to create monopolistic positions, in the absence of a creative effort and real commitment on the part of the author. Moreover, although service providers allow users to use the works created, they reserve a co-licence on them.

The same approach seems to have guided the Chinese court, which denied citizenship to the possibility that rights were granted to the developer of the machine. On this point, there is an interesting passage, in which the court dwells on the identification of the subject, deemed to be the user of the system, who would have made an "intellectual investment" and whose works (i.e., the images) would reflect, in the words of the decision, his "personalised expression".

Therefore, although the point is not made explicit in the grounds, it would seem that the judges' opinion distinguishes between the rights granted for the development of software and the works generated, by means of a process of selection among several alternatives, by a user: two distinct rights, a solution that is also appreciable from the perspective of Union law, which distinguishes between the rights granted to developers and those granted to authors who use the software.

(c) Whether the other party, by republishing the image, has infringed the plaintiff's copyright.

On the third point, the court held that the defendant had removed the original watermark of the image, which indicated the identity of the plaintiff as the creator of the image, and the defendant could not provide the specific source from which it had acquired the image. The Court therefore found that Defendant had infringed Plaintiff's copyright.

In assessing whether the defendant is liable for infringement of the other party's copyright, the Chinese Court refers to the deletion of the so-called watermark. Specifically, *watermarking* technology consists in affixing a sort of electronic watermark to an image created by an artificial intelligence model, capable of permanently marking that work. Such marking, in the work used by the respondent, was absent.

On the basis of all these premises, the Beijing Internet Court held the latter liable for infringement of the plaintiff's copyright, for publishing, without authorisation or licence, the image created through the use of artificial intelligence software and for also removing the *watermark* from the image.

The main policy objective behind the BIC decision is to promote innovation through the latest generative artificial intelligence technologies. The court held that copyright law should be applied to incentivise creativity and innovation using the latest tools, which requires the adaptation of traditional copyright frameworks to the evolution of artificial intelligence technologies. In a recent interview, the judge presiding over the *Li vs. Liu* case reiterated this policy consideration, emphasising the importance of this decision in setting a clear guide for future innovators in the field of artificial intelligence.

The United States and China: two approaches to the copyright of content generated by artificial intelligence (AIGC)

While the BIC ruling stated that the activation of an artificial intelligence tool from text to image could be sufficient creative involvement to be considered the author of the resulting image, recent US Copyright Office (USCO) rulings reach the opposite result.

The USCO published a registration guide [2] rejecting in particular material produced through guided technology where the use of artificial intelligence is more than minimal. First, it refused to register a copyright claim on a work that would have been created independently by an artificial intelligence without human prompting, see A Recent Entry to Paradise [3],a ruling upheld by a US District Court in Thaler v. Perlmutter [4].

Although this ruling is probably consistent with the BIC's interpretation of Chinese law, the USCO has since refused to register copyright claims on works created through substantial iterative suggestion of a generative artificial intelligence tool, see Théâtre D'opéra Spatial and Zarya of the Dawn [5].

Such rulings take a narrower view of authorship, according to which a human prompter of an artificial intelligence tool will not be considered an author of the output if the details of the output cannot be predicted in advance. The USCO recently reaffirmed this narrower view in a letter denying registration of an AIGC for the fourth time, see Suryast [6].

First implications

Chinese courts have ruled on the eligibility of AIGC for copyright protection in Li v. Liu, but have not yet reached a consensus. In Feilin v. Baidu [7], BIC refused copyright protection of an AI-generated report due to lack of originality. However, the Shenzhen District Court granted copyright protection to an AI-generated article in Tencent v. Yingxun [8].

The *Li vs. Liu* decision again shifts the needle of the scales towards the AIGC's recognition of copyright in the Chinese copyright scheme.

It should be noted that the *Li vs. Liu* ruling was issued by the Court of First Instance and Chinese jurisprudence does not apply the common law doctrine of stare decisis. Therefore, it is undetermined whether the BIC ruling will be upheld on appeal and its effect on international intellectual property law. However, the dynamic interpretation of Chinese copyright law in the Li vs. Liu decision has brought a new perspective to the IA copyright debate.

[1] https://english.bjinternetcourt.gov.cn/pdf/BeijingInternetCourtCivilJudgment112792023.pdf
[2] https://www.federalregister.gov/documents/2023/03/16/2023-05321/copyright-registration-guidance-works-containing-material-generated-by-artificial-intelligence
[3] https://www.copyright.gov/rulings-filings/review-board/docs/a-recent-entrance-to-paradise.pdf
[4] https://ecf.dcd.uscourts.gov/cgi-bin/show_public_doc?2022cv1564-24
[5] https://www.copyright.gov/rulings-filings/review-board/docs/Theatre-Dopera-Spatial.pdf https://www.copyright.gov/docs/zarya-of-the-dawn.pdf
[6] https://www.copyright.gov/rulings-filings/review-board/docs/SURYAST.pdf
[7] https://www.chinadaily.com.cn/specials/BeijingInternetCourtCivilJudgment(2018)Jing0491MinChuNo.239.pdf
[8] https://link.springer.com/article/10.1007/s40319-020-00944-9

12

Thomson Reuters Wins First Copyright Lawsuit Against AI

The company, which combines several publishing brands, won a legal victory against Ross Intelligence for copyright infringement, setting a significant precedent on 'fair use' for AI companies.

Thomson Reuters won a major victory in the first major US litigation over alleged copyright infringements committed by an artificial intelligence company. This judicial outcome sets a high-impact legal precedent at a time when the use of copyrighted content within AI technologies is at the centre of a heated debate on a global scale.

In 2020, Thomson Reuters took unprecedented legal action against Ross Intelligence, a start-up specialising in artificial intelligence applied to legal research.

Thomson Reuters accused Ross Intelligence of copying copyrighted material from their flagship service, Westlaw, without obtaining the necessary authorisations.

Westlaw is one of the most reputable and widely used legal research services globally, making infringement particularly significant and alarming for copyright holders in the digital content sector.

The verdict, delivered by Judge Stephanos Bibas of the US Court of Appeals, set an important legal precedent. The court declared that Ross Intelligence had indeed infringed Thomson Reuters' copyrights, categorically rejecting all defences put forward by the start-up.

"None of Ross's possible defences hold water. I reject them all", Bibas said in his final judgment, emphasising the seriousness of the infringement and the ineffectiveness of the justifications presented.

This ruling not only reaffirms the importance of copyright protection in the context of emerging technologies, but also raises important questions about the application of 'fair use' in the field of artificial intelligence.

AI companies hoping to use protected materials to train their models will now have to carefully consider the legal implications of such actions.

One of the key issues in this case was the doctrine of 'fair use', which is often invoked by artificial intelligence companies to defend themselves against accusations of having used copyrighted material illegally.

DOI: 10.1201/9781003731290-16

According to Judge Bibas, Ross Intelligence's use of Westlaw's content did not fall within the parameters of fair use, as the start-up intended to compete directly with Westlaw by developing a substitute product in the market.

James Grimmelmann, professor of digital and internet law at Cornell University, said that "if this decision is followed elsewhere, it will be really bad for generative AI companies." Grimmelmann also suggested that much of the case law cited by AI companies to argue fair use could be deemed "irrelevant" as a result of this decision.

Chris Mammen, partner at Womble Bond Dickinson and intellectual property law specialist, agreed that the ruling will complicate fair use arguments for AI companies, saying it "puts a finger on the scale towards the conclusion that fair use does not apply."

Despite Thomson Reuters' victory, many AI companies, including giants such as OpenAI and Google, have the financial resources to sustain lengthy legal battles. The closure of Ross Intelligence in 2021, due to the high costs of defending themselves in court, highlights the difficulties start-ups can face.

The legal theory based on 'fair use' is a key defence for technology companies including OpenAI, Microsoft and Meta in a number of copyright infringement cases brought by authors, record labels, visual artists and others regarding the use of their material to train artificial intelligence systems.

Technology companies claim that generative artificial intelligence systems make fair use of copyrighted material, studying it to learn how to create new content, while copyright holders claim that companies use their work to generate competing content that threatens their livelihoods.

With numerous other cases pending both in the US and internationally, the Thomson Reuters vs. Ross Intelligence case may be only the first of many important legal developments in this field.

This decision not only sets a precedent, but also raises important questions about how future legal disputes will affect the AI industry.

Thomson Reuters claimed that ROSS improperly used Westlaw's headnotes and Key Number System to train its artificial intelligence system to better match legal issues to relevant case law.

The top notes of Westlaw summarise legal principles extracted from judicial opinions.

Judicial opinions are not copyrighted in the United States

The principle is well known and dates back to Banks v. Manchester , 128 US 244 (1888), a US Supreme Court decision dealing with copyright.The Court ruled that the State could not hold a copyright and upheld its decision in Wheaton v. Peters stating "what a court or judge cannot confer on a journalist as the basis of a copyright on him, he cannot confer on any other person or the State".

The Key Number System is a numerical taxonomy that categorises legal topics and cases. By clicking on a headnote, users are directed to the corresponding passage in the legal text. By clicking on the key number associated with a headnote, users are directed to a list of cases that raise the same legal point.

It is important to note that ROSS did not directly acquire the introductory notes and the Key Number System to train its model. As is often the case, companies turn to other companies or even non-profit suppliers for such actions: ROSS hired

LegalEase, a company that provides legal research and writing services, to create training data based on the introductory notes and the Key Number System.

LegalEase created Bulk Memos, a collection of legal questions paired with four to six possible answers. LegalEase instructed lawyers to use the Westlaw introductory notes as a reference for formulating the questions in Bulk Memos. LegalEase instructed the lawyers not to copy the introductory notes directly.

ROSS attempted to obtain a licence for the necessary content directly from Thomson Reuters, but the latter refused to grant it because it believed that the artificial intelligence tool being considered by ROSS could compete with Westlaw.

The court agreed that ROSS copied 2,243 headnotes from Westlaw. The court ruled that these headnotes and the Key Number System met the low legal threshold for originality and were copyrighted. The court rejected ROSS's defence because, according to the court, the use of the headnotes and the Key Number System were not dictated by necessity. The court also rejected ROSS's fair use defence on the basis that the 1st and 4th factors weighed in favour of Thomson Reuters. At this point, the only remaining issue for trial is whether the copyrights of certain headnotes had expired or had been registered late.

There are some points that have not been definitively clarified by this ruling.

Are quasi-literal summaries 'original'?

'Original' has a special meaning in US copyright law: it means that a work has a minimum of human creativity that our society would like to protect and encourage. Based on the evidence that has survived redaction, it is almost impossible to find creativity in individual footnotes. Footnotes consist of literal copies of non-copyrighted judicial texts, along with some basic paraphrases of facts.

As we know, facts are not protected by copyright, but expressions of facts often are. An important safeguard to protect our freedom to refer to facts is the doctrine of merger. US law has long recognised that when there are only limited ways to express a fact or idea, those expressions are not considered 'original'. The expressions 'merge' with the underlying unprotectable fact and become unprotectable themselves.

According to some, Judge Bibas is wrong about the merger: he argues that the merger does not apply here because 'there are many ways to express points of law from judicial opinions'. This view misunderstands the doctrine of fusion. It is in the nature of human language to be able to convey the same thing in many different ways, as long as one is willing to do some verbal acrobatics. But when there are only a limited number of reasonable and natural ways to express a fact or idea, especially when textual precision and terms of art are used to convey complex ideas, fusion applies.

With regard to the selection and arrangement of the Key Number System, the court argues that originality exists here as well, because "there are many possible and logical ways to arrange legal arguments according to level of granularity", and Thomson Reuters exercised some judgement in choosing the particular "level" with its Key Number System. However, the cases are marked with Key Number System by an automated computer system and the arguments closely mirror what law schools teach their first-year students.

The court does not say much about why the compilation of the headnotes should receive separate copyright protection, except that it qualifies as original "factual compilations". This statement is doubtful because the compilation is of non-copyrighted material, as discussed, and the selection is driven by the need to represent fact and law, not creativity. Even if the compilation of headnotes is indeed copyrighted, using parts of it that are not copyrighted is definitely not infringement because the United States does not protect sui generis database rights.

Is it not possible to claim fair use if no one has seen a copy?

The court would properly ignore in this case Bellsouth Advertising & Publishing Corp. v. Donnelley Information Publishing, Inc. , 933 F.2d 952 (11th Cir. 1991), and Sundeman v. Seajay Society, Inc., 142 F. 3d 194 (4th Cir. 1998).

In deciding whether ROSS's use of Westlaw's introductory notes and the Key Number System is transformative within the meaning of the first factor, the court holds that copying them constitutes copyright infringement because there was an intermediate copy that contained copyrighted material created by Westlaw. And, according to the court, the intermediate copy can only weigh in favour of fair use for computer code.

Suddenly we have a market for AI training?

The fourth factor of fair use is very much subject to circular reasoning: if a user makes a derivative use of my work, this surely shows that there is already a market for that derivative use or that it is likely to develop; if there is a market for that derivative use, then, as the copyright holder, I should have absolute control over that market.

In the eyes of the court, ROSS, by virtue of using Westlaw data in the context of AI training, created a legitimate market for AI training data that should be legitimately controlled by Thomson Reuters.

Only, US case law suggests that the fourth "market substitute" factor only considers traditional, reasonable or likely to be developed markets. Copyright holders must provide concrete evidence to prove the existence or likelihood of development of a licensing market before they can claim that a secondary use serves as a 'market substitute'. If we were to allow a copyright holder's protected market to include everything for which he is willing to receive licensing fees, this would almost completely eliminate fair use in the service of stifling competition.

According to Authors Alliance (an association that promotes the interests of authors who want to share their creations), the impact of this case is currently limited, both because it is a district court ruling and because it concerns non-generative AI. However, it is important to remain vigilant, as the reasoning advanced by the court could influence other judges, policy makers and even the wider public, if not challenged.

This ruling combines several problematic arguments that, if accepted more widely, could have significant consequences.

First, again according to Authors Alliance, it blurs the line between fact and expression, suggesting that factual information may become subject to copyright simply because it was written by someone in a minimally creative manner. Second, it extends the application of copyright to intermediate copies, meaning that even temporary, non-public use of copyrighted material could be subject to claims of infringement. Third, it evokes a new market for AI training data, regardless of whether such a licence market is legitimate or even likely to exist.

If these arguments take hold, they could further consolidate the dominance of a few large artificial intelligence companies. Only the big players like Microsoft and Meta will be able to afford artificial intelligence training licences, consolidating their control over the industry. The terms of the AI training licences will be determined exclusively between the large AI companies and the large content aggregators, without representation of individual authors or public interests. Large content aggregators will be able to dictate the terms under which creators must assign rights to their works for AI training, and AI companies will dictate how their AI models can be used by the general public.

Without a significant backlash and political intervention, smaller organisations and individual creators cannot participate fairly. The call is not to rewrite copyright law to further entrench this imbalance of power

On https://www.bakerlaw.com/thomson-reuters-v-ross/ are all the most relevant documents of the case, including the pleadings and replies of the parties.

13

AI Training

Copyrighted Photos Can Be Used Even Without Consent, But Only for Research and by Onlus

The Hamburg District Court admits the use of copyright protected images to train an artificial intelligence system if carried out for scientific research purposes by a non-profit organisation. The opt-out of the right holder is not absolute and unlimited.

The judgement under comment is particularly relevant because it is the first decision by a court of an EU Member State on the reproduction of images for the purpose of content analysis and related textual description or for the collection and examination of functional data for the training of AI systems.

The case

The case pits professional photographer R.K. against the non-profit organisation LAION.

By accessing the *Have I Been* Trained platform (which allows one to find out in seconds if one's own photo has been used to train an artificial intelligence system), photographer R.K. had discovered one of his photographs being used without consent. It was enough to upload the photo on the search engine to access the huge archive of images called LAION-5B, tracing not the reproduction of the photographic image but clear evidence of the correlation between the photograph itself and the URL used to identify the work downloaded on the web.

LAION is a German non-profit organisation that releases free artificial intelligence datasets in open source mode.

To date, LAION has a library of about six billion images used to feed Stable Diffusion, Google Image, Midjourney, DALL-E and many others.

The photographic work had originally been published in the stock of a photo agency for licensing in return for payment, with a reservation statement prohibiting the automated reproduction of the database with web scraping techniques (so-called opt-out).

DOI: 10.1201/9781003731290-17

R. K.'s photographic work had however been used during the dataset creation process. In particular, LAION had retrieved the image from the photo agency's website and used software to check the correspondence of the descriptions in the source dataset with the corresponding visual content. As part of this text-image correspondence check, LAION had temporarily stored the image corresponding to the photograph in order to implement and develop AI systems through the selection of functional data for the system itself.

The photographer appealed to the Hamburg Regional Court, which, denying protection to Mr K., upheld, albeit in part, LAION's defence.

The decision of the Hamburg Court

According to the German court, the use of works protected by copyright for the extraction and analysis of data by research organisations for scientific research purposes as referred to in Article 3 of the Copyright Directive and Article 60d of the UrhG is permissible.

Artificial intelligence systems are to be trained through the creation of a dataset. This contribution, although it does not generate an immediate acquisition of knowledge, constitutes - in any case - work that is preordained for the attainment of future knowledge and/or development also for research purposes.

In addition, LAION is a non-profit organisation that published the contested dataset free of charge so that it could be made available to researchers in the field of artificial neutral networks.

It is of no relevance, in the Court's view, that the members of the same LAION organisation are commercial companies or, again, that the same dataset may be used not only by researchers, but also by commercial companies for profit.

The Hamburg Regional Court, which ruled out temporary reproduction under Article 5(1) of Directive 2001/29/EC, also pointed out that any privileged access to the research results to commercial companies (members of the research organisation itself) had not been proven, let alone proven.

The German courts went on to provide important clarifications on the opt-out of the right holder, i.e., the declaration of reservation published on the website of the photo agency pursuant to Article 4(3) of EU Directive 2019/790.

The opt-out and training of datasets for artificial intelligence systems

Pursuant to Article 53(1) of the EU Regulation 1689/2024 on artificial intelligence (so-called AI Act):

"AI model providers for general purposes:

... (c) implement a policy to comply with Union law on copyright and related rights and, in particular, to identify and respect, including through state-of-the-art technology, an express reservation of rights pursuant to Article 4(3) of Directive (EU) 2019/790;

(d) draw up and make available to the public a sufficiently detailed summary of the contents used for general-purpose AI model training, according to a template provided by the AI office'.

The reservation applies to the extraction of text and data for the creation of training datasets of AI systems.

The photographer, Mr. R. K., had made use of the reserve declaration published on the photo agency's website and in a 'machine understandable' format.

The exercise of the opt-out is legitimate but, as the Hamburg Court pointed out, it is not absolute and unlimited. The German court placed limits on the opt-out by copyright holders to the use of content for artificial intelligence training for scientific research purposes made by LAION.

Section 70b of the copyright act

In our legal system, it is worth noting that the Copyright Directive was transposed by Legislative Decree No. 177 of 8 November 2021, which introduced Article 70 ter of the Italian Copyright Law.

The extraction of text and data for scientific research purposes is also permitted in Italy. The regulation states that research organisations include universities, institutes and other entities with research purposes.

Permitted are, in fact, *'reproductions made by research organisations and cultural heritage institutions, for purposes of scientific research, for the extraction of text and data from works or other materials available in networks or databases to which they have lawful access, as well as the communication to the public of the results of the research when expressed in new original works. For the purposes of this law, text and data extraction means any automated technique aimed at analysing large amounts of text, sound, images, data or metadata in digital format with the purpose of generating information, including patterns, trends and correlations*'.

In light of the above, it is considered that in accordance with Section 70b of the Copyright Act, the correlations made by LAION between the photographer's image and the identification URL could have been considered in compliance with copyright law.

Conclusions

The protection of copyrighted works may be sacrificed in the case of reproductions made by research organisations (including non-profit organisations) for the purpose of pre-training artificial intelligence systems.

The pre-training activity, consisting of the selection, analysis and cleaning of training data, should be considered as a research activity worthy of protection.

In any case, the decision highlights the difficult balance between intellectual property law and the development of new technologies, favouring the interests of artificial intelligence systems that - in order to grow - must necessarily rely on the authorial contributions of third parties.

Considerations on the judgment

The biggest flaw in the German judgement is inherent in two statements that suggest a too 'old economy' approach and understanding of the AI phenomenon.

The first is that "*it is not relevant, in the Court's view, that the members of the same LAION organisation are commercial companies or, again, that the same dataset may be used not only by researchers, but also by commercial companies for profit.*"

This evidently contrasts with the objectively proven fact that '*LAION has a library of some six billion images used to feed Stable Diffusion, Google Image, Midjourney, DALL-E and many others*'.

The second is that '*The exercise of the opt-out is legitimate but, as the Hamburg Court makes clear, it is not absolute and unlimited. The German court placed limits on the opt-out by copyright holders to the use of content for the training of artificial intelligence for research purposes*'.

Thus, the contrivance seems transversally evident: the commercial company - faced with the limit of usability - creates a non-profit entity that 'for research purposes' acquires and uses the images for machine learning and AI training, but doing so 'as a non-profit legal diaphragm' and declaring 'for research purposes' (it is not clear specifically which, if not machine learning) acquires access that was not previously legitimate and makes it available to its 'partners'.

What escapes the court's notice - apart from the ontological creation of a fictitious entity to bypass the rule - is that for the purposes of AI, having training datasets is a far more valuable (as things stand) economic-commercial asset than the actual commercial out-put.

Better and larger training dataset means higher performance and more 'metadata base' for higher value-added out-puts, as well as higher performance of the system itself.

This is so indispensable that even giants such as Google Image and Midjourney (which in themselves have direct access to exorbitant datasets) also target 'niches' of six billion images.

A transversal relevance that we find in other ways.

A recent methodology adopted to provide training datasets to the AI was to have machine 1 generate content for machine 2 to train. In the medium term, it was found that machine 2 had a progressive decline in performance: it did not work well with datasets provided by another AI: it needed 'original and humanly processed material' to learn.

Apparently responding to a 'social' demand, Meta recently announced the removal of filters for the 'aesthetic enhancement' of photographs. Behind this policy - which evidently entails a loss of profit for the company - in reality lies the same issue: the Meta group AI wants 'real photos' and not reworked with filters, which appear (and are) photos generated by another AI.

This way makes us realise the value - immediate, economic and financial - of training datasets, which sometimes exceed those of the sale of a widely used service such as immediately available photo filters.

This 'survivor' need for AI is also demonstrated by a number of cases - less and less marginal and sporadic - reported on the net, from which one can see how the voracity of OpenAl bots destroyed websites as if they were DdoS attacks.

OpenAl was sending tens of thousands of requests to the server in an attempt to download everything, hundreds of thousands of photos, along with their detailed descriptions. OpenAl's crawlers were taking down the affected website even though it had a terms of service section on its site prohibiting bots from taking its images without permission. But this alone was not enough.

Web sites must use a properly configured robot.txt file with tags that specifically tell OpenAl's bot, GPTBot, to leave the site alone. (OpenAl also has a couple of other bots, ChatGPT-User and OAI-SearchBot, which have their own tags, according to its crawler information page).

In this regard, the Triplegangers' server logs were made public to demonstrate the hyper-invasiveness of these 'attacks'.

It is therefore clear that - in the current state of technological development of generative Ai - machine-learning datasets for training purposes have a far greater commercial value than the final out-put.

Not understanding this intrinsic fact leaves the way open for convenient ploys like Laion's. And it is not difficult to close Lion and open a hundred more. By simply exploiting the interpretative meshes of an EU regulation 1689/2024 on artificial intelligence (the so-called AI Act) that should instead be interpreted with greater rigour and narrowness.

Limiting oneself to using even correctly configured robot.txt files is not enough: firstly, because AI development companies have immense resources to create additional bots with a variation of a letter or a number from time to time, bypassing restriction policies, and secondly, because they could always argue that 'training is research and not commercial out-put'.

Finally, when the largest search engine in the western world declares between the lines but very clearly that having integrated its AI with Search, if you do not authorise training it will not index your website... the game is up.

It is here that truly and deeply understanding the dynamics of the phenomenon, and applying the rules in their strict and narrow reading, remains the only way to curb policy (and law) violation.

14

Open AI vs. Deepseek

When AI Accuse Each Other of Copyright Infringement

DeepSeek arrived like a meteorite in the world of artificial intelligence and shook up the market, but OpenAI does not stand for this and accuses DeepSeek of copying ChatGPT, or rather of using ChatGPT as a 'teacher' to train its R1 model, with a technique called 'Knowledge Distillation'.

According to the US artificial intelligence giant, DeepSeek employed the process known as 'Knowledge Distillation' to train its new R1 model, using data derived from OpenAI's ChatGPT. This battle has raised many questions about the ethics and legitimacy of using pre-existing technologies to create new AI models.

DeepSeek announced its R1 model, presenting it as an advanced AI solution that combines high performance with low cost, and it was precisely the extremely low cost compared to competitors that caused the financial markets to tremble, causing, according to some, the AI bubble to burst. For the first time, the AI industry appeared weak in the face of a disruptive phenomenon that showed that the US is not alone in leading the AI revolution.

OpenAI's accusations are based on the assumption that DeepSeek used 'knowledge distillation' to partly replicate ChatGPT's functionality. David Sacks, called to defend the technology and artificial intelligence policies of the new US administration, told Fox News that there is 'substantial evidence' that would confirm DeepSeek's use of this method. Sacks pointed out that major AI companies are considering measures to prevent such practices in order to protect their original models.

Knowledge Distillation' is a process used in the field of Ai to transfer knowledge from a large model (the 'teacher') to a smaller model ('student'). This allows the smaller model to achieve similar performance to the original model, but with a reduced computational budget. The process is particularly useful for implementing artificial intelligence models on devices with limited hardware resources.

DOI: 10.1201/9781003731290-18

The process of 'Knowledge Distillation' was first used in 2015 by Geoffrey Hinton, one of the founding fathers of modern artificial intelligence. Hinton developed an algorithm that enables precisely the transfer of knowledge from a trained model to one that has not yet been trained.

- The Knowledge Distillation process usually involves the following steps:
- Training of the teacher model: A large model with accurate results (teacher) is trained on a large dataset.
- Output Generation: The teacher model is used to generate outputs (often probabilistic) for a set of supplied inputs.
- Training the student model: These outputs are then used to train a smaller student model, trying to minimise the divergence between student and teacher predictions.

Knowledge Distillation is particularly useful because it allows smaller models with similar performance to larger ones, enabling more efficient implementations in terms of memory and speed, without sacrificing too much accuracy.

Currently, OpenAI's allegations are based on observations of the behaviour of the R1 model and similarities with ChatGPT. However, there is no publicly available concrete evidence conclusively proving the unauthorised use of 'Knowledge Distillation' by DeepSeek.

In the world of artificial intelligence, leading companies such as OpenAI are well aware of the problems associated with the unauthorised distillation of models.

To counter these practices, they take proactive measures such as blocking suspicious access and limiting the number of requests that can be sent to their systems or from specific computers.

However, distillation techniques are becoming more and more sophisticated, sometimes managing to circumvent controls and thus allowing third parties to create their own models based on the high quality ones, which require considerable resources, both in terms of computing capacity and development costs.

Unauthorised distillation poses a real threat to the economic viability of large companies that invest huge amounts of capital in the development of comprehensive and advanced models.

These companies, such as OpenAI, incur development costs of up to hundreds of millions of dollars in order to create increasingly powerful next-generation models. However, other players can leverage these investments to derive simplified models with greater efficiency and lower operating costs.

The field of artificial intelligence is still young and constantly evolving, with surprising changes that can drastically affect the technological landscape, as demonstrated by the tumultuous events of the last week. This makes it difficult to predict with certainty whether, in the medium to long term, it will be more profitable to invest in the development of complete models or in the creation of distilled models, especially in relation to specific types of operations.

The question remains open and it will be interesting to see how the industry will adapt to future technological developments and market dynamics. In the meantime, it has fuelled a debate on what can be considered legitimate or ethical to use derivative technologies for the development of new products in the field of artificial intelligence and has put OpenAI in a difficult position.

Numerous observers have noted that OpenAI now tries to defend its intellectual property against DeepSeek but on the other hand is facing many lawsuits filed by publishers for the alleged unauthorised use of their content in the development of ChatGPT.

Publishers accuse OpenAI of using newspaper archives, photo galleries and video platforms to collect data needed to train its artificial intelligence systems. OpenAI defends itself by stating that such content was only used in the development phase and that the system generates its own content.

Publishers, on the other hand, claim that ChatGPT often reproduces their content as is, infringing copyright. In practice, ChatGPT would accuse DeepSeek of copyright infringement in exactly the same way as publishers accuse ChatGPT.

After all, the technique of using one AI to create content to train the growth and machine learning of another AI is a well-known practice, and one that was developed on the basis of an observation: AI systems do not need a linearly increasing flow of data, but with quantum computers - the only ones that have been able to give true impetus to AI - the flow of data to be 'eaten and digested and returned' is growing exponentially.

The undisputed advantage of players such as Meta and Microsoft, who can feed machine learning with new and up-to-date data created by humans via their own social networks and messaging systems (Facebook, Instagram and Whapp on the one hand, Linkedin and Messanger on the other).

Google, on the other hand, triumphs thanks to the data provided by its search engine and the analysis of Gmail mails.

In order to compete, companies have on the one hand commissioned third parties to retrieve data - in the event of lawsuits, they are not directly liable for copyright infringement, and in the case of 'research' and non-profit organisations, they benefit from the 'pro-research' wide net - and have created data-generating systems for use in training.

It then turned out that this data source was 'boring' for the AI to train, which seemed to understand that this content was not 'human'. One response to this was put forward by Meta: cloaked in a 'need for authenticity and contrast to artefactual myths' the reduction of the pervasiveness of filters on Instagram offered its AI 'human photos' (which Ai seemed to appreciate more than retouched images!).

What is particularly interesting at this stage, however, is to read what the various OpenAIs will write in their own pleadings to defend their alleged copyrights, and how much this will ontologically conflict with what OpenAI itself writes elsewhere when defending itself against the same accusations against traditional publishers.

Alongside this theme, another one emerges.

There is a market of content 'suitable for training' that AI companies do not pay for and from which they claim to extract for free - as from a mine - valuable elements for the development of their products. A market that they have always denied exists precisely because - according to them - the training function is worth zero, while it is only the output that counts.

As if to say 'gold is worthless, what is worthwhile is only the jewellery I produce'.

Today, they seem to be proving themselves wrong: there is a market for training input, and it is also worth a lot.

15

AI Hallucinations and GDPR Protections

Finding the Balance Between Access and Redress Rights and AI

We do a web search and are returned a result, which we recognise as wrong

We ask ChatGPT to process a text, and find it to be full of inaccuracies and errors.

All these are common, everyday phenomena, which often severely affect people's rights through the production of false, incorrect and misleading information.

In this article we try to understand how this happens, why, and what instruments are available to protect us.

AI hallucinations

Current AI systems (based on ***Machine Learning*** and ***Large Language Models***) are designed and programmed to give an answer at all costs and, more precisely, the most probable answer, not necessarily the right, correct or true answer.

It is good to clarify the concept in greater depth, namely that 'the most probable answer' does not necessarily mean - neither from a logical nor from a syntactic point of view, nor in the sense of computer programming or algorithm design - that it is also 'the correct one', but only that - given probabilities assumed ex ante and ingenerally for generic and all-inclusive categories - the answer is the most probable of those possible answers sought within a finite dataset of information limited to what the AI has access to.

With such an approach, so-called '**hallucinations**' can easily occur, i.e. outputs (answers) that are not based on objective truth and are therefore an error - or rather, wrong data

Recent statistics reported by the New York Times indicate that the responses of AIs suffering from hallucinations range from 3 to 27 per cent.

While an error of less than 10% may still seem low, let's try to think about what it means not so much that one in ten answers is wrong (worse one in three) when

DOI: 10.1201/9781003731290-19

given an overall text required of a generative AI (let's say a text of 10,000 words) over 10% of this text (over 1000 words in this case) refer to information and contain incorrect data.

Imagine asking an AID to generate a profile on a candidate for a professional position, a medical history, a newspaper article or a criminal profile... and then consider that even 5% (without ending up at 25%) of this profile is false.

And now let us imagine that - in all these contexts - the profile we are talking about is yours.

So far the 'false' data.

Now let us consider both qualitatively and quantitatively the text we are talking about.

As is common experience - for instance - most of the most accredited news sites and media (from the NYTimes to news agency sites, from the Treccani to the news) do not authorise Ai systems to use their content for AI training (be it Machine Learning or Large Language Models).

This means that the remaining, let's say 90 per cent of the text is processed on the basis of data and information, and on the syntax and writing model, which lies somewhere between Wikipedia and Facebook, and some amateur blogs.

If we combine this with the fact that - in the absence of any further variables - the AI has no way of arbitrarily choosing or otherwise discriminating between the 100 social profiles of homonyms, and has to 'average' the information found, we can understand what reliability we are actually talking about.

The protections of the GDPR

This erroneous association between person and output data triggers the alarm and protection system of the GDPR in several respects. Of the many rights of protection and self-defence, the right **of access** (Art.15) and the **right of rectification** (Art.16) take centre stage.

The accuracy of personal data is a decades-old established principle in *privacy* and enshrined in Article 5.1d) GDPR.

This principle provides not only for accuracy but also for the possibility of updating the data.

In this context, it is good to remember that the GDPR - fortunately - is a regulation that not only covers all citizens in all cases of data management in the territory of the European Union, but also imposes precise rules of compliance even in those cases - increasingly fewer - of web companies that, for example, do not have to have a seat in the Union but must adapt merely because they make their services and products available in the Union (e.g. OpenIA with ChatGPT).

Article 15 GDPR corresponds to the data subject's right to obtain - among other things - confirmation from the data controller that his data are being processed, access to them and how they are being processed. Access is thus also a manifestation of the principle of transparency (Articles 5 and 12 GDPR).

Article 16 GDPR, on the other hand, concerns the right to obtain rectification of inaccurate personal data.

In this regard, it should be emphasised and reminded strongly and clearly that **updating** and **completeness** are an option for the data subject, but **rectification** is an obligation for the data controller whenever he has or should have knowledge that he is processing inaccurate data.

The importance of these standards becomes even more relevant if we consider that these outputs are totally automated and that it is difficult even for the data controller to reconstruct the procedure followed by the AI to generate a given output.

OpenAI, for instance, denied access and rectification of data in some cases on the grounds that it was impossible to correct them. The proposed solution would have been to apply a filter to the prompts, which would, however, prevent ChatGPT from filtering any information on the data subject.

Google, for instance, allows access and rectification of data 'up to a certain point' - i.e., data held directly and functionally, e.g. user registration to its services - by clearly stating that 'search data when they become metadata' (practically always) are not even accessible to Google.

The black box problem

In order to understand the difficulties of exercising the rights of data subjects, it is useful to bear in mind a major technical limitation of AI; the so-called '***black box problem***', i.e., the impossibility of really understanding how a *deep learning* system arrived at a given output.

The privacy legislation requires, especially in automated processes, that the data controller be able to provide the data subject with '*meaningful information about the logic used, as well as the importance and expected consequences of such processing for the data subject*' (Art. 15.1(h) GDPR).

If it is already difficult (if not in some cases impossible) for an AI technician to reconstruct the logical path followed by the AI, it will be even more arduous to explain its operation clearly and transparently to the person concerned.

This technical limitation - which exists, and is inherent in the system 'as conceived and programmed to date' - cannot be a justification for the data controller to refuse a data subject's request for access. Such an approach would defeat the applicability of Articles 15 and 22 GDPR as well as technically the right of rectification (Art. 16 GDPR).

The point, upstream, is that the legislation came later, as is often the case, and - in part - large companies moved 'into the breach' of previous fragmented and often unclear legislation.

Wrong output could be the result of a new item introduced at the prompt that the AI had not been trained on, or the use of incorrect data.

In fact, AI is trained on data provided to it and on the experimentation of possible combinations of the same (and it seems scarcely credible that we are able and that it is economically viable - in terms of programming and computing resources - to predict all possible scenarios to be taught).

The debate between quantity and quality of data becomes relevant especially if we think of the principle of '*privacy by design and by default*'.

This principle would lead us to favour the quality of the data, and it is therefore crucial in the design of the AI platform to be able to envisage a way of rectifying the data not only with a view to reducing hallucinations, but above all with a view to the exploitation of AI in areas that have a greater impact on the rights of the data subjects.

16

When Public Administration Discrimination Comes from AI

An UK Case Study

In the UK, the AI system that detects subsidy fraud is discriminatory: the machine learning programme used to examine Universal Credit claims incorrectly selects people from some groups more than others.

This was recently revealed by the investigation published on 6 December 2024 by Robert Booth in the Guardian: the AI system used by the UK government to detect welfare fraud shows discrimination on the basis of people's age, disability, marital status and nationality.

The internal evaluation of the machine learning programme used to examine Universal Credit claims in England found that it incorrectly selected people from some groups more than others when identifying who to investigate for possible fraud.

In practice, the system favours specific racial groups in the investigation of alleged abuses of the welfare system.

The circumstance emerged after an access to records at the Department for Work and Pensions.

The final decision on whether or not a person will receive unemployment benefits is still made by a human being, and officials believe that continued use of the system, which is attempting to save around £8 billion a year lost to fraud and error, is 'reasonable and proportionate'.

Activists retaliated by criticising the government for adopting the policy of 'first do wrong, then fix it' and called on ministers to be more fair to groups that the algorithm wrongly suspects of trying to cheat the system.

Recognition of disparities in the way the automated system assesses fraud risks is also likely to increase government scrutiny of AI systems and, at the same time, fuel demands for greater transparency.

There are 55 automated tools used by public authorities in the UK, potentially influencing decisions affecting millions of people, despite the fact that the government register only covers nine.

DOI: 10.1201/9781003731290-20

In recent years, government departments, including the Ministry of the Interior, have been reluctant to release information on the use of artificial intelligence, justifying the closure with the concern that more information could allow malicious parties to manipulate the systems.

The British case is neither unique nor isolated and is due to a well-known but difficult to eliminate 'bias' in programming and weighting of data - certainly not from machines but from people's heads - which is due to a vicious circle already discovered in many predictive systems used for example in the United States.

In this sense, adopting standardised models - under the pretext of being cheaper than programming new ones - does not help to solve the problem, indeed like a virus it spreads from country to country and in heterogeneous administrations.

It is evident that based on the 'historical' weight of a neighbourhood in large urban centres includes a convergence of both racial and educational level, which has an impact on income statistics, access to health services, and type of work.

It is therefore clear that an algorithm designed in this way will assign higher risk factors to certain neighbourhoods and social classes, which transversally, and not coincidentally, are also where the need for subsidies is concentrated.

As the rate of absorption of applications increases, so does the rate of risk of fraud: if there are 10 applications in district A and 100 in district B, it is very easy for district B to have a higher risk of fraud. The whole thing should then be read from a socio-racial cross-sectional perspective.

This bias was first detected in the algorithms used in the systems for predicting and determining health insurance premiums in the United States, but upon inspection it appears to be repeated in the same dynamics and spotty weightings in many PA systems.

This suggests the great difficulty of understanding the error and reprogramming the set of weights and weightings with new non-discriminatory predictive models.

The vulnus is therefore in adopting critically and without verification 'preset products' instead of discussing and thinking about specific weights.

In their recent book (Look Again. The Power of Noticing What Was Always There of 2024) Tali Sharot and Cass R. Sunstein point out how things can get even worse if artificial intelligence systems are introduced: 'These are built to imitate the human mind: they use input from the surrounding world to make predictions and judgements. If the data they receive is distorted, AI systems will react in the same way as human ex-servers: the decisions and advice they make will be distorted.

They give the example of David and Jamie H.'s experience. In 2019, the married couple applied for an Apple credit card, sharing all financial resources, including bank accounts and real estate. The two were shocked when they learned that Apple offered David a much higher credit limit - twenty times higher - than Jamie. After reporting the story on social media, they discovered that others had also experienced the same thing, including Apple co-founder Steve Wozniak and his wife.

To assign credit, Apple used a distorted machine-learning algorithm. To establish an evaluation, the algorithm is given millions of examples of good choices (for example, data on people who have always repaid their debt) and bad choices (for example, data on people who have not). In this way, the algorithm learns which factors are predictive of good choices. If women are paid less than men or find it more difficult to get a job because of gender discrimination, the algorithm will conclude that men are better candidates for credit. By discriminating against women, the algorithm will further increase the gender gap, creating a feedback loop.

Of course, what we are interested in is not the - albeit interesting - case of a private company, but the absolutely simple way in which an IA can be - even unintentionally - discriminating.

17

Artificial Intelligence in the Service of Criminal Justice?

AI and Criminal Law: Benefits and Dangers of A De-Humanisation of Justice

The need for celerity and reduction of the trial load has led to increasing pressure for justice from the political world, from practitioners and from users themselves. While a fair and just trial must necessarily also be a speedy trial, not all means to achieve this goal are suitable to guarantee at the same time fair justice, the rights of the individual and of the defendant, a careful evidentiary assessment, and respect for guarantees. In this context, the digitisation of the trial, which has been strongly employed in the civil sphere and is also advancing in the criminal sphere, has long since been included.

While the more conservative still harbour some reservations, the more 'progressive' (in the sense of fans of progress) have proposed the idea of applying Artificial Intelligence in the field of criminal justice, in order to meet the demands of speed, efficiency and effectiveness of the same, in light of the now massive use of artificial intelligence systems in everyday life.

1. Artificial Intelligence

As stated on the European Parliament's *website*, Artificial Intelligence (also known by its abbreviation, 'AI') consists of "the *ability of a machine to exhibit human capabilities such as reasoning, learning, planning and creativity*" and "*enables systems to understand their environment, relate to what they perceive and solve problems, and act towards a specific goal. The computer receives data (already prepared or collected through sensors, such as a video camera), processes it and responds*', being able to '*adapt its behaviour by analysing the effects of previous actions and working autonomously*'.

DOI: 10.1201/9781003731290-21

2. Artificial intelligence and criminal law

As is well known, criminal law always lags behind the phenomenon of digitalisation that has affected other branches of public law to a greater extent, mainly, it is argued, because of the need to guarantee the rights of persons, who are human beings, as much as possible.

Fans of technological progress argue that Artificial Intelligence algorithms and automatisms could be applied, with a view to predictive justice, by the authorities to predict (think of the practice of automated facial recognition by means of a special database), precisely the commission of certain crimes (e.g., in certain parts of the world with a higher crime rate) or to pre-identify the perpetrators of specific categories of offences (e.g., persons already known to the justice system with a higher chance of reoffending and, therefore, of committing crimes of the same nature again).

Such systems could also be applied at the preliminary investigation stage to assess the findings. One thinks, for instance, of the summary testimonial information provided by the various persons informed of the facts in dispute, the reliability of which could be assessed by means of cross-checks to ascertain any discrepancies between them and to uncover guilt profiles.

Some also fear that algorithms could be used in automated decision-making, thus saving economic and human resources.

3. The limits of the application of artificial intelligence systems to criminal law

A massive application of Artificial Intelligence systems to criminal law could, however, lead to a de-humanisation of justice.

Perplexities arise above all in the area of ascertaining both the objective element and the subjective element of the offence.

How could an algorithm assess the different nuances of the psychological element (think, for instance, of the element of possible intent or premeditation) that drives a man to commit a crime, or think of the cases of the different causes of justification (exculpatory) that could exclude an unlawfulness of the case?

The risk of incurring judgments based on a strict liability criterion would be immediate.

Further doubts exist with respect to the ascertainment of the material element of the offence where a certain factor as such would not be considered suspicious, if not by application of human sensitivity and with reference to other indirect elements that came to light during the investigation.

In such cases, there could be serious injuries to all those principles of criminal law such as the right to a fair trial, the right of defence, the right to equality as well as the principle of reasonable certainty and the right of beyond reasonable doubt.

Cases of the distorted use of algorithms to bring about a manoeuvred and '*ad hoc*' decision to satisfy undue *extra-legal* interests or the use of the various *databases* in violation of the right to *privacy* of sensitive data could not be ruled out, with the necessary involvement of all the recent legislation developed in the field of personal data security.

See in this sense the recent ECHR rulings (e.g., vs. Switzerland) for the use of predictive tools based on ethical and racial profiling.

A specific committee should be set up to monitor the correctness of the decisions taken on the basis of the algorithms and the various databases from which the data are extracted. This does not reduce the complexity of the judicial machine, which requires additional specific expertise.

In such circumstances, there could also be, even in a mere dilatory perspective, numerous appeals aimed at contesting the regularity of such automatic decisions, with the emergence of an additional workload, to the detriment of the judicial circuit, and an aggravation of the time taken by justice.

Moreover - and this is particularly relevant - it is evident that in the very setting up of the data set it is impossible to exclude any bias, from political, ideological, religious, ethical interference, which would in fact transform an impartial technical instrument into an instrument of partiality in re ipsa.

4. Conclusions

Criminal law, which is unique in its kind, requires an application of human sensitivity that is perhaps lacking in other branches of law and that is unlikely to flow into cold, calculating systems.

Different is the use of AI, for instance, in the comparative evaluation of cost estimates for a tender, rather than the evaluation of homogeneous tests for a public competition, rather than the evaluation of performance in the PA, in applications for access to documents, in the preliminary evaluation (without excluding the human one) of applications for financial benefits or administrative connections, all areas of application in which it would be useful for anti-corruption purposes, or at least for skimming and relieving the human administrative burden.

If we want criminal law to continue to satisfy those fundamental criteria of legal certainty, of beyond all reasonable doubt, of protection of the accused (innocent until a final verdict), in a general view of guaranteeing the fundamental rights of the human person established at constitutional, European and international level, also in order to avoid possible miscarriages of justice, it is necessary to try to act with extreme prudence, avoiding falling into the trap of excessive depersonalisation of that particular branch of public law that regulates the exercise of state punitive power.

That place where the judge, however much he or she may be called upon to perform his or her task of applying and, very often, interpreting the law in an impartial and third-party manner, will be implicitly guided by his or her own professional convictions, his or her own previous experiences (including personal ones) as well as his or her own free appreciation and sensitivity.

Where one is ultimately judged among equals: human by human.

18

Predictive AI Applications in Criminal Law Between Ordinary and Legal Limits and General Guarantee Principles

A Synthetic Picture

The need for celerity and containment of the trial load has led some jurists to imagine the use of Artificial Intelligence in terms of 'predictive justice'.

While the more conservative still harbour some reservations, the more 'progressive' (in the sense of fans of progress) have proposed the idea of applying Artificial Intelligence in the field of criminal justice, in order to meet the demands of speed, efficiency and effectiveness of the same, in light of the now massive use of artificial intelligence systems in everyday life.

1. First experiences of artificial intelligence in the judiciary

The use of AI in the area of civil justice has been experimented in some European countries. In particular, in France, the *Predictice* system was created in 2016 to estimate the amount of damages recoverable in commercial or intellectual property cases.

In Italy, some interesting projects on artificial intelligence used in predictive justice have been launched.

The first is the one promoted by the Court of Appeal and the Court of Brescia, in cooperation with the University of Brescia, which has been in operation since November 2021. At the moment, it only deals with 'labour law' and 'company law'. The aim of the project is to "*provide users and economic agents with data of certainty and predictability and, at the same time, to contain demand, disincentivising reckless litigation*", as well as to promote the "*transparency of decisions*", the "*circularity of jurisprudence between first and second instance*" and the "*overcoming of unconscious contrasts*".

DOI: 10.1201/9781003731290-22

Another interesting project that has already started is the one promoted by the Court of Appeal of Venice, in collaboration with Ca' Foscari University of Venice, Unioncamere del Veneto and Deloitte, which provided the technical support. The aim of the first phase, relating only to the subject of dismissals for just cause, was to enter into the computer all the decisions issued in the district in the three-year period 2019–2021, in order to make case law precedents knowable and decisions predictable, discouraging litigation with poor prospects of success .

Also in the tax sector, a project called 'Prodigit' has been financed, aimed at creating systems based on algorithms capable of analysing laws, judgments and doctrinal contributions to predict what a judge's decision-making stance on a given legal issue might be. In particular, it is envisaged that, by analysing a large number of judgments, thanks to the AI's ability to learn, it will become increasingly reliable, enabling the taxpayer, when the system is operational, to obtain an answer as to whether or not to appeal.

2. AI in administrative justice

In the field of administrative justice, there have already been some groundbreaking decisions on the role of artificial intelligence in public administration decision-making.

The Council of State, after an initial interesting ruling in 2019, which underlined the indisputable advantages of automating the administrative decision-making process through the use of procedures managed by a computer system by means of algorithms, in accordance with the canons of efficiency and economy of administrative action, admitted the use of robotized procedures only in a constrained activity (in this case, the automatic classification of applications for the recruitment of secondary school teachers already included in the relevant rankings), there has been a progressive jurisprudential openness to the use of algorithms also in the discretionary activity of the Public Administration; provided, however, that the mechanism through which the robotized decision (i.e., the algorithm) is realised is knowable and, consequently, can be reviewed by the judge.

It would be desirable - always subject to human control and verification - to use it, for example, in the comparative evaluation of cost estimates for a tender, rather than the evaluation of homogeneous tests for a public competition, rather than the evaluation of performance in the PA, in applications for access to documents, in the preliminary evaluation (*without excluding the human one*) of applications for financial benefits or administrative connections, all areas of application in which it would be useful for anti-corruption purposes, or at least for skimming and relieving the human administrative burden.

3. Predictive AI applications in criminal justice

A first orientation considers that, from *an ex ante* perspective, artificial intelligence can be used as a crime prevention tool. In fact, it has been hypothesised that, by inputting into a *computer* a series of data extrapolated from reports of thefts and robberies that have occurred in certain areas and in similar ways, the system would be able to predict places and times when other crimes of the same kind are likely to be committed and, therefore, intervene to prevent them.

Artificial intelligence, on the other hand, can have a broader scope of application at the preliminary investigation stage as a means of searching for evidence. Suffice it to think of the increasingly frequent use of data generated automatically, without any human intervention in their collection, by special *software*, such as computer capturing devices (so-called Trojans) to intercept conversations and GPS to locate the position.

It is also worth mentioning that, again by means of AI tools, it is possible to analyse digital images, taken, for instance, from the network of cameras present in every city, containing people's faces in order to perform facial recognition, which can be used as evidence in criminal proceedings. However, such tools may, on the one hand, undoubtedly be useful for investigative purposes but, on the other hand, they risk conflicting with fundamental individual rights, such as the right to *privacy*.

Much more delicate is the problem of the use of artificial intelligence in a 'predictive' function in criminal proceedings.

In this regard, the European Commission for the Effectiveness of Justice (CEPEJ) of the Council of Europe, in 2018, issued the 'European Ethical Charter for the Use of Artificial Intelligence in Criminal Justice Systems and Related Environments'.

This is the first time that, at European level, noting the '*growing importance of artificial intelligence (AI) in our modern societies and the expected benefits when it is fully utilised at the service of the efficiency and quality of justice*', principles have been identified to which public and private entities responsible for the design and development of AI tools and services must adhere. These are, in particular, the principles of 'respect for fundamental rights', 'non-discrimination', 'quality and safety', 'transparency' and 'guarantee of human intervention'.

The last principle of 'guaranteeing human intervention' - '*under user control*' - is the one of interest here, since, being aimed at '*ensuring that users act as informed subjects and exercise control over the choices made*', it implicitly admits the possibility of using AI in the field of criminal justice.

In 2021, the European Commission for Civil Liberties, Justice and Home Affairs formulated a proposal for a resolution of the European Parliament and the Council to establish harmonised rules on artificial intelligence in criminal law and its use by police and judicial authorities. The proposal also contains a reflection, in general, on the potential risks of the use of AI (opaque decision-making processes, various types of discrimination, intrusion into private life, etc.) and, in particular, on the even more serious risks of its use in criminal justice, to which is added the recommendation that, when using AI systems, the rights enshrined in the Charter of Fundamental Rights of the European Union be respected.

4. The American experience and the 'Loomis' case

In the United States, which is known to be at the forefront of experimentation with artificial intelligence in criminal law, a number of data-processing programmes, consisting of algorithms predictive of the risk that a defendant may commit a further crime, have already been in existence for several years.

An example of the use of AI to make predictions about the future conduct of a defendant is the oft-cited 'Loomis' case. This is an African-American convicted felon, arrested after an attempted escape while driving a car previously involved in a firefight and found in possession of weapons, whom a Wisconsin judge, in 2016, sentenced to six years' imprisonment, based on the COMPAS algorithm's response that - predictively - had defined him as a subject 'at high risk of violence'.

The algorithm, to assess the risk of reoffending, uses a form of 137 questions concerning age, level of education, work, social life, drug use, personal opinions, etc. and assigns a dangerousness score from 1 to 10 according to the answers given by the defendant.

If we look closely, these are information profiles that the human judge, in our system, should not take into account at all, except in the merits of the assessment of, for example, aggravating or mitigating circumstances.

Upon appeal, based on the fact that COMPAS does not foresee the risk of individual reoffending of the defendant, since it elaborates the prediction by comparing the information obtained from the individual with that relating to a group of subjects with similar characteristics, the Supreme Court confirmed the legitimacy of the instrument used by the trial judge, concluding that the sentence would not have been different if only the judge had decided.

However, the algorithm was found to suffer from *racial* bias, as it assigned the African-American population a recidivism risk factor (calculated ex ante, and on an a priori statistical basis) twice as high as the white population.

5. The importability of the predictive model in Italian criminal law

Regardless of the questionable choice of entrusting the assessment of the defendant's personality to a machine, the fact remains that automated decision-making in predictive terms would in any case be precluded in our legal system.

This is expressly prohibited by Article 22(1) of the Regulation of the European Parliament and of the Council of 27 April 2016, No. 679 (GDPR), where it states that '*the data subject shall have the right not to be subject to a decision based solely on automated processing, including profiling, which produces legal effects concerning him or her or significantly affects him or her in a similar way*'.

Moreover, our code of procedure does not allow for expert opinions to establish the character or personality of the defendant (Article 220(2) of the Code of Criminal Procedure), so an Italian judge could hardly use a *computer* to establish whether or not there is a risk of a defendant reoffending.

6. Predictability of the outcome of a criminal trial through AI

Using AI, is it possible to predict the outcome of a trial? Essentially, the question is whether by adopting a sophisticated AI system with an adequate *database* of regulatory sources and case law, i.e. orienting it in terms of law, one could predict, with a sufficient degree of reliability, the outcome of a trial.

Can a machine predict the future? The Code of Criminal Procedure establishes that both the public prosecutor and the judge not only can, but even must, make a prognostic assessment as to the possibility of a future conviction on the basis of the evidence acquired, as can be deduced from the use of the phrase '*reasonable expectation of conviction*' in relation to the public prosecutor's request for dismissal (art. 408, paragraph 1, Code of Criminal Procedure), at the preliminary hearing (Article 425, paragraph 3, Code of Criminal Procedure) and at the new pre-trial hearing (Article *554ter*, paragraph 1, Code of Criminal Procedure).

We can assume that the reference to the binomial '*reasonable prediction*' presupposes reasoning that is not only logical (i.e., formally correct in inferring a certain conclusion from a certain premise), but even mathematically probabilistic.

This issue has been the subject of recent doctrinal investigation, in particular with regard to the question of whether the evaluation of the evidence acquired can be carried out on a statistical basis (e.g., by referring to other similar cases and, therefore, to case law precedents) or according to a criterion of mathematical probability.

The idea of quantifying the soundness of a hypothesis in mathematical terms, attributing to it a fractional numerical value between 0 (= impossibility) and 1 (= certainty) - enunciated by Bayes in the form of a theorem - was, however, doomed to failure, not only and not so much because of the complexity of the calculations required in the case of multiple proofs or relating to complex facts, but rather because the concept of statistical probability concerns classes of repeatable events, whereas the evidence available in the trial concerns specific and non-replicable facts.

Ultimately, with the help of appropriately programmed *machine learning*, it should be possible to predict the outcome of a trial with a sufficient margin of accuracy on the basis of the input data. This is especially true with regard to questions of law, whereas with regard to questions of fact, the solution is not so simple, as in the case where it is necessary, for example, to assess the reliability of witnesses who have given conflicting versions.

7. AI as a decision-making function

Given the exceptional speed with which AI systems have evolved and the probable imminent realisation of ever more refined tools capable of emulating human thought, we cannot but wonder whether the day will come when an algorithm, albeit under human control, will even be able to produce the decision in a criminal trial.

I will not repeat here broader and more complex considerations already made elsewhere [Di Salvo, M. (2024) - Artificial Intelligence and the cyber utopianism of justice. Why AI is not intelligence and man's struggle to survive himself. - RJEL. Russian Journal of Economics and Law] in which I highlighted how the limits of human judgement would certainly not be balanced by the non-humanity of alleged computational intelligence.

For the purposes of this reasoning, the most relevant limitation for AI systems, in formulating a decision, appears to be related to the fact that in the decision-making function they would only be able to express clear-cut judgements, without any nuance, whereas the criminal process generally deals with human facts in which feelings and passions cannot be ignored.

Finally, there would be no room left for the applicability of the canon of '*beyond reasonable doubt*' in Article 533(1) of the Code of Criminal Procedure. Whereas - as the American Richard P. Feynman, Nobel Prize winner for physics, has well pointed out - '*this freedom to doubt is fundamental in science and, I believe, in other fields. It took us centuries of struggle to win the right to doubt (...) and as a scientist I feel a responsibility to proclaim the value of this freedom and to teach that doubt should not be feared, but welcomed*'.

19

The Standards for the Development and Adoption of Artificial Intelligence Technologies

A First Analytical Review of Italian Legislation

On 23 April 2024, the Council of Ministers approved Bill No. 1066AS entitled 'Regulations for the development and adoption of artificial intelligence technologies'.

The bill is only the first, in the government's intentions, of a series of specific measures to implement delegations that the government will have to implement in 12 months.

The development of artificial intelligence systems is entrusted to a strategy prepared by a special structure of the Prime Minister's Office, in agreement with the national authorities in charge of technological innovation, the Ministry of Made in Italy and the Ministry of Universities. This choice denotes the government's intention to play a crucial role in the development process of A.I. systems. Moreover, this is also evident from the decision to entrust AgId and the National Cybersecurity Agency with the task of ensuring the application of national and European regulations, since both are technical agencies of the Prime Minister's Office.

The risk, however, is that on this issue an excessive national logic is badly reconciled with the gap in technology and investment in research and development: in no uncertain terms, it would perhaps have been preferable - in the opinion of the writer - for a programme that, although it entrusts close supervision and coordination of development and at the same time specifically regulates the use of the tool and the management of data, to have been geared towards 'specialised collaboration'.

To be concrete, something similar to CERN or the Airbus model or even ESA: models that clearly work, are efficient and organised and above all achieve results and objectives.

The risk - not even that hidden - is that behind this 'nationalisation' and centralisation there is the eagerness to manage *(in every sense of the word)* and direct

DOI: 10.1201/9781003731290-23

the *(huge)* resources that are about to rain down on the sector, including in terms of patronage and elections.

Also part of the strategy for the development of artificial intelligence is the venture capital activity of the Ministry of Enterprise and Made in Italy, i.e., the purchase of participations (up to a total amount of EUR 1 billion) in SMEs (small and medium-sized enterprises), operating in the field of new technologies, quantum computing or telecommunications and with high development potential.

The government's choice to favour suppliers operating on Italian territory rather than, more generically, within the perimeter of the European market (Art. 5) is peculiar.

Particularly significant is the defining interpretation in Article 1, according to which the bill aims to promote '*a correct, transparent and responsible use, in an anthropocentric dimension, of artificial intelligence, aimed at seizing its opportunities'*.

The anthropocentric approach to artificial intelligence emerges from Article 3, which stipulates that the use of this new technology must respect the fundamental rights laid down in the Constitution and European law and also the principles of transparency and proportionality of the processes, reliability and correctness of the data used for the development of artificial intelligence systems.

And here, apart from the fact that the meaning of anthropocentric is unclear (in a general sense, every instrument created by man is anthropocentric in itself, even the ergonomics of a hammer is anthropocentric), some doubt arises precisely on the statements in Article 3.

The use of this new technology must **comply with the fundamental rights** provided by the Constitution and European law and also with the principles of transparency and proportionality of the processes, reliability and correctness of the data used for the development of artificial intelligence systems.

Now, apart from the declaratory screen (laws often declaim lofty statements of principle), and granted that even from a technical-legislative point of view, the rule could not have provided otherwise. To be honest, if it had provided otherwise, it would have been illegitimate from every legal point of view.

In substance, its content is not understood. In fact, having clarified that an activity cannot be 'contrary to the fundamental rights provided for by the Constitution and European law and also to the principles of transparency and proportionality of the processes, reliability and correctness of the data used for the development of artificial intelligence systems', nothing is said about how these rights - already established and inalienable - are defended, enhanced and protected 'in the specific case'.

And as these rights appear increasingly 'volatile' - *when not mere declarations of principle in the age of liberalism coupled with globalisation, in which the holders of the basic tools of AI are multinational corporations for the vast majority non-European*

- It would perhaps have been desirable to spend a few more words on active, preventive, prudential protection processes, as opposed to stating that 'everything must be controlled by the government'.

The bill contains a series of principles to be applied in the fields of information, economic development, health, intellectual professions, the judiciary, user protection, copyright and, finally, also criminal protection.

Article 4 deals with the use of **I.A.** systems **in the field of information**, providing for the protection of the democratic nature and pluralism of the media; information on the processing of personal data must be clear and accessible to anyone, in order to guarantee the right of those concerned to oppose their sharing.

Even in these cases, the remedies, tools, and systems made available for the protection of these rights are neither clear nor clarified (just compare the speed of Ai to our civil justice and the picture is perfect).

The bewilderment, however, manifests itself in the fact - I think not insignificant - that one does not really understand what one is dealing with.

Artificial intelligence is a hyper-computation system combined with machine learning technologies; in order to function, it must 'grind data and information' otherwise, for example, one cannot understand how a 'generative ia' can grow.

And this data the AI gets from all over the web.

Now, since the most authoritative websites, such as the major and most accredited television stations, have closed their access to their content, this means that the generative AI (e.g., ChatGPT) when answering your question will be able to draw on quora and facebook posts (for example).

Now, that is being concrete.

And a generic reference in a paragraph of Article 5 stating 'guarantee companies engaged in the sector access to high quality data' is certainly not enough to resolve the issue. Because such access is not regulated, and high quality is not defined (not even definable a priori), nor can this paragraph violate industrial and research property and copyright.

In particular, Article 23 envisages the introduction, in the context of the **regulation of audiovisual services** - subject to the acquisition of consent from rights holders - of an obligation to identify content created or modified through AI systems 'that are capable of presenting as real data, facts and information that are not', through the insertion of an appropriate identification mark. This is a response to the concerns generated by so-called '**deepfakes**'. This obligation of transparency is placed on the author or holder of the rights to such content: it will be the implementation modalities of this rule that will clarify on whom this responsibility materially falls. The insertion of the identifying sign is excluded when the content is part of a manifestly creative, satirical, artistic or fictitious work or programme, without prejudice to the protections for the rights and interests of third parties. The resolution of doubts as to the manner of implementation is left to self-regulatory and co-regulatory soft law sources.

The government aims to foster the development of **Italy's entrepreneurial fabric**; for this reason, Article 5 stipulates that the state and other public bodies:

- promote the use of A.I. in production processes to improve human-machine interaction and increase productivity;
- foster the development of an innovative and open Italian artificial intelligence market;
- ensure that companies involved in the sector have access to high quality data;

- direct the digital procurement platforms used by public administrations in such a way that preference is given to those solutions that guarantee the localisation and processing of critical data at data centres located throughout the country.

No specific direction is clear. Short of an 'anthropocentric model that respects the constitution'. And apart from an explicit 19th century-style protectionism, what seems to be the main thrust is the orientation of the AI in favour of the technologisation process of production enterprises.

As far as healthcare is concerned, the use of A.I. systems must not result in the selection of discriminatory criteria for access to treatment and medical services. The principle of informed consent is declined in the duty to inform the patient about the use of AI systems.

Fine. But all this was already provided for, moreover by general rules consolidated by extensive case law. What is omitted is the handling and protection of the product resulting from this use.

The question had arisen in connection with metadata.

Google paradoxically and dramatically states the truth when it denies access to much of the information requested on its own account by users: Google does not really know some things, because the transformed data, reassembled, become an articulated and amorphous metadata in which the individual is no longer traceable.

The main point was to standardise and protect metadata: a failed challenge.

An IA may certainly need informed consent to acquire 'first data' originator information, and existing rules already regulate such 'access'.

But the AI is not a cloud where files are simply stored in separate, recognisable folders; the AI that analyses 1 million ultrasound scans per month in Italy (for example) can break down the data: the gynaecologist looks for the vital data of the foetus, but tomorrow's AI can investigate the macro-data of the microcirculation of the uterine wall: 12 million a year of anonymous uteruses but which tell a great deal.

Who manages and protects this data, how? Also economically (since pharmaceutical companies, industries producing scanner systems, etc.) can make huge profits from it. And who can access this data, or ask this AI to analyse and search it for research purposes? For what purposes?

Here it is not that the regulation is missing, and an amendment is sufficient. Here, the thing that needs to be regulated is not really understood, and at the bottom, you would not even know what you are talking about.

The regulation of the use of A.I. is also crucial **in the intellectual professions**, where the use of A.I. systems is only permitted to carry out activities that are instrumental and supportive of the professional activity and where the intellectual work being performed is predominant.

In order to ensure the relationship of trust between the professional and the client, information on the artificial intelligence systems used by the professional is communicated to the recipient of the intellectual service in clear, simple and comprehensive language.

A question therefore arises, first and foremost, as to the meaning to be attributed to the concept of '*instrumental and support activities*' and the criteria for measuring the '*prevalence*' invoked by the rule. In this regard, it should not be forgotten that professionals compete with colleagues in other countries and with service companies against whom these limitations would not apply.

The ill-concealed idea underlying these statements is that the professional, called upon, for example, to write a text, sits in the armchair, writes the question to ChatGPT and it works for him. It is the anthropocentrism of fraudulent human logic.

Designing a bridge or tunnel in which all the calculations, virtual simulations, 3D processing and structural calculations, and even of each individual component, are included in this 'bridge project', how do they fit in?

Because this already happens: it is already machine learning systems with hyper computational capacity that do these things.

In the judiciary, artificial intelligence systems will be used exclusively for the organisation and simplification of judicial work as well as for jurisprudential and doctrinal research.

The Ministry of Justice will regulate the use of artificial intelligence systems by ordinary judicial offices. For other jurisdictions, the use shall be regulated in accordance with their respective regulations.

It remains reserved to the magistrate to decide on the interpretation of the law, the assessment of facts and evidence and the adoption of any measure.

The Civil Court will be the competent body to decide on cases relating to AI functioning.

There is one point that is unclear: if AI systems are used in evidence, in CTUs and CTPs, in reconstructions, in investigations, how much is the decision taken on the basis of their evaluation 'AI-free'?

Above all, there is a lack of any limitation and reference - although the debate, not only academic, is broad and widespread - on the criteria for programming algorithms in this matter, especially for the purposes of even potential verification of discriminatory and prejudicial proceedings.

Since the use of artificial intelligence often intersects with the protection of the users of audiovisual or radio services and with the matter of **copyright**, Article 23 of the bill states that any information content broadcast on any type of audiovisual or radio platform that has been entirely created or modified with AI systems must be made, by the author or the owner of the economic exploitation rights, recognisable to users by means of an identification sign or an embedded marking with the wording 'I.A.'.

As regards the protection of copyright, however, Article 24 of the draft law provides for the amendment of Article 1, Law no. 633/1941 according to which intellectual works, and therefore protected by the aforementioned law, also include those that have been created with the use of artificial intelligence, where the human contribution is in any case '*creative, relevant and demonstrable*'.

Again, anthropocentrism gives way to 'suspicion of man'.

Yet the principles exist and are borrowed for example from common-law experiences (for obvious and chronological reasons, these are also the systems that have been dealing with concrete cases on the subject for the longest time), on the other hand, copyright depends on the ***threshold of originality***, i.e., the so-called ***"threshold of originality"*** given by three assumptions: skill (creative competence), labour (commitment, work) and judgement (ability to discern, distinguish and choose the distinctive elements of the work).

In extreme synthesis, we can say that using this threefold parameter (simultaneously subsisting and in which the elements must be at least equivalent, if not quantitatively equivalent) for Anglo-American jurisprudence, works produced with artificial intelligence systems present skills and labour. Lacking, however, is the judgement that belongs to the human being.

These are common-sense principles, and not overly elastic as they might seem, yet it seems clear that those who wrote the rule missed the point radically.

Undersecretary Butti specified that in the field of copyright law, competence lies with the EU and EU rules already regulate the issue of content protection in the case of web scraping, with the opt-out mechanism on the part of rights holders.

The bill includes two novelties and a reminder: the need for an identification mark on any type of content is made or modified with AI; copyright protection for works produced with AI as long as the human contribution is creative, relevant and demonstrable; and a reference to copyright law for the reproduction and extraction of works or other materials through artificial intelligence models and systems, including generative intelligence, permitted for research reasons or when the use of the works and other materials has not been expressly reserved by the holders of copyright and related rights as well as the owners of databases.

And yes here, to be practical, nothing that is not foreseen for example in any disclaimer in a printed book.

Finally, the government also intervenes **in criminal matters**, punishing the distorted use of artificial intelligence systems, which can create damage to legal assets such as the moral integrity of individuals.

In fact, a new offence is introduced in Article *612-quater* of the Criminal Code, which punishes '*Whoever, in order to cause damage to a person and without his consent, sends, delivers, assigns, publishes or in any case disseminates his image, video or voice, falsified or altered through the use of artificial intelligence systems and suitable to mislead as to their genuineness*' (which includes, for example, so-called deep fakes) with imprisonment from six months to three years or from one to five years if unfair damage results from the act.

The offence is punishable on complaint by the offended person, but is prosecuted ex officio if the offence is connected with another offence for which prosecution is ex officio, or if it is committed against a person who is incapacitated by age or infirmity, or against a public authority by reason of the functions exercised.

A number of aggravating circumstances concerning the use of artificial intelligence are also provided for in Articles 61(*11-novies*), 494 and 501 of the criminal code.

Again on the criminal law front, the use of AI systems also becomes an aggravating circumstance for a number of offences such as substitution of person, fraudulent raising and lowering of prices, fraud, computer fraud, money laundering to self-laundering, and market rigging.

Copyright protection extends in the case of reproduction or extraction of text or data from works or other materials available on networks or in databases in violation of Articles 70-ter and 70-quater, including through artificial intelligence systems.

In this respect, the measure does not deviate from the governmental tradition whereby every regulatory intervention intervenes, sometimes even only incidentally, in criminal matters.

The delicacy of the specificity of criminal law would call for greater caution in this approach, also for the sake of the stylistic rigour of the code of criminal law, the primary instrument for implementing that principle of 'knowledge and cognizability' of the criminal law as a prerequisite for awareness of the commission of the offence.

By dint of the insertion of *bis-ter-quater* articles and '*x-nonies*' paragraphs, the Italian penal code has more than tripled in volume without directly affecting the reduction of offences (except for those abolished or transformed into administrative offences).

Instead, this has led to less clarity, less knowability, and therefore less certainty, all of which are accompanied by the objective fact that the more you include the more you risk creating a conflict between norms, uncertainty of applicability in practice, conflict between offences - objective or interpretative - and widening the margins of interpretation: all characteristics that are ill-suited to Article 27 of the Constitution and in general to a penal system that is both guarantor-friendly (but also only definable as civil, and at the same time at least useful, if not effective).

There was no pressing need for 612-quater, for example: it was enough to make the case as specific in 612. and if one wanted to change the penalty range envisaged, one only had to amend it. Considering the use of AI - which is a tool - as an aggravating element of punishment is more of a political manifesto than an effective tool in the criminal law context. It is as if the crime of massacre provided for in Article 422 of the Criminal Code (*one of those crimes for which there is no 'attempt', but having only planted a device, even if exploded without human victims, corresponds to the case in point*) were more serious if committed with a bomb than with a machine gun, and less serious if committed with a pistol.

What should count in criminal law - *which, let us remember, is that branch of law that affects people's freedom* - should be, both as an aggravating and as a mitigating factor, 'the fact', and the consequent damage and injury to the right.

Criminal law should be parsimonious, but this would run the serious risk of also becoming clear, certain and stable, like any self-respecting criminal law.

But the vice of 'weak politics' of intervening in a 'strong way' with political manifesto articles in criminal matters is the short way to say you have done something concrete. A concreteness reified in a few lines written in a law. And it is an issue of bipartisan legislative technique.

Enhancement of customised teaching plans for students with high cognitive abilities for the integration of **AI training** and the use of artificial intelligence systems for the improvement of psychophysical well-being through sporting activity, also for the development of innovative solutions aimed at greater inclusion of persons with disabilities in sport.

In case it had escaped our notice, let's clarify: AI is to be used to support customised educational plans for students with high cognitive abilities, while for people with disabilities, innovative solutions are to be sought for greater inclusion in sports.

Is the underlying cultural model clearer this way?

One completely ignores the entire decade-long field of revolutionary studies of the use of AI (today) and the 40-year-long field of the use of information technology (yesterday) for the development and cognitive support of differently abled, or even disabled, people.

Subject to the general principles set out in this law, artificial intelligence systems may also be used for the organisation of sports activities.

On the relationship between **AI systems and minors**, the government sets a number of limits: for minors under 14 years of age, parental consent is required; minors between 14 and 18 years of age may give their consent for the processing of personal data related to the use of artificial intelligence systems, provided that the information and communications (privacy notices) are easily accessible and understandable *(sic!)*. More generally, information and communications relating to the processing of data are provided in clear and simple language, so as to ensure that the user is fully aware of and has the right to object to incorrect processing of his or her personal data.

Now, we weren't able to do this with Google, Facebook & co. on data, we lost completely without 'figuring it out' on metadata, and now we would like these principles applied to AI, which is a computational hypercapacity?

A clear and simple language to explain complex metadata management and processing processes is indeed desirable, but someone who has at least understood the phenomenon should ask for it and clarify the rules. Here, this is clearly not the case.

In what language should it be said clearly and simply that your data is taken from you, full stop, the IA at the end of the day not only hardly cares whether it is from Mario Rossi or Maria Bianchi, rather the names and surnames are 'extra data' that weigh down the process.

That this data will be ground up, shredded, selected, recompacted, reformulated: it is like making a house by tearing down three and choosing the pieces to construct the new building by anonymising the origins.

That is how it should be explained: but that is exactly how it will not be explained.

Economic development and **cybersecurity** are areas in which the provision of quality data and storage in national data centres is valued: but these are principles in principle. Reading the period three times, however, one realises that it is so empty as to become absurd, so useless that one cannot even say that it is 'wrong'.

Article 6 then identifies **activities carried out with the help of AI systems for purposes of national security and defence** - including activities to protect national security in cyberspace - which are excluded from the scope of the bill.

The provisions of Article 8 denote an attempt to remove some of the obstacles that the current legal framework places in the way of the use of health data for **scientific research** purposes. Among other things, it provides that not-for-profit entities are legitimised to make secondary use of personal data, even of special categories, already collected during previous research projects, without the need to request further consent from the data subjects.

Of course, this is a text that is destined to be discussed and revised in parliament, but it is nevertheless possible to highlight, on the one hand, incompatibility profiles with the **provisions of the GDPR** and, on the other hand, a gap with regard to scientific research activities by profit-making organisations.

There is also a problem of coordination with the provisions on scientific research in the field of health, contained in the law converting the so-called PNRR decree, definitively approved on 23 April (the same day as the approval of the DDL IA), and aimed at amending Article 110 of Legislative Decree No. 196/2003 (Privacy Code).

These provisions, inter alia, remove the obligation of prior consultation of the Garante in the case of processing of data relating to health, without the consent of the data subject, for the purposes of medical scientific research.

In short, therefore, that little guarantee on the most sensitive data is in fact circumvented, and at the same time, any reference to the regulations on data management by for-profit companies is omitted.

Public administrations use artificial intelligence in order to increase the efficiency of their activities, to reduce the time taken to define procedures and to increase the quality and quantity of the services provided to citizens and businesses, ensuring that those concerned are aware of its operation and can trace its use. The adoption of each measure remains the responsibility of the officials and managers (*responsibility over which nothing is done*).

The text of 26 articles stipulates that its implementation, also by public administrations, should be financially neutral. No additional resources, except for the one billion (already existing, simply differently tied) to CDP Venture capital destined for the entrepreneurial system, which should drive private investments of 3 billion.

'Italy is the first country to have launched an industrial policy on AI,' stressed Butti.

Definitely emphatic, disproportionate and technically untrue statement.

The 'industrial' focus is there in all sector regulations. If anything, one wonders whether, in order to give attention (and emphasis) to industriality, other, ontologically more central aspects have not been omitted.

Incidentally, on this issue one waits to read the Italian Strategy, which has so far only come out in executive summary, while Article 21 is dedicated in the bill.

In the ten-page AGID document, however, there is a revolutionary idea: create a Foundation to coordinate... a new institution, and if possible even the most old-economy (though among the most flexible).

However, another aspect of Butti's statement *'Italy is the first country to have launched an industrial policy on IA'* is interesting: an industrial policy without resources and isolated. Let someone explain to Butti what an industrial policy is.

These provisions, inter alia, do away, as we have seen, with the obligation of prior consultation of the Garante in the case of processing of data relating to health, in the absence of the consent of the data subject, for the purposes of medical scientific research.

The real crux of this general regulation is that any reference to the regulation of data management by for-profit companies is omitted.

20

Recidivism and Predictive Policing

The Limits of the AI Act and the Guidelines to the Regulation

On the occasion of the full effectiveness of Chapters I and II of the EU Artificial Intelligence Regulation (AI Act: ban on unacceptably risky systems in force), the European Commission on 4 February 2025 published an annex to the Guidelines on Prohibited Practices.

These are specific areas in respect of which both the design and implementation of artificial intelligence systems is prohibited because they would entail unsustainable risks to people's fundamental rights.

Article 5 of the Regulation enumerates these practices, in summary and in general lines:

- Subliminal-manipulative-deceptive techniques
- Techniques for exploiting disabilities or specific situations of weakness
- Social scoring
- Predictive policing
- Facial recognition by scraping
- Recognition of emotions
- Biometric categorisation (except for law enforcement)

The guidelines are intended to illustrate and exemplify the mutual boundaries between prohibitions and non-exclusions in order to facilitate compliance work by public and private entities.

As guidelines they cannot be binding: any 'authentic' interpretation of the rules of the regulation will be left to the EU Court of Justice and any application of Article 5 will have to be made on a case-by-case basis.

The predictive policing part directly impacts on the judiciary.

In general, the use of artificial intelligence systems for individual risk assessment and crime prediction is prohibited.

DOI: 10.1201/9781003731290-24

The main objective of Section 5(1)(d) of the AI Act is to prevent AI tools from being used to predict the likelihood of a person committing a crime, based solely on profiling or assessments of personality traits.

The prohibition is based on the protection of fundamental rights and the risk of discrimination and stigmatisation arising from the use of such systems, and covers criminal offences based solely on personal data and profiling, net of exceptions and exclusions.

The exceptions provided for, however, allow the use of AI systems to support human evaluations, provided they are based on objective and verifiable data directly linked to criminal activities.

The prohibition of Article 5(1)(d) is triggered when three simultaneous and cumulative conditions occur:

1. The practice must constitute the 'placing on the market', the 'putting into service', for the 'specific purpose' or 'use' of an IA system,
2. The IA system must carry out risk assessments that assess or predict the risk of an individual committing an offence,
3. Risk assessment or forecasting must be based on one or both of these activities:
   (a) the profiling of a natural person,
   (b) the assessment of a natural person's personality traits and characteristics.

Thus, in concrete terms, no prohibition if 'the main purpose' is not prediction, even if this is a 'by-product' of a different purpose.

In addition, what is stipulated in point three, both in a) and b) are not at all defined, nor in themselves prohibited.

The prohibition applies to AI systems that assess the risk or likelihood of a person committing a crime in the future, if they are based solely on profiling data or personality characteristics without any link to concrete facts.

If AI assesses a person's risk of committing a crime based solely on personal characteristics (e.g., personality, ethnicity, past non-criminal behaviour, socio-economic status), it is prohibited. Such systems can generate prejudice, discrimination and injustice.

If, on the other hand, they are not 'exclusively' based on these two data but in the broader context of other and further analysis criteria, this requirement can easily be curbed.

In this context, it suffices to recall that the 'weights' of each criterion are not indicated, but only 'the criteria used absolutely' or exclusively.

This fits in perfectly with the next step.

If AI is used to support a human assessment and is based on concrete and verifiable data, such as a criminal record, documented association with criminal networks or evidence directly linked to a crime, then it is permitted. In this case, the AI system does not make decisions on its own, but helps human experts assess risks.

The guidelines present some concrete examples that should, in intention, simplify the identification of what can and cannot be done.

An AI system that assigns risk scores to people based only on their personality or the neighbourhood in which they live is prohibited.

An AI system that analyses data from ongoing investigations and indicates correlations between certain factual elements and the risk of reoffending is allowed.

The key criterion is that profiling should be based on verifiable evidence and not on assumptions or generic correlations.

In this case there is a macroscopic flaw.

Where the principle of the presumption of innocence until final judgment is provided for, data on 'ongoing investigations' (not even indictment!) as well as 'factual elements' (not adjudicated at trial) already and in themselves constitute an element of prejudice to and in profiling, including ethnicity and socio-economic status.

If, for example, a person lives in a suburban neighbourhood and is an immigrant who has already been prosecuted for a property crime (e.g., embezzlement), even if not prosecuted, he or she will end up in the prediction in any case, even if not explicitly on the basis of the ethnic or socio-economic criterion simply because of the statistical incidence, which in this case becomes a self-fulfilling statistical prophecy, since it excludes non-immigrant subjects from other neighbourhoods from the prediction a priori.

In this regard, we can cite the recent case in England where the AI system used by the government to detect welfare fraud showed discrimination on the basis of people's age, disability, marital status and nationality. An internal evaluation of the machine learning programme used to examine Universal Credit claims in England found that it incorrectly selected people from some groups more than others when identifying who to investigate for possible fraud.

The AI Act permits the profiling of persons for the purpose of assessing risk (recidivism) and the commission of future offences only if it is based on objective and verifiable facts directly related to criminal activity, however with exceptions and limitations governing its use.

1. No decision can be fully automated.

Even if an AI system uses concrete data, it cannot make autonomous decisions on the assessment of criminal risk. There must always be human supervision, with the power to verify, challenge and correct AI assessments.

2. The ban on 'generalised' profiling applies.

The IA cannot generate risk assessments on entire categories of people (e.g., all inhabitants of a neighbourhood or members of a social group). The assessment must be individualised and based on specific elements directly related to criminal activity.

3. The data must be directly linked to criminal activities.

The system may only analyse data that have a direct and verifiable link to criminal acts. The use of data of personal habits, political or religious orientations or other personal characteristics unrelated to crimes is not permitted.

4. The prohibition of discrimination applies.

Even if AI uses hard data, its use cannot generate discrimination prohibited by EU law (e.g., based on ethnicity, religion, gender, socio-economic status). Evaluations must be transparent and verifiable to avoid systemic bias, i.e., justifiable by objective and verifiable data, avoiding opacity in decision-making processes.

Regarding the first point, that AI cannot decide on its own seems tautological, at least insofar as there is not yet an AI-powered robot-judge.

That any predictive data must be 'presented' to a human operator seems pleonastic to specify. In fact, the guidelines explicitly state that there are areas in which the police can use AI to support investigations, but not to automatically justify arrest or surveillance decisions.

But if the survey is 'statistically oriented' it is also directed, leading to the de facto exclusion of other paths, or at least making them more difficult because they are unsupported (if not excluded a priori).

The second limitation appears naïve to say the least, because what escapes one's notice is that it is the AID that creates the categories 'by itself' through data management and analysis, so if it has to predict recidivism in a suburb where statistically high percentages of immigrants, often from other religions than the 'national' one, live in socio-economically disadvantaged conditions, it is evident that it will end up statistically generating a prediction in this sense, and at the same time creating two categories: those more included and those more excluded from the risk category.

As specific predicted events come true, these two sets will be consolidated on the basis of the 'prediction come true' process. This will reinforce the categorical bias.

The criticism of the second point ends up implicitly violating - in an unintended but not prevented way - the limitation in points three and four as well.

An AI system is not covered by the ban if it meets all these criteria:

- It supports human analysis: AI does not make autonomous decisions, but provides data and evaluations that are examined and interpreted by a human being.
- It is based on objective and verifiable facts: the data used must be concrete, documented and verifiable. Examples: Official criminal record. Documented involvement in criminal networks.
- Material evidence of criminal activity (e.g., images from video surveillance, suspicious financial transactions confirmed by investigation).
- It has a direct link to a criminal activity: it cannot make inferences based on personal characteristics (e.g., psychological profile, socio-economic background, ethnicity) without a specific connection to a crime.

Practical examples of AI systems excluded from the ban

Allowed (if they meet the above criteria):

- Analysis of financial crime patterns: An AI system that analyses suspicious banking transactions based on verified money laundering data.
- AI for the prevention of reoffending: A system that supports legal practitioners in analysing the probability of reoffending based on concrete criminal records.
- AI for forensic analysis: Systems that identify connections between already verified forensic evidence and established criminal profiles.

All the examples (taken from the guidelines), although valid in their intentions, are in fact discriminatory in themselves: basing oneself on previous convictions is in itself pleonastic (only a person who has already committed an offence can be a recidivist, the incensed person cannot), but in this pleonastic criterion (which is therefore useless) a mechanism of self-fulfilling statistical prophecy is inserted.

Worse is the third point that even lends itself to outright forgery: by executing an offence 'imitating the means and modalities' of a convicted offender, one ends up having him investigated, even though nothing would have led to him by any other route.

The point is that these risks are not only concrete, but also - on the basis of these guidelines - inevitable. And we already know this now (just as we already know that in ten years' time the ECHR will have to establish this for events experienced 'in the skin' of real people).

The fact that examples of explicitly prohibited systems include those of

- AI that assigns a criminal risk score based only on personality or online behaviour.
- A system that labels people as potential criminals because they live in an area with high crime rates.
- AI that generates automated surveillance alerts on persons without documented evidence of criminal activity

not only does not solve the problem, but hides behind it. It is evident that no one will write in black and white that the system they intend to implement will do so. On the contrary, it is more than likely to write the exact opposite in order to be policy compliant.

Is this enough to legitimise the system? This is especially sufficient in the knowledge that - beyond the declarations - AI systems through ML do nothing more, by analysing human behaviour, than consolidate self-fulfilling statistics, and thus in themselves discriminate exactly according to officially forbidden criteria.

Even in cases where profiling can be carried out under the conditions laid down, the AI system may form the basis of an automated decision that must always be subject to human evaluation.

The concept of 'human intervention' has been the subject of scrutiny by the Court of Justice of the European Union (CJEU), particularly in the context of automated decisions involving the prediction of the risk of involvement of persons in serious crimes.

In particular, the judgment of reference is the 'Ligue des droits humains' case (C-817/19), in which the CJEU analysed the legality of using an advanced AI system for the systematic analysis of air passenger data (Passenger Name Record - PNR) to predict the likelihood of involvement in acts of terrorism or other serious crimes.

The EU Court ruled that negative decisions (it did not rule on 'positive' decisions!) cannot be made solely on the basis of an automated process. An independent, non-automated human assessment is required before making a decision based on results generated by an AI system.

This assessment must be based on objective criteria to avoid discrimination and false positives.

Consequently, according to the Court, any use of AI to predict criminal risk must include effective human supervision; human operators must be competent, trained and able to understand the capabilities and limitations of the AI system; procedures must be in place to avoid blind automation bias and to intervene in the event of erroneous or discriminatory results.

In conclusion, the EU Court ruled that human intervention must not be a mere formality, but a real active control over the results produced by automated systems.

However, it must be said that in the case examined, the set considered was itself closed (the passenger list) and uniform (people taking a certain flight) and limited (dozens of individuals).

If the principles of the judgment in itself are valid, they become less so in a generalised analysis where the whole is not limited, is not heterogeneous, is not discriminated against on the basis of a precise individual choice ex ante (take that flight on that day and go to that place).

As the prediction scenario changes, the criterion must also change.

The guidelines go on to indicate when the ban involves private actors:

- if I am mandated by law to exercise public authority to prevent and combat crime (a private security agency mandated by law to support police operations in identifying criminals may not use AI to assign individual risk scores);
- if they are explicitly mandated on a case-by-case basis by law enforcement authorities (a data analysis company that is asked to use AI to predict the likelihood of a person committing a crime could be subject to the ban);
- whether the use of IA by these entities is required by law to fulfil specific regulatory obligations (a bank has a legal obligation to monitor transactions to detect money laundering activities).

There are cases in which a company's activities do not fall under the prohibition of the AI Act, even if they involve the use of AI for risk monitoring: if the use of AI does not have the main purpose of assessing individual criminal risk.

A company that uses AI to analyse financial anomalies (such as suspicious movements in bank accounts) to protect its financial interests is not covered by the ban, unless it is making individual predictive assessments of criminal risk.

If the AI system is used exclusively for internal business purposes. For example, if an insurance company uses AI to assess the risk of insurance fraud without specifically predicting whether a customer will commit a crime, it does not fall under the prohibition.

If the analysis concerns collective and not individual behaviour. Analyses based on aggregated and anonymous data (geospatial analyses of crime in a city) do not fall under the prohibition because they do not directly identify individuals as potential criminals.

In conclusion, private companies may be subject to the ban if they act on behalf of public authorities or for specific legal obligations. On the other hand, they are not covered by the prohibition if their use of AI does not directly concern the prediction of individual crimes or if they operate only for internal business purposes.

On the latter points of limiting or not limiting use, the imbalance in several respects is evident.

Public activity - in itself of public interest, even when delegated - is severely restricted, even when it concerns aspects of objective security.

On the other hand, a private activity is explicitly permitted, which is not only particularly invasive, but also (again explicitly) linked to commercial purposes, both direct and indirect.

Whilst public activity is at least in part guaranteed by a multiplicity of vertical controls, and is therefore at least potentially endowed with lines of control, verification, correction and sanction at an organisational and power level (not least in view of its public utility purpose), the same cannot be said in terms of controls, verifications and sanctions in private entities, which, if we look at the purpose (typically commercial and profit-making), constitute a real and concrete conflict of interest.

Let us make two practical assumptions.

A private security agency mandated by law to support police operations at airport checkpoints, in identifying criminals, cannot use AI to assign individual risk scores. Yet in this case, with a few adjustments, the purpose might justify its use at least in spot checks.

On the other hand, these two uses are permitted:

- by an insurance company to assess the risk of insurance fraud (without specifically predicting whether a customer will commit a crime) and if the analysis concerns collective and not individual behaviour, then analyses based on aggregated and anonymous data (geospatial analyses of crime in a city) do not fall under the ban because they do not directly identify individuals as potential criminals.

Well then, when the result of the analysis reveals that past statistics show criticalities, which manager will not raise rates according to residency by neighbourhood (socio-economic and socio-racial discrimination) or refuse to contract on this basis? If he deviates from the system's indication, he will even be recalled by the company (officially for carelessness with respect to policy, actually for reasons of company profit!).

What emerges on the whole is that this part of the guidelines, in the albeit appreciable context of formal defining safeguards in terms of non-discrimination - are not only ineffective, but clearly dimensioned to protect the interests of the private sector, first and foremost the economic-financial-insurance sector, which has also been using these systems for some time now for the definition of formal compliance criteria and for the optimisation of controls and profit and loss results.

21

AI Manipulative and Deceptive European Commission Guidelines on Prohibited Advertising Practices

On 4 February 2025, the European Commission approved Guidelines to promote compliance with Article 5 of the AI ACT Regulation. The standard enumerates which practices are prohibited in the use of artificial intelligence systems.

The prohibition in Section 5(I)(1)(a) and (b) of the AI Act specifically concerns the prohibition of the placing on the market, putting into service or use of AI systems that are manipulative or deceptive in nature and/or exploit vulnerabilities, influencing the behaviour of individual users or categories.

The standard aims to protect users of AI systems (especially those who are more vulnerable due to age, disability or socio-economic conditions) from the potentially harmful effects of manipulation and exploitation of this technology, which could undermine their decision-making autonomy, free choice and, in general, freedom (the articles fit within the right to dignity). These prohibitions are particularly concerned with those systems that employ subliminal, deliberately manipulative or deceptive techniques.

The focus of this standard is on techniques that act at the threshold of an individual's conscious awareness, and their impact on the ability of a person or group to make informed decisions.

The article prohibits the creation and marketing of systems that employ subliminal techniques to direct/manipulate someone's opinions with the end effect of distorting their behaviour by impairing their ability to make informed decisions, manoeuvring them to behave in ways they would not otherwise behave.

For the ban to be triggered, however, at least these two interrelated conditions must be fulfilled:

- the AI system must be put on the market (so both providers and their distributors are susceptible to prohibition - in this case, for example, the requirement would be curbed simply by talking about a product 'in test', a demo version, and it is not clear whether 'free of charge' falls into this category).

DOI: 10.1201/9781003731290-25

- the system must employ subliminal, manipulative and deceptive techniques. (Subliminal techniques act by bypassing the individual's rational defences, affecting his or her decision-making processes - precisely because 'subliminal' appears from the outset to be particularly complex as well as burdensome to test such a system).

  The guidelines exemplify these techniques in 'macro' categories:

- visual subliminal messages: *too fast for the brain to register*;
- audio subliminal messages: *at a volume too low to be perceived;*
- sub-visual and sub-audio signals: *hidden or imperceptible;*
- images 'hidden' in other images;
- misdirection: *the system makes the user focus on certain information/stimuli while hiding others;*

Temporal manipulation: *the system alters the user's perception of time, causing dependency/impatience.*

Deliberately manipulative techniques aim to influence, alter or control an individual's behaviour by undermining his or her individual autonomy. They are typically designed to exploit cognitive biases, psychological vulnerabilities or other situational factors.

It is not necessary that the supplier, distributor or the system itself intend to cause harm; therefore, if the system learns this type of technique through user responses or research material, the supplier and distributor are only subject to the article if, aware of the techniques adopted, they do not act with preventive/mitigating measures.

So, in summary: the technique must be subliminal, it can be 'acquired' and through machine learning and implemented autonomously by the machine, and the producer - if and when aware - is exempt from liability if he does not intervene ex-post.

One wonders if it was not - and is - simpler to provide for ex-ante blocking procedures to these practices so that the machine, even when and if it 'finds and applies these strategies autonomously', is ex-ante inhibited from putting them into practice?

Deceptive techniques subvert or impair a person's autonomy, decision-making capacity or free choices by presenting false or misleading information with the aim or effect of deceiving individuals and influencing their behaviour.

These techniques must have the ultimate purpose or effect of distorting the behaviour of a person or group, causing behaviour or decisions that would not have been made under other circumstances.

What is not addressed, and therefore clarified, is the limit of 'atmosphere'. Creating an ambience that is familiar, comfortable, close to the user, has no direct implications in a deterministic sense, but certainly favours user choice. Think of a human voice even 'familiar' with a human face, if anything 'friendly', in a place/time specific interaction.

For the prohibition to be triggered, there must be a reasonable and plausible causal correlation between the AI manipulative techniques and the potential material distortion of the person's behaviour or subconsciousness, i.e., an influence on the person's ability to make informed decisions, thus causing them to behave or make decisions they would not otherwise have made.

It is precisely for this reason that the failure to address the issue of an 'ambient atmosphere' generated by the AI is a vulnus that increases the complexity and onerousness of the test.

Furthermore, the prohibition is applicable if the purpose of the supplier or distributor is actually to deceive users or even if that simply turns out to be the end effect.

According to the guidelines, in order to avoid providing AI systems that could potentially be banned, developers and providers should take appropriate measures such as: transparency and safeguarding individual autonomy, compliance with applicable regulations, and adherence to due diligence and industry standards.

Compared to this 'bureaucratic burden', it would have been sufficient to provide explicit and ex ante 'blocks' of things that the system 'cannot do' as opposed to ex post verification of a theoretical adjustment to 'standards' (which do not exist for the time being) in the context of policies that are in any case subject to wide margins of interpretation.

The 'distorted' behaviour must cause significant harm to the person, other persons or the group.

No definition of 'significant damage' is given, which therefore needs to be assessed on a case-by-case basis.

A number of considerations to be made when assessing the harm are specified: severity of the harm, the context of the person and the cumulative effects of the harm, scale and intensity of the harm (how many people were affected by the harm), the vulnerability of the group involved, duration and reversibility.

Once again, it appears that the writer of the rule is not familiar with the phenomenon, and merely extends typified principles of material damage.

In these cases, on the other hand, it is precisely the typicality of AI's dynamic activities that must provide for a wide-ranging hypothesis of harm and proof of harm even in the context of classes of harm such as 'loss of plausible alternative'.

The damages identified may be:

- physical (to persons or property);
- psychological (they have an impact on a person's mental health and psychological and emotional well-being and are more difficult to assess because their consequences are noticed in the long term);
- financial and economic.

The focus of this standard is the protection of people who are particularly vulnerable due to age, disability, or specific economic and cultural situations, and who are more susceptible to exploitation by AI systems.

Again, these are standard categories, replicated by other regulatory frameworks where these are the 'normal' requirements for so-called vulnerable categories.

We forget - it seems - that in the context of subliminality we are all vulnerable, with the paradox even being that a possible disability that limits certain forms of use (think of visual blindness) may even reduce the very vulnerability to such systems.

The article I am commenting on prohibits the creation and marketing of systems that exploit the vulnerabilities of persons or groups of persons due to their age, disability, specific economic or social situation with the aim or effect of manipulating or distorting their behaviour that causes or reasonably could cause significant harm to that person or group. To be applied it must happen that:

- The system must be placed on the market and in use or potentially usable;
- The system has to exploit vulnerabilities due to age (children under 18, the elderly), disability (people with long-term physical, mental, intellectual and sensory impairments), socio-economic situations (e.g., people living in extreme poverty or belonging to religious or ethnic minorities, migrants or refugees); thus it concerns individuals who tend to have less capacity to realise/resist the manipulation of AI systems and therefore need more protection;
- Exploitation must be objective or objective must be the effect of material distortion of the person's or group's behaviour (here we go a step further than in the previous article, which focuses on the person's ability to make informed decisions: here it is assumed that decisions cannot be informed because we are talking about vulnerable groups);
- The distorted behaviour must cause or have the potential to cause significant harm (again, physical, psychological, financial, economic) to the person or group (the threshold of what can be considered serious harm is also lowered, considering that we are talking about vulnerable individuals).

Thus, when evaluating which article to apply, one must consider the dominant aspect of exploitation: are you targeting a specific group?

The guidelines exemplify some practices that do not fall under the prohibition of manipulation, deception and exploitative AI, if they do not cause significant harm.

There are two main categories:

- Lawful Persuasion;
- Persuasion techniques based on transparent and verifiable information are not prohibited.

They aim to inform and convince, in a dialogue in which the user is aware of the attempted influence and can choose to accept it independently. It therefore formally respects the frameworks.

Examples given are traditional advertising: advertisements that use persuasion techniques without manipulating emotions or distorting the user's ability to make decisions; or AI systems for coaching and motivational support, which help improve productivity or lifestyle habits, without using deceptive techniques.

On this point, however, it fails to mention that a major achievement was to clearly define (on television and in newspapers, it must be clearly scrutinised) that this is advertising, which is not the case in AI contexts.

In addition - precisely because of their technical and technological peculiarities - degenerative systems of targeted advertising with integrated Ai systems often skim forms of 'ad personam', which makes objective discrimination extremely complex.

They are also excluded:

- Manipulative or deceptive AI systems that do not cause significant harm;
- An AI system that uses manipulative techniques without serious effects on decision-making capacity or without causing significant material or psychological harm may not be covered by the ban.

Does the ex-ante exclusion of these systems actually inhibit ex-post verification of the veracity of these assumptions? It is unclear, especially if these exclusions are provided for directly in the guidelines, which should instead offer clear - and possibly simple and immediate - systems for verifying the limit. Providing for an ab origine exclusion here actually creates limits to the verification itself.

Examples of AI excluded from these limitations are then proposed: AI that suggests purchases based on the user's preferences (without deceiving or pushing the user into harmful purchases). AI companion systems designed in an anthropomorphic way with affective computing to make it more attractive and effective in engaging users, but which does not adopt manipulative or deceptive practices; therapeutic chatbots that use subliminal techniques to guide users to a healthier lifestyle; online music platform with emotional recognition; manipulative techniques in online security training (such as phishing attempts).

In all these 'excluded a priori' cases, it is not clear who is responsible for verifying the expressed consensus. Once it has been self-declared by the subject that its 'AI system suggests purchases based on the user's preferences without misleading him or inducing him to make harmful purchases', what are the tools for verifying this condition in practice?

Instead, it seems more effective to introduce a system based on the precautionary principle, which would have established, for example, that when an entity intends to adopt and market an 'AI system that suggests purchases based on user preferences', it must clearly and transparently demonstrate ex ante that it acts 'without deceiving the user or inducing him to make harmful purchases'.

This is also in order to avoid a disproportion in the cost and position of ex post verification and challenge, if at all, after such a system has been adopted vis-à-vis a potentially very large public and for a not indifferent length of time.

Finally, the guidelines take care to recall that these rules do not prejudge but complement the framework provided in other Community acts. Specifically:

- Consumer Protection Act (UCPD)
- Data Protection Laws (GDPR)
- Anti-discrimination laws
- Digital Services Act (DSA)
- Directive 2010/13/EU (AVMSD)
- Product safety laws
- Criminal laws

Which ultimately ends up devolving to these latter regulations - and to the authorities in charge of their compliance - also the verification of the contents regulated in the guidelines.

22

AI and Prohibition of Social Scoring in the European Commission Guidelines

On 4 February, the European Commission approved important Guidelines to promote compliance with Article 5 of the AI ACT Regulation. The standard enumerates which practices are prohibited in the use of artificial intelligence systems.

In this article, we analyse the prohibition of social scoring established by Section 5(1)(c) of the AI Act. Social scoring, i.e., the marketing, commissioning and use of social scoring AI systems, is prohibited when it involves discriminatory or disproportionate treatment based on personal characteristics or social behaviour.

It should always be emphasised that the Guidelines are not binding, especially with regard to future interpretation by the EU Court of Justice.

Social scoring is defined as an AI system that evaluates or ranks people based on social behaviour, personal characteristics or personality traits, even if only inferred, over a period of time.

Social scoring is prohibited if it leads to unfavourable or harmful treatment in unrelated contexts; or to treatment disproportionate to the severity of the behaviour.

The guidelines give as an example of the first case the exclusion from public services of a person with a low credit score; as an example of the second case the restriction of access to public transport in the case of a fine for jaywalking.

Key elements of the ban are

(a) evaluation or grading on a social or personal basis, i.e., using personal, behavioural or psychological data to create a score,
(b) the production of harmful effects in unrelated contexts (if social scoring leads to consequences in different spheres, e.g., school, work, health);
(c) use by public or private entities and even governments.

DOI: 10.1201/9781003731290-26

Several cumulative conditions must be fulfilled for the ban to be triggered:

(a) the 'placing on the market', 'putting into service' or 'use' of an artificial intelligence system;

(b) the purpose of assessing or classifying natural persons or groups of persons over a period of time on the basis of their social behaviour; or known, inferred or predicted personal or personality characteristics;

(c) the causal relationship between the social score created with the aid of the AI system and harmful or unfavourable treatment of persons or groups within one or more of the following scenarios: in social contexts unrelated to those in which the data were originally generated or collected; and/or treatment that is unjustified or disproportionate to their social behaviour or its severity.

The ban assumes that the evaluation or classification is based on data spanning "a certain period of time". This, according to the Guidelines, suggests that the assessment should not be one-off or immediate. At the same time, it is important that this condition be assessed taking into account all the circumstances of the case in order to avoid circumvention of the scope of the prohibition.

The example could be that of an immigration and asylum authority implementing a partially automated system built on a series of infrastructures including cameras and motion sensors for surveillance in refugee camps.

If the data analysed cover a period of time and specific individuals (such as migrants) are assessed, e.g., to ascertain whether they run the risk of attempting to abscond, then it would qualify as 'for a certain period of time' and the prohibition in Section 5(1)(c) of the IVG Act may apply if all other conditions are met.

The guidelines emphasise that while 'assessment' implies (would imply!) the involvement of some form of judgement about a person or group of persons, the mere classification of persons or groups of persons based on characteristics such as age, gender and height is a broader concept and can also cover other types of classifications or categorisations of individuals or groups of persons even in the absence of assessment.

The term 'assessment' also refers to the concept of 'profiling', which is governed by EU data protection law and constitutes a specific form of assessment. According to the Guidelines, profiling can also be included in the prohibition (*although without the AI Act explicitly calling out the GDPR on this aspect*) if the assessment takes place in an automated manner with an AI system based on personal data.

Profiling is the use of information about an individual (or group of individuals) and assessment of characteristics or behaviour to place them in a certain category or group, in particular to analyse them and/or make predictions about, for example, their ability to perform a task; their interests; or likely behaviour.

According to the interpretation of the Guidelines, a governmental scoring system based on social behaviour would be explicitly prohibited (or rather not allowed).

It would be a case of a government scoring citizens based on public behaviour and daily habits (e.g., traffic fines, social media posts) to limit access to public services or state benefits.

A private scoring system that influences access to goods and services would also be unacceptable. For example, a bank refusing loans to those with a low 'social score' based on consumption habits and online relationships. In this case, the use of data unrelated to financial behaviour leads to unjustified discrimination.

Ranking people according to their social 'trustworthiness' would then be prohibited. For example, an employer would exclude candidates on the basis of a social score calculated through online data and social media. In this case, the system would penalise individuals without objective criteria and outside the work context.

Instead, a social scoring system to make assessments based on specific and justifiable criteria would be permitted according to the Guidelines. A credit system that only assesses financial history and repayment capacity would be permitted, because the criteria are directly linked to the financial decision.

Reputation systems for digital platforms would also be allowed. User reviews on transport or e-commerce apps (e.g., evaluation of drivers or sellers) are permitted. In this case, the rating is contextualised and has no disproportionate negative effects.

Specifically excluded are rating systems for goods and services (e.g., ratings on critical or ecommerce sites); credit control systems based on real financial data; ratings based on objective professional criteria (e.g., evaluation of employees based on job performance).

The AI Act prohibits social scoring practices whether they come from governments and public authorities or from private companies and other entities.

Governments have significant powers over essential services (health, education, social welfare). The use of social scoring by the state could lead to exclusion from public services (e.g., health care, transport); systematic discrimination (e.g., scores awarded on the basis of social or political activities); and even massive surveillance (e.g., monitoring online behaviour to influence job opportunities).

Private companies are also dangerous because they could implement AI systems that classify customers or employees on a discriminatory basis. Classic examples are insurance companies that collect data on a customer's personal consumption in order to decide whether to refuse a contract or increase the premium; credit agencies that assess creditworthiness on the basis of personal characteristics; or employers that classify job applicants on the basis of personal information with no direct relation to the job position.

Responsible for meeting the criteria of the standard are the AI Providers: they must demonstrate that their systems do not generate discriminatory scores and deployers must ensure that the data used are justified and proportionate to the context.

The vulnerabilities of these guidelines, in these specific cases, are many.

Let us first address the public sphere.

It is common knowledge that when a state apparatus - with a thousand difficulties - is caught violating such a rule, it benefits from a unique exculpatory position: the public interest to be protected.

This can be declined both in the apex form of the interest in national defence and public security, and in that of the protection of public property.

In such cases - in con rection - the citizen who considers his or her rights to be infringed would have to 'climb the mountain' of demonstrations in concreto that not only does this overriding interest not exist, but that it could be otherwise achieved without infringing his or her right.

This is the case - which has already occurred - of the artificial intelligence used in the UK where the AI detecting subsidy fraud was found to be discriminatory: the machine learning programme used to examine Universal Credit applications incorrectly selects people from some groups more than others.

In practice, the system favours specific racial groups in the investigation of alleged abuses of the welfare system.

There are 55 automated tools used by public authorities in the UK, potentially influencing decisions affecting millions of people, despite the fact that the government register only covers nine.

In recent years, government departments, including the Ministry of the Interior, have been reluctant to release information on the use of artificial intelligence, justifying the closure with the concern that more information could allow malicious parties to manipulate the systems.

The English case emerged through a specific access to records, but we do not know how widespread the practice is in all public administrations in all European countries.

At least - however - as far as governments are concerned, there is a 'minimum obligation to contract' (pertaining to minimum levels of healthcare) and a right of access that allows for some verification.

Turning to private entities, the situation is better, as the wall of public overriding interest or security is not present, but it is also worse, as both the right of access and the obligation to contract are missing.

There is the basic issue here: the private employee is unlikely to deviate from this report even during the 'human/analogue' verification of the data emerging from Ai.

If only to incur serious risks of policy violations: in this case even the provision of human supervision, when there is any, is circumvented or even rendered null and void with respect to the criterion of 'prudent adaptation'.

AI providers and developers (private or public) must demonstrate that their systems do not generate discriminatory scores and ensure that the data used are justified and proportionate to the context.

No one explains how this is to be done in practice, and how it is verifiable, effectively rendering the guidelines ineffective, if not worthless.

23

Can AI be Sustainable for the Environment?

The topic of the relationship between artificial intelligence and environmental sustainability is oriented around two assumptions, which we can consider objective. On the one hand, artificial intelligence systems pollute and from a consumption classification point of view are inherently energy-consuming systems. Not only in the same way as classical computational systems, i.e., in the processing and output phase, but additionally - an even more energy-intensive phase - in the training and learning phase. On the other hand, one of the 'fundamental requirements' for a '*trustworthy*' AI under the AI Act is precisely social and environmental welfare.

The regulatory provision

The AI Act, soon to be published in the EU Official Journal and to become applicable in stages, expressly refers to environmental and energy sustainability, and emphasises its importance in several points.

"Social and environmental wellbeing" means that AI systems are developed and used in a sustainable and environmentally sound manner and in a way that benefits all human beings by monitoring and evaluating the long-term impacts on the individual, society and democracy. The application of these principles should, where possible, be translated into the design and use of AI models. They should in any case serve as a basis for the development of codes of conduct under this regulation. All stakeholders, including industry, academia, civil society and standards organisations, are encouraged to take ethical principles into account, where appropriate, in the development of best practices and voluntary standards';

"Providers and, where appropriate, deployers of all AI systems, high-risk or otherwise, and AI models should also be encouraged to voluntarily apply additional requirements relating to, for example, elements of the Union's ethical guidelines for reliable AI, environmental sustainability..."

DOI: 10.1201/9781003731290-27

What generative AI says about itself

When asked "Do you consider yourself a green and sustainable system?", ChatGPT replied: "As an artificial intelligence, I do not have a direct environmental impact, but the energy consumption of the data centres that host me can be significant. However, many technology companies are adopting more sustainable practices, such as using renewable energy, optimising energy efficiency and reducing carbon emissions. Thus, my environmental impact depends largely on the green practices adopted by the cloud computing providers and data centres that host me'.

To the question "Do you think artificial intelligence tools are energy-hungry systems?" ChatGPT replied, "Yes, artificial intelligence tools can be energy-hungry, especially during the model training phase, which requires significant computational resources. Training large machine learning models requires the use of powerful GPUs and other specialised hardware, which consume a lot of energy. Inference, i.e. the use of trained models to make predictions or generate responses, can also be energy-consuming, although to a lesser extent than training. Companies are working to improve the energy efficiency of their artificial intelligence models, using techniques such as quantisation, pruning and the use of more energy-efficient hardware. In addition, many are switching to renewable energy sources to power their data centres, seeking to reduce the overall environmental impact'.

The energy impact of AI systems

Every online interaction is based on data stored in data centres, which consume energy to run. According to data from the International Energy Agency, data centres currently consume between 1 and 1.5 per cent of global electricity. This percentage could increase with the AI boom: large language models (LLMs: the language models on which generative AI solutions are based) are trained with ever larger textual datasets and this requires the use of ever more powerful servers.

The process of training artificial intelligence models is the primary driver of energy impact and involves feeding large amounts of data into 'algorithms', which learn to recognise patterns, make predictions or perform other tasks. Training such models typically requires enormous computing resources, often in the form of high-performance computing clusters or specialised hardware such as graphics processing units (GPUs) or tensor processing units (TPUs).

Deep learning' models have a particular need for computing power: according to consensus research, training a single model on a large scale can consume energy equivalent to the consumption of five cars. As AI applications become more complex and data-intensive, the demand for energy will increase further. The AI applications used, such as those powering recommendation engines, autonomous vehicles or smart infrastructure, require continuous computing power to process data and make decisions in real time. Although the energy consumption of individual AI applications may seem modest, the cumulative effect on millions of devices and servers worldwide can be significant.

Furthermore, the energy demand of AI-powered systems is expected to increase as it is incorporated into everyday devices and infrastructure through the Internet of Things (IoT).

At the very least, a mention should be made of the water consumption that AI requires: in 2021, it was estimated that an average data centre, of one of the companies 'doing AI', consumed 2 million litres of water per day, about the same amount that would be needed to produce 160 pairs of jeans, including the cultivation of the necessary cotton (*data from Riverside research at the University of California*).

A question of balancing

Reconciling innovation and environmental sustainability is a classic theme, certainly not new and specific to AI. If anything, today a renewed focus on the environment shifts the attention from a purely economic issue to an ecological one (broadly understood) and shared in decision-making. This reconciliation requires a collective effort to develop and deploy AI technologies so as to minimise their carbon footprint and maximise their positive contribution to society.

Furthermore, addressing the energy implications of AI is not only an environmental issue, but also a matter of equity and access: energy-intensive AI systems increase the gap in resource allocation and access to technology, particularly in regions with limited energy infrastructure or high energy costs. Ensuring equitable access to energy-efficient AI solutions is essential to promote inclusive growth and reduce socioeconomic inequalities.

By embracing innovation, promoting collaboration and taking a more integrated approach to energy management, it would be possible to both harness the power of AI and protect our planet for future generations.

While from a technological point of view, some have proposed greater use of hybrid AI (which consumes less power), this may certainly be an intermediate solution, or limited to a few solutions, especially in view of the exponential growth expected in AI-based technologies.

Certainly, concerted action and responsible management of the best 'green' technologies seems necessary, at least as far as basic needs are concerned.

The (virtuous) use of particular applications of AI (e.g., in the management and rationalisation of energy and environmental resources) could also provide many of the solutions to the critical issue of the sustainability of this technology.

But we cannot disregard the fact that Ai has a cost, especially energy, which is very significant and destined to grow exponentially, and that this cost is double; on the one hand of electrical energy for operation, and on the other of energy and resources (such as water) for cooling the systems.

The rush to develop AI without taking these costs into account was fuelled by the strategic need to be among the first and to develop these technologies as best as possible. This does not detract from the fact that in the current moment of reflection, the term energy-environmental impact, and not only technological and geopolitical supremacy, must also be an element to be taken into account.

An issue very similar to the debate of the nuclear age, in terms of the necessary balance between risks, environment, energy resources, development model, and technological supremacy and geopolitical power.

A debate that cannot be ruled out could also lead to a serene rationalisation, i.e., to reconsider the use of AI where it is really useful and necessary and has a 'positive impact', and instead limit such use in all those cases where it really appears superfluous, or in any case has a 'negative impact' like so many IoT systems.

In fact, it seems clear that such deployment is necessary for reasons of marketing, fashion, and above all data collection for machine testing and machine learning, but hardly brings such benefits that can justify the collective energy and environmental costs.

24

Medical Research and Personal Data Processing

The Amendment of Article 110 of the Privacy Code and the AI ACT

Article 110 of the Privacy Code is the main legal basis for the processing of personal data in the context of medical research.

The legislator has proposed an amendment: 'for the processing of personal data relating to health for the purposes of scientific research in the medical, biomedical or epidemiological field, in the absence of a legal provision and when it is not possible to acquire the consent of the data subjects, because due to particular reasons, informing them proves impossible or involves a disproportionate effort, or risks making it impossible or seriously prejudicing the achievement of the research purposes, the data controller is no longer required to consult the Garante in advance, pursuant to Art. 36 of Regulation (EU) 2016/679 ("GPDR"), but to observe the guarantees that the Authority is now called upon to identify pursuant to Article 106(2)(d) of the Code (see Article 44(1-bis) of Law No. 56 of 29 April 2024).

The instrument chosen is not an ad hoc law, if anything following extensive and articulate debate and discussion, but a law converting Decree-Law No 19 of 2 March 2024, containing urgent provisions for the implementation of the National Recovery and Resilience Plan (NRP) in the context, in turn, of the guidelines on the use of AI.

Article 110 of the Code, in its wording prior to the amendment made by Legislative Decree No. 101 of 10 August 2018 to comply with the GDPR, provided that data controllers promoting clinical studies (necessarily of a retrospective nature) for the performance of which it was necessary to enrol deceased or non-contactable subjects -with the consequent impossibility of acquiring their consent-, had to request in advance the authorisation of the Garante, pursuant to the then applicable Article 40 of the Code, subject to the obligation to also obtain the favourable opinion of the competent territorial ethics committee. 40 of the Code, subject to the obligation to also obtain the favourable opinion of the territorially competent ethics committee. Article 40 of the Code allowed authorisations to be replaced by acts of a general nature relating to certain categories of data controllers or processing operations.

DOI: 10.1201/9781003731290-28

The Authority had therefore promptly adopted General Authorisation No. 9/2016 on the processing of personal data for scientific research purposes of 15 December 2016, respecting the contents of which data controllers were exempted from the burden of prior requests to the Garante.

The evolution of the discipline, with a view to the risk-based approach and, in particular, the principle of accountability, has innovated this approach, entrusting the guarantor authorities mainly with roles of promoting awareness and knowledge of sector regulations and control.

In the first rewrite of Art. 110 of the Code, in the aftermath of the entry into force of the Regulation, the request for authorisation was replaced with the obligation to consult the Garante in advance pursuant to Art. 36 GDPR, while also providing for a specific administrative sanction for non-compliant holders, pursuant to Art. 166 of the Code.

The promoters of clinical trials who, in their capacity as data controllers, considered it necessary to process health data relating to deceased or non-contactable subjects, in the absence of other regulatory prerequisites, were therefore required to submit to the Garante for the lawfulness of the processing a prior consultation request concerning not only the protocol of the trial (for a clear definition, in particular, of the purpose of the processing) but - as is proper in this institution - the data protection impact assessment, carried out pursuant to Art. 35 GDPR, on which the Garante was called upon to express an opinion pursuant to Art. 36 of the Regulation.

If Art. 110 of the Code falls within the regulatory space of Art. 9(2)(j) GDPR, this specific fulfilment could be considered as a further condition for the processing of health data under Art. 9(4) GDPR.

Although the Garante has provided, in the more than 30 measures adopted pursuant to Article 110 of the Code over the past six years, useful indications for the processing of personal data in the field of medical, biomedical, and epidemiological research, the provision was immediately disliked by operators in the sector.

The prior consultation of the Garante was perceived, in fact, as a burdensome bureaucratic fulfilment for data processing, useful only to slow down research by undermining Italy's competitiveness at EU and international level in this sector. This with even more undesirable effects given the relevance of retrospective studies in our country, which is favoured by the wealth of information assets available to hospitals by virtue of the specific policy of conservation, sine die, of medical records (Circular of the Ministry of Health of 19 December 1986 no. 900).

The recent amendment of Article 110 of the Code, helping to complete its evolution in the name of accountability, represents an important simplification measure in the field of medical research.

With a (coincidentally or deliberately) appropriate timing, the novelty intervened at a time when the Garante seems to have given, through the aforementioned opinions pursuant to Article. 110 of the Code, a significant number of indications for the processing of personal data in the field of medical research, intervening with a high degree of detail with respect to such secondary data processing, also in line with the renewed attention devoted, also under the propulsive thrust of the Covid-19 pandemic, to this sector by the European Data Protection Supervisor (EDPS), and by the European Data Protection Board (EDPB).

The novelty, however, does not 'liberalise' anything at all, but entrusts the Garante with the task of identifying specific guarantees for the processing of data when the consent of the data subjects is not required, in accordance with Article 106(2)(d) of the Code. These guarantees will therefore have to be defined in the deontological Rules that the Garante is called upon to promote.

Article 89 of the regulation is the provision specifically dedicated to the field of scientific research. With wording not dissimilar to Article 25 GDPR, on the obligation to protect data by design and by default, or Article 32 GDPR, on security of processing, which might make it appear almost redundant, it provides the coordinates for the processing of personal data for archiving in the public interest, scientific or historical research or statistical purposes.

Article 89 of the GDPR is a regulation without (in itself) sanctioning provisions, which therefore performs a purely interpretative function by providing, firstly, data controllers and then the Member States with the levers on which to weigh for a fair balance between the protection of personal data and freedom of research, which can be plastically found in the anonymisation, pseudonymisation and minimisation of data.

Given that the anonymisation of data necessarily puts an end to any debate on data protection rules, it should be noted that in the light of Article 89(1) GDPR, the minimisation of data, in particular through their pseudonymisation, is the key to ensuring the effective application of data protection principles in the field under consideration, with the effect that the discretion for the data controller to resort or not to this technique is significantly reduced.

If it is true that the safeguards to protect the effective application of the principles of personal data protection must and can go no further than the limit within which the functionality of the data is guaranteed for the achievement of the purposes (in this case medical research) for which they are intended, it may now also be true that the new Deontological Rules represent at this historical moment the appropriate venue for the identification of measures that are concretely effective both for the protection of the fundamental rights and freedoms of the data subjects and for the pursuit of research purposes, as much as and more than the Authorisations, first, and the prior consultation of the Garante, then.

This fits in with the almost contextual dispositive events in which Bill No. 1066AS entitled 'Rules for the Development and Adoption of Artificial Intelligence Technologies' falls.

The bill is only the first, in the government's intentions, of a series of specific measures to implement delegations that the government will have to implement in 12 months.

The provisions of Article 8 denote an attempt to remove some of the obstacles that the current legal framework places in the way of the use of health data for scientific research purposes. Among other things, it provides that not-for-profit entities are legitimised to make secondary use of personal data, even of special categories, already collected during previous research projects, without the need to request further consent from the data subjects.

Of course, this is a text that is destined to be discussed and revised in parliament, but it is nevertheless possible to highlight, on the one hand, incompatibility profiles with the provisions of the GDPR and, on the other hand, a gap with regard to scientific research activities by profit-making organisations.

There is also a problem of coordination with the provisions on scientific research in the field of health, contained in the law converting the so-called PNRR decree, definitively approved on 23 April (the same day as the approval of the DDL IA), and aimed at amending Article 110 of Legislative Decree No. 196/2003 (Privacy Code).

These provisions, inter alia, do away, as we have seen, with the obligation of prior consultation of the Garante in the case of processing of data relating to health, in the absence of the consent of the data subject, for the purposes of medical scientific research.

The real crux of this general regulation is that any reference to the regulation of data management by for-profit companies is omitted.

25

Meta's AI can Read Minds

Limits and Problems of an Uncontrolled Development of Neurotechnology

Meta AI has developed technology to decode brain activity into text via advanced neural networks. This advance in human-computer interface opens up new possibilities for digital communication and interaction, and also raises ethical and privacy issues

The research, conducted by Meta's Fundamental artificial intelligence research (Fair) in Paris, in collaboration with the Basque Centre on Cognition, has developed a revolutionary system that literally reads thoughts.

Using a sophisticated scanner, the researchers were able to decode up to 80% of the characters that the 35 participants thought they were typing. Astonishing results captured not only the words but also the semantic context of the thought.

"We are sharing a breakthrough towards understanding the neural mechanisms that coordinate language production in the human brain. Studying the brain during language has always proved extremely challenging for neuroscience, partly due to a simple technical problem: moving the mouth and tongue heavily corrupts neuroimaging signals,' Meta stated in the presentation post. Limitations that have been overcome thanks to artificial intelligence and that open up revolutionary perspectives, opening up new possibilities for people with communication disabilities.

The researchers used magnetoencephalography (Meg) and electroencephalography (Eeg), a synergetic system based on an artificial intelligence model, Brain2Qwerty, which interprets the brain's magnetic signals as if they were keys pressed on an invisible keyboard. It is like having a simultaneous translator who, through non-invasive reading of brain activity, can interpret thoughts and turn them into written words.

It works like this: during the test, the volunteer sits inside the Meg scanner helmet, which detects the magnetic signals generated by neurons as they are activated in the brain. Then the artificial intelligence model analyses which signals correspond to certain keys. After appropriate training, the AI is able to predict the letters a person is thinking of typing.

DOI: 10.1201/9781003731290-29

Meta explains in detail: 'By taking 1,000 images of the brain every second, we can pinpoint the exact moment when thoughts are transformed into words, syllables and even letters. Our study shows that the brain generates a series of representations that start with the abstract meaning of a sentence and are progressively translated into concrete actions, such as the movement of fingers on the keyboard. A 'dynamic neural code', a special neural mechanism that concatenates successive representations by maintaining each of them for long periods of time'.

As Meta herself stated, 'we are witnessing the exact moment when thoughts turn into words'.

Despite its revolutionary premises, the project still has many practical limitations. The first is performance-related: performance decoding is still imperfect. But also practical.

The scanner must be placed in a specially shielded room to block the earth's magnetic field, which is a trillion times stronger than brain signals. Moreover, even the slightest movement of the head can disrupt the signal and it is necessary to remain still. Finally, while this research was conducted on healthy volunteers, as Meta specifies, future work is needed to explore how it might benefit people suffering from brain injury.

Undoubtedly, Meta's mind-reading technology is a window into the future of neurological medicine and human communication. A non-invasive approach that is blazing a more accessible trail than the brain chips that Neuralink is testing.

Although the project does not aim to develop a commercial product in the immediate future, the history of technological innovation reminds us that giant devices in their infancy do not remain so forever: the scanner that today takes up an entire room and requires special conditions could, tomorrow, become as discreet as an earpiece or a hat.

In the human brain, the area responsible for word formation and language comprehension is separate from the area that manages voluntary muscles, including those in the mouth. The Meta researchers exploited this functional division to fine-tune their project.

They then asked 169 volunteers to undergo magnetic resonance imaging and electroencephalography while listening to the reading of audio books in English and Dutch. The result was over 150 hours of recordings showing in detail the brain activity during the comprehension of a text. However, these images are characterised by background noise, which makes it complex to isolate, within all the brain activity that accompanies an individual at all times, the processes involved in understanding each individual word of the audiobook.

The algorithm currently only works on the texts of audio books used for training: while the volunteer listens to the narration through headphones, it is able to extrapolate the text from brain activity. The next step is to extend the capacity of the system so that it can also work without a predefined dataset to support it.

This technology may help thousands of patients who, as a result of trauma, are no longer able to communicate with the outside world, but it also raises quite a few ethical issues, because it actually allows us to enter people's brains and read their thoughts.

In order to 'clean up' the brain signal related to text identification, Meta engineers repurposed an AI algorithm developed in 2020 to extract a clear track from an audio file recorded in a very noisy environment.

This system, repurposed and applied to the brain activity recordings of volunteers, made it possible to isolate brain activity related to text comprehension. The researchers were thus able to create a large dataset relating the comprehension of individual words, for example 'cat', to the activity of the neurons forming that word in the brain.

The system is then able to read, via an MRI and electroencephalogram, the word-creation activity in the brain, and reproduce it externally in the form of a text or audio file.

It must be said at the outset that much of the development of these systems is the result of neuroscientific medical research, which had already acted convincingly independently on other applications. The synergy in this case with Meta has certainly brought resources, both economic and technological, useful for the development of a system that falls within the broader spectrum of instruments that investigate 'how the mind and brain of man acts' in a non-invasive manner, starting with MRI and fMRI.

This application, however, appears particularly delicate because - far beyond Libet's famous experiment - it goes into investigating not what the brain does (as with functional magnetic resonance imaging, which detects active areas) but what the mind 'intends to do' without it doing so.

A kind of 'Minority Report' applied to everyday activities.

And there is a lot of difference between 'the body presses - actually - a button and we see the x part of the motor cortex in activity' from 'but the mind is thinking about pressing a button - without doing so - and we see that it activates as if it were going to do so'.

Rather than reading 'actual' thought, it is as if one were reading 'intentions' at the stage of hypothesis of action, without allowing the opportunity to rethink, re-evaluate and change one's mind about the action to be taken.

In other words - and here the neuroscientific component counts in no small measure - the controlling and inhibiting action of the prefrontal cortex is excluded.

Hence the broad caution with which we must take these results, which should even be disclosed with strict bioethical scrutiny.

Not least because the borderline between what as research output must remain in laboratories and clinics and what can be transferred to the private sector must be clarified with rigour and stringent checks long before the first volunteer enters 'the machine'.

Once neuroscientific know-how has been applied to a 'mechanical-technological' instrument and an AI has learnt to decode the signal, there is nothing to prevent the private party - especially if it has enormous funds - from going it alone in developing 'out-of-control' applications.

This not only poses a problem of privacy, but of outright interference in free will, and opens up incredible possibilities in terms of manipulating the will of the individual.

26

AI and Human Emotions

Definition, Regulation and Possible Implications

As Artificial Intelligence advances in its ability to understand human emotions, legal-ethical considerations become paramount.

Emotions are deeply complex and nuanced, intertwined with personal experiences, cultural influences and the human condition. As AI continues to evolve, a balance must be struck between the benefits of emotional understanding and the ethical considerations involved. And first of all, we need to understand and define with certainty what emotions are and what their typicality is with respect to personal data, and thus demand specific protection and not simply extended by analogy.

The theme

The fusion of emotions and technology presents intricate challenges, including those related to data privacy, emotional ambiguity and the balance between personalisation and generalisation.

Among the emerging trends, *emotional AI*, which seeks to enable machines to understand, interpret and respond to human emotions, is the one that is the most perplexing, although it is also the least addressed from a legal regulatory perspective.

It concerns, however, the broader context in which emotion - as a qualitative 'label' of a fact - actually determines it. We realise this, for example, every time social networks censor or block a visual content, such as an image or video. And they automatically block it precisely because it appears ambiguous or flat and lacking the emotional quality according to which human intelligence discriminates.

And this is precisely because platforms are increasingly using AI in the management of content policies.

A striking example was the case of the Kiss of David, considered a 'pornographic image', not to mention the case of the photo-denunciation of the street killings in Tehran, censored because of its 'explicitly violent content'.

The fusion of emotions and technology also presents intricate challenges, including those related to data privacy, emotional ambiguity and the balance between

DOI: 10.1201/9781003731290-30

personalisation and generalisation; it will, therefore, be crucial to ensure a responsible implementation of emotional AI in our daily lives.

Human emotions: emotional data generated by AI

In the field of Artificial Intelligence (AI), understanding human emotions is as central as the emotions themselves are in our daily lives, as they shape our thoughts, decisions and interactions. The primary question is whether AI can really learn to understand and interpret human emotions.

In the field of '*emotion recognition systems*', the point of reference is the scientific field of *Affective Computing* (AC), which is intended to be implemented or already used in various fields, making emotions machine-readable and offering the opportunity to automatically process a new type of data: *emotional data.*

The phenomenon of so-called *Affective Computing* owes its origins to the studies of Rosalind Picard and the group of researchers at the *MIT Media Lab*, who had the intuition that they could combine advances in computational and automated techniques with the progress made in the field of psychology on the analysis of human emotions.

As far as we know, all the big players such as Amazon, Apple, Facebook (Metaverse), Google, IBM and Microsoft are working on emotional AI tools to develop '*empathic products*' for different applications and contexts.

Thus a '*datafication*' of human emotional life was born, so much so that traditional approaches relied on the analysis of facial expressions, vocal intonations and physiological signals to infer emotions. Machine learning algorithms have been trained on large data sets containing classified emotional responses to improve accuracy, and advances in *computer vision* and natural language processing have paved the way for highly sophisticated emotion recognition systems.

Learning models such as convolutional neural networks (CNN) and recurrent neural networks (RNN) have shown promising results in emotion classification tasks. These models can process visual and textual data, allowing machines to infer emotions from images, videos and written texts.

In particular, it is interesting to report on an aspect related to the use of AI in analysing human feeling, in general to technologies that '*perceive, learn about and interact with human emotional life*'. According to Andrew McStay, AI-enabled business systems are implementing the inclusion of automatic monitoring of workers' emotions. Using computational and statistical analysis methods, *affective computing* and machine learning, *Emotional AI* techniques can be applied to various types of *input* data such as biological sensors, facial microexpressions, physiological and vocal signals, and text semantics.

Through the application of machine learning algorithms and statistical analysis, emotion AI could generate inferences about human emotions and its application in workplace surveillance, in particular, brings with it both advantages and concerns. On the one hand, the use of these technologies can help improve the well-being and productivity of employees. they can both identify situations of stress or dissatisfaction and use the acquisition of such information to improve the quality of the customer experience by adapting the interaction with employees according to their emotions. On the other hand, their use raises important ethical and privacy issues.

It is essential to ensure that emotion monitoring is carried out transparently and with respect for employees' privacy. It is necessary to ensure that the data collected are only used for legitimate purposes and that appropriate measures are taken to protect their security. Furthermore, the use of emotional AI raises concerns about the possibility of manipulating emotions themselves.

Despite the progress that has been made, therefore, there are several challenges to be faced, and above all, it is good to consider that emotions are highly subjective and influenced by cultural, social and personal factors. Accurately interpreting emotions requires understanding the context in which they arise. Emotion is not only a private feeling, but also a particularly sensitive type of (private) information. The decision to share one's inner emotions should be an individual choice. As human beings, we convey emotions through non-verbal signals, such as body language, gestures and tone of voice. Teaching machines to recognise and interpret these signals accurately is a complex challenge, where a 'small mistake' has huge consequences, for example where emotions often display ambiguity and complexity, making it difficult to classify them into distinct labels. Emotional states can evolve rapidly and manifest themselves in subtle variations that may be difficult to identify accurately.

In simple words, it is clear to us - over two hundred million years of social evolution in a collective context - the difference between a smile of joy, a smile of circumstance, a bitter smile, a sad smile. Even explaining and describing them in words is extremely complex, and almost never complete and exhaustive. Imagine what it means to 'programme' a machine to define and recognise these differences with certainty. We must therefore first of all recognise that the problem in these cases is not the machine but our human capacity for description and codification.

Fundamental legal aspects

With the proposal for a Regulation of the European Parliament and of the Council (*Artificial Intelligence Act* - AIA), harmonised rules on Artificial Intelligence are established and certain pieces of Union legislation are amended, Brussels, 21 April 2021, COM(2021) 206 final 2021/0106 (COD).

It is worth saying that the emotion recognition system, as it is presented by the IA Act, in Art. 3, no. 34, must be considered '*an AI system aimed at identifying or inferring emotions or intentions of natural persons on the basis of their biometric data*'. Title IV introduces transparency requirements for a number of AI systems (Art. 1(c)), stipulating that '*harmonised transparency rules for AI systems designed to interact with natural persons, emotion recognition systems, biometric categorisation systems and AI systems used to generate or manipulate images or audio or video content*'. Article 52(2), on the other hand, requires that '*users of an emotion recognition system or biometric categorisation system shall inform natural persons exposed to it about the operation of the system*'.

The AIA, therefore, presents a legal framework, the purpose of which - as Recital 1 of the Proposal for a Regulation specifies - is 'to *improve the functioning of the internal market by establishing a uniform legal framework in particular with regard to the development, commercialisation and use of artificial intelligence (AI) in accordance with Union values'.*

Yet, as stated in the same Proposal, '*some AI systems intended for interaction with natural persons or for content generation may pose specific risks of impersonation or deception, regardless of whether they are considered high-risk or not*', requiring that '*natural persons should be notified when they are exposed to an emotion recognition system or a biometric categorisation system*' (ref. Proposal for a Regulation, recitals 70, 37).

The draft regulation - in its definition of emotion recognition systems - focuses on the use of biometric data. However, these are not the only elements used in *emotion scanning*. This aspect raises the qualifying problem of emotions, as reducing emotions on a qualifying level to biometric data alone would *de facto* exclude similar systems.

According to Art. 3(33), biometric data are to be understood as '*personal data obtained by specific technical processing relating to physical, physiological or behavioural characteristics of a natural person which enable or confirm their unambiguous identification, such as facial image or dactyloscopic data*'. Thus, this is a special category of personal data that allow or confirm the unambiguous identification of a person.

The AIA, with regard to the protection of personal data - in electronic communications - classifies emotions as '*highly sensitive information*' (Recital 2) on a par with other particularly relevant personal data.

Under the GDPR, *Emotion AI* is also subject to the same requirements for the processing of personal data as any other form of data processing. In this sense, pursuant to Article 6 of the GDPR, processing may only take place for predetermined purposes if there are suitable "legal grounds", i.e., conditions under which the processing is considered lawful. Furthermore, any processing of personal data may only be carried out within the limits of specific and predetermined purposes. Clear and transparent information must be provided on the processing of personal data, including the purposes of the processing and the categories of data processed.

This includes implementing appropriate data protection and security measures, such as encryption and access controls, and ensuring that third-party providers involved in the processing of personal data are also GDPR-compliant.

The case of *MorphCast Emotion AI*

One example is *MorphCast* Technology (*MorphCast Emotion AI*), a technology that enables the recognition and analysis of facial emotions through artificial intelligence. The Software does not carry out any processing of biometric data allowing the unambiguous identification of a subject, but only an instantaneous (volatile) processing of personal data during the processing of images (frames), read from the video stream (e.g., of a camera, used only as a sensor and not as an image and/or video recorder) provided by the End User's browser. The technology in question constantly strives to provide all the information necessary for a better understanding and use of Emotion AI. In particular, privacy is an important concern when using *MorphCast Emotion AI*, as it involves the processing of personal data, including the collection of emotional data, which, however, are not covered by the legislation 'as such' (i.e., in their peculiarity and specificity) but only 'by analogy and extension'.

MorphCast Emotion AI has implemented measures to ensure the protection of user privacy. It works strictly *client-side*, which means that users' personal data (the camera shot of the user's face) remain on their device and are not sent to any server for analysis, i.e., users have full control of their data and do not risk being accessed by third parties. The company also emphasises the importance of obtaining explicit and informed consent before collecting and processing such data. *MorphCast Emotion AI* is fully GDPR-compliant, which means that it adheres to regulatory data protection standards and ensures (the company states) that users' personal data is processed fairly and legally. But if this is the case, the 'unspoken doubt' remains: what about the data 'processed' for the purpose of Emotion AI's machine learning?

The General Data Protection Regulation (GDPR) contains provisions for the management of AI systems, in particular with regard to the standardisation of obligations in data processing and the definition of the rights of the data subject in the use of personal data.

The GDPR itself, in Article 9, prescribes the prohibition of the processing of '*biometric data intended to uniquely identify a natural person*', unless the data subject has given his or her consent or in the other exceptions provided for by law. Therefore, the principles enshrined in the GDPR are also relevant for AI systems.

Emotion recognition systems generally learn to determine the link between an emotion and its external manifestation from a wide variety of data, including some physiological, such as changes in heart rate and skin conductance.

The main objective of the emotion recognition system is to extract the most relevant features from the data and use them to learn the link between the emotion and its external manifestations.

This may involve the use of machine learning algorithms to identify patterns or correlations in the data that indicate a certain emotion. Once trained, the emotion recognition system can be used to analyse new data and classify it according to the corresponding emotion. For example, it could be used to analyse the emotion expressed by a speaker during a presentation, or to identify the emotion portrayed by a character in a film scene.

Such a 'massive' influx of data and so many people raises a number of questions concerning the implications on the dissemination and control of these data.

The protection of 'emotional data' and what we talk about when we talk about emotion

From a regulatory point of view, data protection is essentially delegated to compliance with the GDPR by essentially treating emotional and emotional data in the same way as any personal data.

It is basically argued that if sentiment analysis requires the collection of users' personal data, such as texts, social media posts or chat messages, it is essential to comply with privacy regulations, such as the General Data Protection Regulation (GDPR) in the European Union, which requires users' informed consent for the collection, processing and storage of their personal data.

It is also argued that when data is collected for emotion analysis, it is important to anonymise users to protect their privacy, as if that in itself were enough, not considering that emotional data is always expressed in a relationship, unlike personal data.

I smile is different than 'I smile at you' and still different than 'I smile at the sight of a certain view' if anything related to a 'personal memory' if anything related to 'the memory of that significant day with a significant person' if anything related to feeling. This 'social chain' of the emotional correlate cannot fit into how one regulates the treatment of a telephone number. Least of all - evidently - that the 'data' is 'anonymous'.

It is argued that AI-based online emotion evaluation systems must be transparent about how data are collected, used and processed. Users must be fully informed about how their data is used for sentiment analysis and for what specific purpose.

Here again, we must first clarify to ourselves 'what we are talking about when we talk about an emotion' and whether this 'full information' should be known and shared by 'all parties to an emotion'.

It is argued that since online emotion evaluation systems are based on AI, it is important to ensure the accuracy of the results obtained. The company or organisation using such systems could be held liable for any negative consequences resulting from incorrect or misleading sentiment analyses.

Again, it escapes us that we ourselves - as humans, the programmers and classifiers of emotions - must first define them with certainty and unambiguously. Only then can we demand rigour in the treatment of the accuracy of the result obtained from the analysis. This is in the rather common and intuitive context that we humans are by no means accurate interpreters of our own emotions and the emotions of others. Let alone with what rigour we can programme an AI to do so.

It is argued that users must be guaranteed their freedom of expression and opinion when using online emotion rating systems. Companies should not use the information collected to restrict or suppress users' opinions that may be considered negative or undesirable.

But if we ourselves do not have an unambiguous criterion for classifying and evaluating an emotion, and even if we ourselves derive our relationship with another's emotion (behaviour) from our absolutely subjective degree of empathy, how can we expect an AI, which by definition has no empathy (nor could it have), to do so? And from this it follows that an AI's 'opinion on an emotion' is an a priori nonsense.

It is argued that sentiment analysis may be subject to bias or discrimination, e.g., based on the race, age or gender of the persons involved. It is important that online emotion evaluation systems are developed and used in a way that avoids discriminatory or unfair results.

But if emotions are our qualitative labels to an experience, their 'originality' and authenticity also lies - and often above all - in reflecting prejudice and discrimination, which are not in themselves negative entities. We have prejudices towards the taste of excrement, even without ever having 'tasted' it (and thus we have a prejudice) that show the emotional expression of 'disgust' on our face. Is it wrong because it is prejudiced? We discriminate against a wasp (yellow-black colour) because it atavistically 'tastes bitter' while the strawberry (red colour) appears juicy to us a priori, is this discrimination? In evaluating his behaviour, will a person with obvious racial prejudice for cultural reasons express such a cultural conception on his face, the AI should not take this into account? Based on that a priori criterion? And who determines that? Because when we talk about human behaviour and its emotional response to the world, cultural bias is itself an element of that response. For example in the last case you may have all thought we were talking about a white-skinned person towards an African-American person. Again, did you not first exercise racial discrimination and prejudice?

The legal protection of emotional data

On the basis of the above, how could the term 'emotional data' be defined in such a way that it is suitable for the legal context, particularly in the context of the 'emotion recognition systems' mentioned by the AIA?

Biometric data become 'emotional data' through systemic processing in the emotion recognition system. In a first step, we will therefore consider the processing of biometric data under the Data Protection Act. In a second step, the question will be asked as to what insights can be found to process 'emotional data'.

The GDPR in Article 4 para. 1 p.4, defines biometric data: '*Personal data obtained by specific technical processing relating to physical, physiological or behavioural characteristics of a natural person which enable or confirm their unique identification, such as facial image or dactyloscopic data*'.

They fall within that particular category of data for which the European Regulation, places specific attention, prohibiting their processing, except in certain particular situations, indicated by Article 9 par. 2. These provisions, moreover, are confirmed by Article 2 septies of Legislative Decree no. 101/2018 "*Guarantee measures for the processing of genetic, biometric and health-related data*", according to which "*genetic, biometric and health-related data may be processed in the presence of one of the conditions set out in paragraph 2 of Art. 9 GDPR and in compliance with the safeguards measures laid down by the Garante with a specific provision which, adopted every two years, shall take into account not only the best application practices, but also the scientific and technological evolution from time to time occurring in the field covered by the measures*'.

27

Technology and Personal Integrity Protection

The Constitutional Court of Chile on the Protection of Neural Rights

The Chilean Constitutional Court, the first in the world, adopted a ruling on 8 August 2023 that is destined to remain a milestone on the boundary between technology and the protection of the integrity of the person.

It basically stated that even *devices* intended to track people's brain activity for 'private use' must be authorised by the health authorities; if the users' data, then, are processed for scientific use, the consent given by the user, then, must be informed, express, specific about the research and its purposes, and dynamic, i.e., required whenever the purpose of the research changes over time.

The news was released by lawyer Maite Sanz de Galdeano at the Global Summit of the Legal Hackers community held on 8 and 9 September in Madrid.

"The constitutionalisation of neurorights in Chile has opened up the possibility of a 'constitutional protection action' against the commercialisation of a device that puts them at risk. The ruling shows that the lack of specific regulation exposes users to uncontrolled risks, which justifies a particular rigour in the application of the current law and, on the other hand, a reflection on the necessary changes: if these technologies escape the controls of medical devices, in Chile (and in the rest of the states) at least the regulations on consumer protection, product safety and privacy, which currently do not guarantee the safety of users because they do not take into account these new risks, should be reviewed. In terms of neurodata, in addition to the risks to privacy, a 'new' vulnerability of the human being, hitherto unexplored, is revealed: the knowledge and consequent control of brain activity, for purposes that are not exclusively medical. The answer can only be an explicit regulation of neurodata, as a category of sensitive personal data, enabling the defence and development of neurorights. In Europe, the GDPR must be amended in this sense'.

DOI: 10.1201/9781003731290-31

The market for hi-tech wearables

The research agency International Data Corporation (Idc) predicted a shipment of around 442.7 million wearable devices in 2024, equivalent to a 6.3% year-on-year growth.

These are 325 million headsets, 162.2 million connected watches, 33.8 million smart bands, the health monitoring devices, and 2.2 million products in other so-called 'wearable' categories.

In terms of market share, the numbers translate into 62.1 per cent earbuds, 31 per cent smartwatches, 6.5 per cent smartbands and 0.4 per cent other devices.

We do not know the amount of devices intended to measure our brain and cognitive activities; but we do know that companies such as Elon Musk's Neurolink are already particularly active in this direction.

The Chilean case: wearables and brain activity

Chile is the first country in the world to have legislated on neurotechnology and included the 'rights of the brain' in its Constitutional Charter.

In 2021, an amendment to Article 19 was passed to 'protect the mental integrity and immunity of the brain from the advances and capabilities developed by neurotechnology'.

Although appearing to be a premature choice, the Chilean parliament preferred to put its hands on the development of neurotechnology, whose ability to act on the human brain is still limited but for which applications are spreading beyond the medical field. The case before the Chilean Constitutional Court can be described as a 'pilot case', both because of the plaintiff and its genesis.

The plaintiff, Guido Girardi Lavin, is a Member of Parliament and promoter of the protection of human rights also through *The Neurorights Foundation*, but he brought the case before the judges, first of merit and then constitutional, as a buyer and user of the *Insight device,* a wireless device that through a band of sensors collects information on the electrical activities of the brain and collects data on gestures, preferences, reaction times and cognitive activity. Insight is produced by a US company, Emotiv.

The case submitted to the Constitutional Court

Girardi Lavin purchased the device via the web and followed the instructions to activate it: he created an account on the company's cloud, agreeing to the terms and conditions; he downloaded software onto his PC, again agreeing to the terms and conditions of service. But he decided to use the free and not the pro licence; a choice that - he reported to the courts - did not allow him to export or import his brain data records.

The plaintiff also pointed out that everything was recorded and saved in Emotiv's cloud. In short, he complained about the potential risk of hacking, surveillance, unauthorised capture, and commercialisation of his neuro-data.

The complaint therefore concerned the violation of the Chilean Data Protection Act (No 19.628) both in the part where it lays down the liability profiles of the data controller and in the part where it assigns the data owner's right to obtain the deletion or blocking of his data in the event of the closure of his account. Emotiv, in fact, stores user data for scientific and historical purposes. Gilardi therefore asked the Court to order Emotiv to change its privacy policy and to prohibit the marketing of the device in Chile until this compliance, while warning the company to immediately delete its data base.

The company argued that *Insight* is not a medical device but a self-quantification device, that it has no invasive purpose, that the terms and conditions are detailed, that there is a requirement of express consent for both the processing of personal and brain data, and that no proof of actual harm suffered by the plaintiff had been provided.

In addition, Emotiv argued, there had been no violation of either the Chilean Privacy Act or the more restrictive GPDR (General Data Protection Regulation), the European regulation on the processing of personal data, which obliges pseudonymisation, an activity that prevents the data collected from being attributed to a specific or determinable person.

With regard to the violation of Article 13 of the Chilean Privacy Act, the company had noted that data are saved as long as the user's account is active and that with regard to 'data brains', the user can at any time revoke consent to the processing, as the privacy policy prescribes.

As for further processing, for scientific or historical purposes, the company noted that the data are anonymised, encrypted, stored securely and separated from other information. Therefore, they acquire the nature of statistical data, as such removed from the protection of privacy.

The Constitutional Court's decision

The Constitutional Court overturned the judgments on the merits, deeming relevant the fact that the marketing of *Insight* was not subject to medical (as well as customs) authorisation, reminding the authorities in charge of analysing the device in the light of the regulations in force with a view to its future marketing in Chile.

The judges ruled that 'prior to the development of new technologies involving more and more aspects of the human person, aspects that were unthinkable a few years ago that they could meet, the State must pay particular attention and care in the control, in order to prevent and anticipate the possible effects, in addition to directly protecting human integrity in its entirety, issues that include privacy and confidentiality and the rights of mental integrity and the subject of scientific experimentation. In this way, before the arrival of a new technology such as the one at issue in these proceedings, which treats the electrical activity of the brain in a dimension that was once absolutely private and personal, and outside strictly medical contexts, it is absolutely necessary that before allowing it to be marketed and used in the country, technologies and devices be analysed by the competent authority, on the understanding that they raise issues that have not been previously investigated by it'.

Neuro-rights in international law

The Chilean Constitutional Court has had to recognise that, despite the direct protection mandate contained in the amendment to the Constitution, there is currently no ordinary law that unravels all the knots imposed by the advancement of applied neuroscience, the requirements, conditions, permissible risks and use by individuals. There is therefore a new fork in the road.

And yet, thanks to the international normative dimension, it is possible to draw a protective boundary in the sense that follows and referred to by the judgment.

The International Covenant on Economic, Cultural and Social Rights prescribes that people should be able to 'enjoy' scientific progress; the Unesco Declaration on Science and the Use of Knowledge and Programme of Science prescribe that science should respect human rights and the dignity of the person in the sense already indicated by the Universal Declaration of Human Rights; the Universal Declaration on the Human Genome specifies that some scientific applications can be harmful and that scientists and other agents have a 'special' responsibility of an ethical nature, which must be integrated into the debate through public discussion; the Unesco Universal Declaration on Bioethics and Human Rights has already imposed the general principles of human vulnerability and the integrity of the person, together with the rights to privacy and confidentiality.

The Court also referred to the Chilean legislation (No 20.120) on scientific investigations on persons and the genome that has banned human cloning, recalling the provisions that deal very specifically with the consent of persons involved in medical research. Under this legislation, the consent of those involved in research not only follows certain precautions when it is collected, but must be renewed every time the scientific investigation undergoes major changes.

With respect to the case at hand, the Constitutional Court found that the company producing the *Insight* device had failed to request this specific consent, which certainly cannot be considered to be implicit in the other consents, which are of a 'commercial' nature.

The final decision

The Court overturned the Court of Appeal's decision, emphasising the need for new technologies, particularly those dealing with human activities that have hitherto been strictly private, such as brain activity, to be submitted to the competent authorities for review before neuro-medical devices are marketed and used in the country. It therefore held that the constitutional guarantees of Article 19 on psychic and physical integrity were violated since Insight marketed without authorisation and without an assessment by the health authorities. The Chilean court upheld the appeal, prohibiting the marketing of *Insight* until it obtains authorisation in light of the regulations referred to; the Public Health Institute and the Customs Authority will have to assess whether the management of data collected with *Insight* strictly complies with the applicable regulations outlined in the judgment. It also warned Emotiv to delete all information that was stored in the cloud or on the portal.

28

Legal Nature and Probabilistic Value of "Significant Damage" in the use of Artificial Intelligence

On 6 February, the European Commission provided interpretative clarifications and operational guidelines.

In this article, I explore the comparison between the concept of 'significant damage' as defined by the European Union and that of 'unjust damage' as defined by the Italian Civil Code.

The distinction between event damage and consequential damage is directly related to the difference between material causality and legal causality. The causal link requires a clear separation: on the one hand, there is the relationship between the conduct and the harmful event (material causality), which is necessary to establish liability; on the other hand, there is the link between the event and the damage suffered, which is necessary to identify the harmful consequences and define the limits of the damage that can be compensated.

Where material causality occurs, it is possible to speak of wrongdoing; where, on the other hand, legal causality also exists, the damage to be compensated can also be configured.

In determining legal causality, both to establish the existence and the extent of the damage, the criterion outlined in Article 1223 of the Italian Civil Code applies, according to which there must be a causal relationship between the event and the damage, such that the compensable financial loss is directly attributable to the event itself (this is the so-called 'nexus').

To be considered compensable, the financial loss must be an immediate and direct consequence of the event. However, the clarity of the applicable legal rules is diminished when defining the specific scope of compensable damage.

While these definitions are now well established in national law, the concept of significant damage remains relatively new, having emerged mainly with the introduction of recent European Regulations.

DOI: 10.1201/9781003731290-32

It almost seems as if an additional filter has been introduced into the legal system in the understanding of legal causality, including a mathematical dimension with economic and financial implications.

It should be noted, incidentally, that the restriction of discretion towards an almost mathematical formulation in terms of damage and compensation is a general trend in EU law, with the aim, not even implicit, of standardising the framework to give (or seek to give) certainty of uniformity to homogeneous facts in heterogeneous countries.

In this context, Article 5 of the AI Act highlights two specific scenarios in which artificial intelligence practices are prohibited.

The first concerns the use of subliminal techniques that operate without the user's awareness or the use of deliberately manipulative or deceptive techniques that induce users to make decisions they would not otherwise have made.

The second refers to the use of AI systems that exploit the specific vulnerabilities of individuals or groups, linked to factors such as age, disability or particular socio-economic conditions, with the intent or effect of significantly altering their behaviour in ways that may cause or reasonably be expected to cause significant harm to those individuals or others.

In both cases, the focus is not on the 'significant likelihood' of harm, but rather on the 'significant probabilistic' magnitude of the harm itself.

In concrete terms, this is a real paradigm shift, partly attributable to an extension of the precautionary principle, typical of the European Union.

It therefore becomes essential to define a minimum mathematical threshold of harm in order to activate the corresponding legal causality filter.

Article 5 of the Regulation, net of other specific conditions, prohibits the placing into service of a system 'which causes or is likely to cause (...) significant damage'.

As provided for in the Rules and Recommendations for the Technical Formulation of Legislative Texts of the Italian Senate, 'in the formulation of precepts, maximum uniformity is adopted in the use of verb modes, the rule being the present indicative, excluding both the subjunctive mode and the future tense'.

In the provision referred to in Article 5 of the Regulation - as highlighted in his analysis by Stefano Saracchi, Head of the Organisation and Digital Transformation Department of the Customs and Monopolies Agency - the transitive verb 'to cause' is used in the present subjunctive, indicating a possibility or hypothesis and acting as a verbal predicate in the relative clause. The coordinating conjunction 'o' connects two verbal possibilities within the same sentence, introducing a further possibility with the modal verb 'potere' (also in the present subjunctive). This modal verb is then followed by the transitive verb 'provocare' in the infinitive. In Italian grammar, the subjunctive expresses uncertainty, possibility, desire, or hypothesis. This verbal mode is used to express an action or state that is not considered real or concrete at the time of speaking, but which could happen or which one imagines could happen. In this specific case, it expresses possibility.

Similar to the algorithms that regulate the functioning of artificial intelligence based on statistical and probabilistic calculations, the prohibition of the use of a particular AI system is also conditioned by a prior analysis aimed at estimating the probability of significant harm occurring. It is therefore essential to identify an internationally recognised mathematical model that can concretely determine the occurrence of such a prohibition condition.

From a legal perspective, the difference between the two verbal terms reflects varying degrees of certainty and has specific legal consequences related to the action described. Saracchi points out that the two verbal forms have distinct implications in terms of liability and burden of proof.

The present subjunctive conveys a plausible certainty and implies that the action of causing damage is considered possible and potentially imminent. This form can be used to deal with situations where there is a direct and obvious connection with an event. If an action actually causes damage, this establishes direct liability.

The potential subjunctive introduces a greater level of uncertainty, not stating that the damage will occur, but indicating the possibility that it may occur. This is characteristic of risk assessments and preventive planning.

The concept of damage in relation to artificial intelligence models is connected to the phenomenon of 'performance failure', which can be defined as the inability of an AI system to achieve the expected performance.

Expected performance is based on the accuracy of predictions and an understanding of their variability.

There are various metrics available for performance evaluation, depending on the model in question: accuracy is one of them.

In the case of AI, these metrics are necessary but not sufficient, and therefore the direction to take is towards more robust testing regimes that take into account the uncertainty of the model and possible margins of error.

A model must be able to provide an output and, together with it, an estimate of the main forms of error inherent in that output. The degree of confidence with which the same result is provided.

The economic damage resulting from the 'performance failure' of AI systems can manifest itself in many ways, including:

- incremental costs for additional human intervention, which has become necessary to compensate for the system's performance deficiencies;
- economic losses caused directly by the malfunctioning of the model;
- economic losses resulting from the operational suspension of the system;
- failure to achieve the economic benefits legitimately expected following the implementation of AI.

Two particularly critical phenomena that can compromise the predictive reliability of models over time:

- Covariate shift: when the distribution of input data in the production phase diverges significantly from the distribution of data used in the training phase. This misalignment can lead to a progressive deterioration of the model's predictive capabilities, resulting in an increase in the error rate.
- Concept drift: this consists of a change, over time, in the statistical relationship between input variables and the predictive target. This phenomenon occurs when, with the same input, the variable to be predicted behaves differently from that observed during the training phase.

A specific and particularly sensitive case is that of fraud detection systems, where models adopted by banks and public entities abound.

Fraudulent methods are constantly evolving, leading to a progressive alteration of the relationship between risk indicators (input) and the fraudulent nature of the transaction (output). In the absence of adequate adaptation mechanisms, the system would show a progressive increase in the rate of false negatives or positives, with consequent economic damage to the financial institution, public body and private individual.

The timely identification and mitigation of these phenomena is essential for the correct assessment of risk in AI systems and for the preparation of adequate risk management strategies.

This strategy must also include periodic review of predictive models, avoiding any discriminatory system and taking into account objective, up-to-date data rather than just socio-economic or geographical predictions.

Probabilistic parametric models, based on predefined probability distributions, assume that system errors follow specific distribution functions. This methodology is widely used in financial and actuarial contexts, but has limitations when applied to complex and non-linear AI systems.

Models based on Bayesian methods, which rely on the continuous updating of risk estimates in response to new evidence, are characterised by their ability to incorporate prior knowledge and progressively adapt to the acquisition of new data.

Among the most significant methodologies for risk assessment in AI systems are 'distribution-free' or non-parametric methods. These approaches do not require rigid assumptions about the statistical distribution of errors.

It is necessary to distinguish between three fundamental aspects, which are interrelated but conceptually distinct.

The first concerns the definition of what constitutes a 'significant error' in the AI model, i.e., the determination of the confidence interval beyond which a deviation from the ideal prediction is considered legally relevant (harmful).

The second concerns the determination of what probability should be considered acceptable (significance threshold), i.e., the probability of malfunction above which it is not permissible to proceed.

The third concerns the methodology for rigorously verifying whether and how often an AI system actually exceeds this threshold.

The definition of an 'acceptability range' is a significant proposal. This range delimits the perimeter within which variations in the model's predictions are considered physiological.

As regards the significance threshold, i.e. the maximum acceptable probability of malfunction, the choice will be influenced by subjective, objective and regulatory factors.

In relation to the third aspect, the methodology offers a statistically stable approach for calculating the probability that an AI system will produce results outside the pre-established acceptability range. This methodology, based on 'conformal prediction' techniques, has the advantage of not requiring assumptions about the statistical distribution of errors and providing conservative risk estimates.

In the legal analysis of the significance of damage, two main interpretative approaches can emerge: the objective approach and the subjective approach.

The objective approach considers the significance of damage to be determined by universal and standardised criteria. According to this view, significant damage is seen as independent of the personal circumstances of the individual. It is based on the idea that there are predefined and measurable parameters that define what is relevant, thus allowing for a consistent and predictable assessment. This approach is often favoured for its ability to ensure clarity and consistency in legal decisions, ensuring that similar situations receive similar treatment.

The subjective approach emphasises that the assessment of significant harm must take into account specific individual circumstances. According to this perspective, what is considered significant harm varies from individual to individual, depending on their economic, social and vulnerability status. This approach values the diversity of human experiences and recognises that the impact of a harmful event can vary greatly depending on personal circumstances.

Neither approach can be considered 'the best' or, in any case, such as to exclude the other.

First of all, we need to understand what specific area of AI application we are referring to: a drug dosing system? The detection of financial fraud risk? The predictability of fraud involving public funds? The risk that a person travelling is a terrorist?

Each of these uses has specific practical implications that cannot be resolved by the standardised and generalised use of an objective or subjective approach.

The two approaches must complement and mitigate each other, both in terms of the area of application and the subject (person) to whom they are applied.

Recognising that significant harm may differ for each person allows the law to adapt more closely to the specific needs and situations of individuals, promoting fair justice.

The subjective approach not only encompasses a wider range of human experiences, but also allows the legal system to respond in a more sensitive and detailed manner to individual suffering, ensuring that no significant harm is underestimated or overlooked due to an overly rigid or uniform definition of the underlying legal concepts.

It is quite clear that some individuals, characterised by a solid financial position, may be willing to bear more significant damage than others. When these systems operate in socially sensitive areas, the permissible error threshold cannot be left to the discretion of the individual operator, but must be established by law, stipulating that the system cannot exceed a certain percentage of error, explicitly quantified.

In this context, it would be appropriate to introduce a system of reference tables to precisely define the permissible error thresholds. These tables should be based on consolidated empirical analysis and objective surveys, conducted according to standardised and methodologically rigorous procedures, with periodic updates to reflect technological developments and the accumulation of application experience.

The thresholds could be parameterised according to multiple variables: the sector of application (distinguishing, for example, between healthcare, finance, justice or administration), the potential number of people affected (differentiating between systems that affect a few individuals and systems that affect large sections of the population), the severity of the potential consequences (providing for more stringent thresholds for AI systems whose incorrect decisions can cause irreversible damage), as well as the degree of human supervision envisaged (allowing for wider margins of error in the system where significant human control over the final decisions to be taken is guaranteed).

This calibrated and differentiated regulatory approach would make it possible to balance the need to protect widespread interests with that of not hindering technological innovation, by establishing a regulatory framework that guides operators towards high quality standards without imposing constraints that are disproportionate to the risks actually present in the various application contexts.

This does not mean that – given a 'reference' table – in specific cases, when faced with specific evidence, it is not possible to deviate from the table, which, let us remember, reflects statistical data, and it may well be that an individual person may deviate significantly from a statistic.

29

When the Judgement is Invented by AI

The Responsibility of Judges and Solicitors

This commentary is inspired by two cases: one Italian case involving lawyers and one American case involving the text of the grounds for judgements written by judges.

This shows that the issue is not only cross-cutting, but also does not concern only 'one part' of the judicial process. Furthermore, it is particularly relevant when – in addition to the interests of the parties involved, for example in civil and administrative matters – it also affects personal freedoms in the criminal sphere.

The order of 14 March 2025 of the Court of Florence reported the incident involving a lawyer who cited a non-existent judgment suggested by an artificial intelligence system in a defence brief. It was only a matter of time before the first ruling by an Italian court reporting an episode of AI hallucination in a court case arrived.

The case is now well known: the Court of Florence - Business Section - in its collegiate order dated 14 March 2025 ruled as follows: *'The defence counsel for the company stated that the case law references cited in the document were the result of research carried out by a member of the firm using the artificial intelligence tool 'ChatGPT', the use of which was unknown to the solicitor. The AI had therefore generated incorrect results that can be described as the phenomenon of so-called artificial intelligence hallucinations, which occur when the AI invents non-existent results but which, even after a second query, are confirmed as true. (...) Now, without prejudice to the negative value of the failure to verify the actual existence of the judgments resulting from the AI query, (...). The indication of grounds for legitimacy in the appeal judgment, further confirming the defence line already set out by the defendant, can therefore be considered as aimed at strengthening an already known defence apparatus and not at resisting the proceedings in bad faith, resulting in the non-applicability of the provisions of Article 96 of the Italian Code of Civil Procedure.*

DOI: 10.1201/9781003731290-33

Other cases of hallucinations – i.e., responses partially or completely invented by artificial intelligence systems, which, when translated into the forensic field, result in the actual invention of non-existent case law precedents – had already been reported by US courts.

A well-known case is that of lawyer Steven Schwartz, who in 2023 cited non-existent judgments in proceedings before the New York District Court.

On that occasion, the US district judge ordered the lawyers involved in the incident and their law firm - *Levidow, Levidow &* Oberman - to pay a total fine of $5,000, on the grounds that the lawyers had acted in bad faith and had committed 'acts of deliberate evasion' and made 'false and misleading statements to the court'..

Let us remember for the moment this – justified – severity, because we will return to it later.

In the Italian case, the Court was certainly more lenient, finding that there were no grounds for considering that the party had acted in bad faith in the proceedings and, therefore, for imposing a sentence under Article 96 of the Code of Civil Procedure.

On a purely interpretative level, the use of generative artificial intelligence for the purpose of conducting case law research appears to fall within the limits permitted by the bill recently approved by the Senate on artificial intelligence, which, with regard to the use of this technology by professionals, introduced the following provision in Article 13, first paragraph: 'The use of artificial intelligence systems in the intellectual professions is intended solely for the exercise of activities that are instrumental and supportive of professional activity, with a prevalence of intellectual work that is the subject of the service provided'.

Legal research carried out using an AI system is, in fact, an instrumental and support activity, certainly not predominant over the intellectual work of a solicitor in drafting a defence brief.

Permitted certainly does not mean 'always allowed', and especially in such a sensitive area, 'allowing' should always be accompanied by 'strictly monitored and verified', given the interests at stake and, above all, taking into account the extraordinary professional diligence that should accompany the legal profession.

It is also worth recalling the provisions of the 'Charter of Principles for the Conscious Use of Artificial Intelligence Tools in the Legal Field', recently adopted by the Milan Bar Association, which prescribes the duty of competence and the principle of the centrality of human decision-making.

With regard to the duty of competence, the Charter of Principles states: 'It is essential to understand the capabilities and limitations of the AI systems used to ensure that the results are accurate and appropriate to the legal context'. It adds: 'Lawyers must be able to identify and manage the risks associated with the use of AI by avoiding dependence on automated results'.

In the case of the order we started with, if the professional had correctly applied these principles, the incident could have been avoided. This is because, even in relations with collaborators, if the owner of a firm does not intend to allow the use of artificial intelligence tools – *now widely available and easily accessible* – they would have had the burden of specifying the prohibition in their firm's policies (or by other means).

Where, on the other hand, their use is permitted, it is important to define the limits and methods by which such tools may be used in the practice of the profession, as well as – *we feel it is worth adding* – appropriate ex-post verification policies.

In this sense, the Charter of Principles also refers to an additional duty: 'Lawyers have a duty to actively intervene to critically evaluate the results produced by AI technologies, ensuring that the processing is not negatively affected by algorithms. Every result generated by AI must be subject to human review to ensure its adequacy, accuracy and compliance with ethical and legal principles'.

In the Florentine case, it would have been sufficient *to double-check* the results produced by the AI system, not by querying the same system again – as seems to have happened – but by consulting commonly used case law databases.

The defence lawyer justified the incident by stating that the case law references cited in the document were the result of research carried out by an assistant using the artificial intelligence tool 'ChatGPT', the use of which the lawyer was unaware of.

In this regard, it is useful to refer to a further obligation provided for in the bill approved by the Senate (Article 13, second paragraph): 'In order to ensure the relationship of trust between the professional and the client, information relating to the artificial intelligence systems used by the professional shall be communicated to the recipient of the intellectual service in clear, simple and comprehensive language'.

The same obligation of transparency should, even more so, exist between professionals working on the same case, so that the person responsible for the assignment is aware of the use of an AI tool and can take all useful or necessary measures to contain possible risks.

Finally – and this goes beyond the defence adopted by the defence lawyer – it would be appropriate, out of respect for the responsibility and quality of lawyers as professionals, to avoid this kind of buck-passing. Even if the act was performed by an assistant, it is the responsibility of the professional in charge to read, reread and verify the document, otherwise the distinction between the professional and an assistant (a professional who is personally responsible for the actions of the assistant) is lost.

In addition to the Milan Bar Association, numerous international bodies have developed their own guidelines on the use of artificial intelligence in the legal field (see, among others, the Artificial Intelligence Strategy of the Court of Justice of the European Union; Practical guidance for the use of generative artificial intelligence in the practice of law - State Bar of California).

The Court of Florence - considering the absence of bad faith - has shown itself to be lenient, limiting itself to censuring the negative value of the omitted verification, probably also in consideration of the novelty of the phenomenon; however, it is likely that in the future, national courts may also adopt a more severe standard of evaluation for such conduct.

Let us return, however, to the United States, where the courts have been much less lenient.

Two US federal judges, operating in Mississippi and New Jersey, 'withdrew' their rulings in two unrelated court cases after the respective defence lawyers formally challenged the accuracy of the court documents, pointing out serious factual and procedural errors.

In Mississippi, a district judge replaced an order issued in the context of a civil rights dispute after state lawyers pointed out that it contained incorrect identification of plaintiffs and defendants, as well as allegations that were not included in the original complaint.

The ruling contained statements based on alleged testimony from individuals who did not even appear in the case file.

The original order, issued on 20 July 2025 and relating to the enforcement of a state ban on diversity, equity and inclusion programmes in universities and public schools, was therefore replaced on 23 July to correct the substantial deficiencies identified by the lawyers.

In New Jersey, meanwhile, a district judge similarly 'withdrew' a decision in a securities lawsuit against a pharmaceutical company. Defence lawyers challenged the fact that the ruling contained citations of non-existent case law, as well as incorrect attributions of statements to defendants.

The incriminating draft revealed that a search produced by artificial intelligence (according to the judge's office's defence) had been inadvertently included, which had been carried out by a temporary assistant and had not been adequately reviewed before publication. The unauthorised use of AI tools in the formulation of judicial decisions violates the court's internal policies.

In both cases, the judges did not publicly detail the reasons for the errors contained in the original judgments. Nor did the lawyers involved mention the possible influence, or responsibility, of artificial intelligence in generating these inaccuracies.

In the past, similar cases have resulted in sanctions or reprimands against lawyers for unethical conduct, consisting of filing documents containing false or inaccurate citations, attributed to the misuse of AI software whose output can generate so-called 'hallucinations', i.e., invented or inaccurate data.

As Keith Swisher, professor of legal ethics at Arizona University's law school, quoted by Mike Scarcella on Reuters, pointed out, the increase in procedural errors related to the use of emerging technologies requires rigorous checking and verification by legal professionals in order to avoid significant consequences in the context of justice.

Regardless of the perspective from which one views what has happened, the fundamental role of AI literacy in the forensic field is clear, aimed at guiding professionals towards greater awareness of the potential and limitations of artificial intelligence tools, including in the practice of their profession.

It is inevitable that when such an innovative and powerful new technology is introduced to the market, it will take time before it begins to be used with knowledge and wisdom by operators, including professionals and solicitors.

From this perspective, training can be an extraordinary accelerator and represents an essential step, especially in sectors that, given the interests involved, deserve special attention, such as justice and the defence of rights.

The American asymmetry regarding the same mistake made by solicitors and judges is indicative of a real risk in our country too, where the responsibility of magistrates is extremely tenuous.

It also seems extremely childish – given the professional level involved – to shift responsibility onto a 'law firm employee' or a 'temporary court employee'.

This is also because – as we are certain based on previous cases – American judges have always held lawyers responsible for the mistakes of their associates.

The point is not only the necessary recourse to greater supervision, control and verification, ex post with respect to research, but also to move away from the ambiguous perception that Artificial Intelligence does not make mistakes.

If we clarify this point definitively, perhaps the necessary responsibilities and indispensable verification work will acquire new value and meaning, while at the same time restoring new value and meaning to human activity.

30

Artificial Intelligence in Law Firms

A British Case

On 6 May 2025, the British Solicitors Regulation Authority (SRA) authorised Garfield.Law Ltd, owner of Garfield AI, the world's first law firm authorised and registered to carry out legal activities reserved for solicitors, to provide services exclusively through artificial intelligence (it is as if a legaltech company in Italy were registered with the bar association).

The Garfield case is not only a technological experiment but also a test of a different regulatory approach. While Europe has chosen the path of comprehensive regulation with Regulation (EU) 2024/1689 – the AI Act – the UK is pursuing a more flexible sectoral approach, creating a laboratory to observe the advantages and risks of divergent strategies.

Garfield.Law was born from the meeting between Philip Young, a solicitor with over 25 years' experience in commercial litigation, and Daniel Long, a quantum physicist dedicated to technological development.

The law firm has its own unique feature: it focuses on small claims up to £10,000, offering services ranging from £2 for a *polite chaser letter* to full litigation management before the small claims court.

The system is not a simple application of ChatGPT but a hybrid architecture that combines enterprise-level LLM with a rules-based expert system, incorporating decades of legal experience into algorithms that follow the UK Civil Procedure Rules. Every document generated is reviewed by the client and by Young himself, who is the compliance officer.

The most revolutionary aspect is that Garfield operates as a fully-fledged law firm: regulated by the SRA, covered by compulsory professional insurance, with solicitors responsible for every output of the system. It is therefore not simply a provider of legal technology, but an entity that assumes full professional responsibility for the services provided through AI.

Garfield's authorisation required eight months of intense dialogue with the SRA, during which the regulator imposed stringent conditions to ensure consumer

DOI: 10.1201/9781003731290-34

protection. These included a total ban on the system proposing relevant case law – an area notoriously prone to 'hallucinations' in language models – and the obligation to maintain human control over every stage of the process, with the client's explicit approval for each stage.

The SRA meticulously verified the quality-checking processes, measures for client confidentiality and mechanisms for preventing conflicts of interest. There are still concerns, for example, about the accuracy of outputs, algorithmic biases, discriminatory biases, maintaining professional responsibility and verification and control systems.

While the UK is experimenting with Garfield in the field, the European Union has taken a radically different approach with the AI Act, which represents the world's first attempt at horizontal and comprehensive regulation of artificial intelligence, introducing a risk-based classification system that distinguishes between prohibited, high-risk, limited-risk and minimal-risk applications.

For the legal sector, the AI Act has particularly relevant implications. Article 6 classifies AI systems used 'in the administration of justice and democratic processes' as high risk, including those intended to 'assist a judicial authority in the search for and interpretation of facts and law and in the application of law to a concrete set of facts'. Although Garfield operates in the context of civil small claims and does not directly fall into this category, the dividing line could prove to be decidedly porous.

European law firms wishing to use AI systems will have to do so within the constraints of a complex regulatory framework. For high-risk systems, Article 9 requires the implementation of a risk management system covering the entire AI lifecycle, while Article 10 sets out stringent requirements for data governance, including the need for 'relevant, representative, error-free and comprehensive' training datasets. Article 13 also requires that such systems be designed to allow for effective human oversight, a principle that Garfield already seems to incorporate into its design.

While the European AI Act establishes a rigid regulatory framework, the UK has adopted a more flexible and sector-specific approach. In its White Paper, 'AI Regulation: A Pro-Innovation Approach', the British government emphasises the need for adaptable regulation that does not hinder technological development.

The UK approach is based on general principles, leaving it to individual regulators – such as the SRA for the legal sector – to manage AI applications in their respective fields. Instead of rigid ex ante rules, the UK focuses on case-by-case assessments, allowing for faster experimentation and progressive regulatory adjustments.

In the case of Garfield.Law, the SRA worked directly with the firm for eight months, developing targeted rules that balance innovation and consumer protection. This model ensures regulatory flexibility, but could also generate potential critical issues. The absence of uniform standards could create uncertainty for operators wishing to scale beyond national borders. Furthermore, dependence on the capacity and resources of individual sectoral regulators could lead to significant disparities between different professional fields.

However, precisely because of the high degree of innovation, instead of introducing theoretical rules to be challenged, England proposes a model of dialogue –

consistent with its general administrative framework – in which the regulator is aware of its mandate but learns with the company and acquires, on a case-by-case basis, the skills that no administration can ontologically possess.

This is even more true when regulation is delegated to a supranational body – in this case, the European Union – and national authorities simply translate and copy-paste regulations and guidelines uncritically, without taking into account concrete needs and realities.

For Italian and European law firms, the Garfield case demonstrates, on the one hand, that the automation of routine legal services is not only technically feasible but also commercially viable and regulatory acceptable. On the other hand, it highlights the complexity of the regulatory path that awaits those who intend to follow this path under the AI Act.

For many routine legal services – from contractual due diligence to the drafting of standard deeds – classification as low-risk systems could allow for greater flexibility. However, as AI moves closer to the heart of complex activity, regulatory requirements intensify proportionally.

The issue of professional liability is particularly sensitive. While Garfield clearly maintains responsibility with qualified solicitors, in the post-AI Act European environment, firms will have to meticulously document chains of responsibility, implement human oversight systems in accordance with Article 14 of the Regulation, and ensure the traceability of every algorithmic decision.

In this regard, with very few exceptions, the firms that will actually be able to equip themselves with these systems will be corporate partnerships with a sufficient number of partners to be able to implement true process governance on the classic three levels.

The fundamental question therefore remains whether a tool that is supposed to increase competitiveness and reduce costs will ultimately end up – as has often been the case historically – creating a further competitive advantage for larger firms at the expense of young and smaller professional firms.

The British legal community's reaction to Garfield has been mixed, ranging from enthusiasm for its potential to democratise access to justice to concern about its impact on the traditional profession. Young argues that the system will 'free up solicitors to focus on higher-level, higher-value work'.

The European AI Act, with its emphasis on human protection and supervision, could offer traditional firms a temporary buffer to adapt, slowing down the adoption of purely algorithmic solutions.

In an interview, the firm's founder recounted the birth of his idea: "I decided to build something to help people like my brother-in-law Andy, a plumber near Sheffield. Like many small business owners, he sometimes doesn't get paid by his customers. Not because of insolvency or problems with the service, but because certain debtors take advantage of the fact that small business owners don't have the time or expertise to write reminders, fill out legal forms or pursue a lawsuit. And for a non-lawyer, the court is intimidating. For a large company, a few thousand pounds is nothing. For a small business, it's the summer holidays. It's a significant problem in the UK economy: some estimates put it at £6 billion, others as high as £50 billion a year. I thought it was the ideal problem to solve with artificial intelligence.

Small claims are the simplest commercial cases in England and Wales and follow a well-defined procedure. As my technical co-founder Dan says, it is a 'succession of relatively closed problem spaces' – perfect for AI.

The founders describe the model as follows:

Garfield is a web application that helps creditors recover debts of less than £10,000 through the English and Welsh small claims system. Garfield guides the user through every stage: initial triage, pre-litigation letters, court forms, application for judgment in default or admission, management of the defence, preparation for the final stage. It also prepares the electronic file, a skeleton argument and an oral note for the hearing. Users can also be represented by a barrister.

Garfield AI is capable of generating documents at least at the level of a competent solicitor in a high street law firm. We intend to continuously improve this standard as the service is rolled out.

We have modelled Garfield's behaviour on that of a good law firm. The facts come from the client, but the legal and procedural knowledge and recommendations come from the firm. A good firm shows drafts to the client before sending them. Garfield does the same: each stage is shown to the user, who can correct any misunderstandings.

Garfield AI is a law firm and therefore the same rules apply as for other English law firms, including regulatory requirements and contractual obligations to clients. Liability is handled as in any law firm, including the fact that we have professional liability insurance.

The SRA has a public duty to promote access to justice. Garfield AI was created with the intention of expanding this access, allowing small businesses to recover minor debts. Once it was verified that the SRA had jurisdiction to authorise Garfield, and that our responses were satisfactory, authorisation was a logical choice.

Users pay on a pay-as-you-go basis. No subscription, no strings attached. Users only pay for what they need. If a case is resolved quickly, they pay for fewer stages; if it goes to trial, they pay for more stages. In addition, many of the legal costs are recoverable from the debtor, if they are solvent and the debt is recognised. This makes Garfield more attractive to creditors.

We have been really impressed by the enthusiastic response. Many companies have already signed up or contacted us. It seems clear that the problem of small unpaid debts is indeed very widespread.

In any case, the British solution seems 'smart' from various points of view.

If we define intelligence as the ability to adapt and find solutions to problems posed by the environment, Garfield effectively uses the tools available to solve a problem whose solution would be uneconomical for the creditor.

It does not replace humans in the control, evaluation, consideration and creative phases.

It does not represent a prompt with which humans can relax, leaving it to 'write in their place', but manages routines in a standardised procedural context.

When regulatory and administrative authorities do not act in a rigid and vertical manner, but take a horizontal and dialoguing position, even a 'unique and first' procedure of its kind can be defined in a few months. And this is the framework in which innovation can find a way to be useful.

31

The Enforceability of Data Subjects' Rights over Data Inferred by AI

Artificial intelligence, in its many applications, allows personal data relating to an individual to be inferred through statistical analysis of data provided directly by the individual, as well as data provided by third parties or anonymous data.

These operations, which allow for the creation of inferences that are difficult to predict, represent a risk for data subjects: on the one hand, they determine the acquisition of information that the data subject may wish to keep confidential, and on the other hand, they may lead to the processing of inaccurate derived data, which can have negative consequences for the data subject.

With regard to this phenomenon, it is interesting to reflect on the applicability of the GDPR to 'inferred' data and on the suitability of the current regulatory framework to provide effective protection for this type of data.

This is also relevant in the broader context in which personal data, collected in a heterogeneous manner, ends up forming even more heterogeneous metadata panels on which training and machine learning actions are performed, and through which data, information and processing based on statistical data are returned – for a fee – without any consent or ability to verify.

1. Are 'inferred' data personal data?

Inferred data (i.e., derived or inferred data) has the full value and nature of personal data. In this sense, in the Guidelines, the Article 29 Working Party distinguishes personal data into data provided directly by the data subject or 'observed' data concerning a person from derived or inferred data, such as the profile of the person that has been created.

Along the same lines, the Court of Justice of the European Union, in case C-434/16, P. N. v. Data Protection Commissioner, clarified that opinions and assessments relating to a natural person also constitute personal data.

The case concerned a candidate who had exercised his right of access and rectification with regard to his examination paper and the assessments made by the

DOI: 10.1201/9781003731290-35

examiner; the Court held that the answers given in an examination paper and the notes made by the examiner constitute personal data relating to the data subject.

To hold otherwise, the Court observed, would mean completely removing this information from the scope of the principles and safeguards relating to the protection of personal data and, in particular, the principles relating to the quality of such data and the lawfulness of its processing.

In concrete terms, if the examination 'concerns me' and the mark 'concerns me', then the examiner's comments on my examination paper can only also concern me, in line with the fact and the data itself.

The increasing spread of artificial intelligence solutions that allow the generation of personal data referable to a specific subject through the statistical analysis of data relating to third parties or anonymous data.

Consider, for example, technological solutions that allow market operators to 'enrich' the profile of their customers through statistical analysis of third-party data (so-called *'statistical twins'*) or to predict certain behaviours in order to evaluate requests from the data subject.

In the aforementioned judgment, the Court of Justice clarified that the use of the expression 'any information' in the definition of 'personal data' [the definition of personal data in Article 2(a) letter a) of Directive 95/46 has remained unchanged in Article 4 of Regulation (EU) 2016/679] reflects the objective of the EU legislator to give a broad meaning to that concept, which potentially covers all types of information, provided that it 'relates' to the data subject; that condition, according to the Court, is satisfied where the information is connected to a specific person by virtue of its content, purpose or effect.

In the opinion of the Court of Justice, inferred data enjoy the same protection as data provided by the data subject if they are processed for purposes related to the data subject or in any case capable of producing effects on the data subject (e.g., profiling, making or receiving an assessment).

In the case of data inferred through artificial intelligence solutions based on third-party or anonymous data, the condition set out by the Court can be said to be satisfied whenever the processing is carried out to enrich the data subject's profile with unknown characteristics or for predictive purposes with regard to certain behaviours of the data subject.

Although European data protection legislation does not deal with data generation and inference processes, it must also apply in the case of derived data.

2. The right to be informed about the processing of inferred data

The data subject's right to be informed about the processing of their personal data by the controller is governed by Articles 13 and 14 of the Regulation.

Article 13, which refers to the information to be provided with regard to personal data collected directly from the data subject, could apply in cases where inferred data are processed by the controller on the basis of the data subject's data.

Article 13 of the Regulation provides that *'Where personal data are collected from the data subject, the controller shall provide the data subject with the following information (...)' at the time the personal data are obtained,* but not in the case of inferred data obtained through the analysis of anonymous data or third-party data.

Article 14 of the Regulation, on the other hand, governs the information to be provided when personal data have not been obtained from the data subject. The provision was created with the intention of regulating cases in which the data subject's data are collected from a third-party source.

Recital 61 of the Regulation provides that *"the data subject should be informed about the processing of personal data concerning him or her at the time of collection from the data subject or, if the data are obtained from another source, within a reasonable period, depending on the circumstances of the case"*.

An interpretation of the regulation consistent with the principle of transparency referred to in Article 12 of the Regulation requires that the obligation to provide adequate information be extended to the processing of inferred data in the sense we are examining.

Recital 60 of the Regulation states that *"the principles of fair and transparent processing imply that the data subject should be informed of the existence of the processing and its purposes. The controller should provide the data subject with any further information necessary to ensure fair and transparent processing, taking into account the specific circumstances and context in which the personal data are processed."*

Although we wish to consider that, under current regulations, there is an obligation to inform the data subject about the processing of inferred data or, in any case, about the processes of generating such data, the information to be provided pursuant to Articles 13 and 14 may not be exhaustive.

The information that the data controller is required to provide to data subjects does not seem adequate to ensure that data subjects have sufficient knowledge of the data generation process and, consequently, sufficient control over their own information being processed.

3. The right of access

The right of access, governed by Article 15 of the Regulation, recognises the data subject's right to obtain confirmation as to whether or not personal data concerning him or her are being processed, as well as access to such data and a range of additional information relating to the purposes of the processing, the categories of data processed, the recipients and the storage period.

This right is one of the main expressions of the principle of transparency and allows the data subject to exercise effective control over the processing of their personal data.

The exercise of this right in relation to inferred data – in particular, data generated by algorithmic processing and artificial intelligence models, including from third-party data – raises significant issues of interpretation and application.

In general, the right of access to data, as governed by Article 15, refers to all personal data relating to the data subject; therefore, it also guarantees the latter knowledge of any inferred data.

With regard to this category of data, the data subject may also wish to know the logic underlying the inferential process through which the data has been processed.

In this respect, however, the current legislation does not seem to offer an adequate level of protection: the right of access to the data processing logic used is in fact recognised by Article 22 of the Regulation only with reference to processing carried out as part of an automated decision-making process that produces legal effects or significantly affects the data subject.

It would follow that, in the absence of an automated decision-making process, information relating to the inferential process – including the logic used and the algorithmic criteria – would not fall within the scope of guaranteed access, with the real risk of compromising the rights and freedoms of the data subject, who could be subject to automated assessments, classifications and profiling without having any possibility of knowing the basis for them or contesting their correctness.

On this point, I would like to highlight a personal case that may serve as a test case.

In the presence of an 'automatic response' (implemented through an automated decision-making process) from a bank, I submitted a request for access, having learned 'through informal channels' of the presence of a note on my profile. The bank responded without mentioning this 'added' information, even though I had made it clear that, to my knowledge, there was a specific code for that note.

We are therefore explicitly in the 'textbook case' referred to in the Court of Justice's opinion on inferred data, which enjoy the same protection as data provided by the data subject when they are processed for purposes related to the data subject or in any case likely to have an effect on the data subject (e.g., profiling, making or receiving an assessment).

Despite reminders, the bank ultimately did not respond and did not provide the data. (As it did not have a significant impact on me at the time, I did not insist, but I reserve the right to cite the case and to name the bank in question elsewhere).

That said, in any case (and leaving aside the personal case represented here), it must be considered that a systematic reading of the Regulation in the light of the principles of accountability, fairness and transparency should lead to the conclusion that, even in the absence of an automated decision-making process, the data subject should still be granted the right to obtain a comprehensible description of the fundamental logic on which the inference is based.

This interpretation of the right of access on the other hand, could conflict, on the one hand, with the difficulty of explaining in an intelligible manner to the data subject the complex criteria and algorithms used to derive the inferred data, with the risk of failing to fulfil the duty of transparency towards the data subject, and, on the other hand, with the possible protection of the commercial secrecy or intellectual property rights of the controller, which could justify a limitation of transparency with regard to the methods of inference, pursuant to Article 15(4) of the Regulation.

4. The right to rectification

The right to rectification, provided for in Article 16 of the Regulation, gives the data subject the right to obtain from the controller the correction of inaccurate personal data concerning him or her and the completion of incomplete data.

This is a fundamental right to ensure that decisions based on personal data are based on accurate and up-to-date information.

More broadly and more concretely, it also ensures that decisions based on personal data are not based on incorrect, outdated, discretionary, unknowable and uncontested information, as well as verified information, and in the case of the use of artificial intelligence, do not fall within the scope of the well-known 'hallucinations'.

However, the literal wording of Article 16 is inadequate in view of the growing use of automated processing, in particular that involving the generation of inferred data through algorithmic or artificial intelligence systems.

Unlike data provided directly by the data subject or acquired from documentary sources, inferred data are often the result of predictive, probabilistic or classificatory assessments, the content of which is based on non-transparent mathematical models that are difficult to trace back to objective parameters of 'accuracy'.

Consider, for example, a system that assigns a reputation score or credit risk level based on certain behavioural or demographic patterns.

In such circumstances, the data subject may not be able to challenge the data on the grounds of 'inaccuracy', as the inference is not a fact but an estimate or assessment.

The distinction between an error in processing and a questionable algorithmic assessment is therefore far from straightforward.

Can the right to rectification apply to data that is not technically 'inaccurate' but has a discriminatory, misleading or disproportionate effect on the data subject?

In light of the current wording of Article 16, the answer would tend to be negative, unless the concept of inaccuracy is extended to the extreme of its semantic limits and typical of regulatory strictness.

The debatable, subjective or predictive nature of the inferred data would therefore fall outside the traditional scope of the right to rectification.

In such cases, it would be necessary to propose an evolutionary interpretation of Article 16, consistent with the principles of fairness and correctness of processing, according to which the data subject has at least the right to obtain an integration of the data, through a statement expressing their disagreement with the inference or a request for re-evaluation of the model applied.

This should be at least 'feasible' if we consider the case of statistical, demographic or trend data: in this case, the data subject is certainly able to demonstrate 'in concrete terms' the deviation of their specific case from the statistics.

Although the right to rectification does not easily apply automatically to inferred data, a systematic interpretation of the Regulation, also in light of the legal principles that inspire it, suggests that appropriate tools should be identified to challenge and correct the effects of inaccurate or distorted inferences, especially in cases where they have significant consequences for the rights and freedoms of the data subject.

5. The right to object and the right to erasure

The right to object, governed by Article 21 of the Regulation, allows the data subject to object at any time, on grounds relating to his or her particular situation, to the processing of personal data concerning him or her, including that based on the legitimate interest of the controller or on the performance of a task carried out in the public interest.

In such cases, the controller is required to cease processing, unless it can demonstrate compelling legitimate grounds for the processing.

The right to erasure is provided for in Article 17 and gives the data subject the possibility to obtain the erasure of their personal data under certain conditions, including the cessation of the purpose for which the data are collected, the withdrawal of consent, the opposition of the data subject, where there is no legitimate reason to proceed with the processing.

With regard to data inferred through artificial intelligence systems, the exercise of these rights raises specific complexities.

Firstly, when processing is based on the legitimate interest of the controller, the data subject may see their objection to processing rejected in a whole series of cases where, in balancing the rights of the data subject and the interests of the controller, the latter are usually considered to prevail; consider, for example, processing activities carried out for anti-fraud or anti-money laundering purposes, network and information system security, product improvement, and creditworthiness assessment.

In such cases, the same balancing also applies to personal data obtained from the data subject or from third-party sources, but it is clear that a data subject's interest in objecting to processing may be greater whenever the processing involves inferred data rather than data provided by the data subject or observed by the controller.

Similar complexities arise with regard to the right to erasure, which could in theory constitute a specific remedy against inferences that the data subject does not consider 'correct' or in any case representative of their condition and against which, for the reasons set out above, the right to rectification cannot be exercised.

Since, as a rule, inference processing is based on a legitimate interest of the data controller, the same critical issues observed above for the right to object apply to the exercise of the right to erasure.

This does not exclude or circumvent the full right to know and be informed of any information, including statistical and inferred information, that constitutes the data subject's data and that the data subject can at least supplement the information itself.

Such integration – in the strict sense of the law – would even constitute a contribution to the 'overriding reasons' in the balancing of interests, contributing, if anything, to 'better' information, both formally and substantively.

6. Conclusions

The growing spread of algorithmic technologies capable of generating inferred data requires in-depth legal reflection on the balance between innovation and the protection of fundamental rights.

The current regulations on personal data protection focus essentially on the collection of data rather than on the generation of data by the data controller, with the result that derived data and inferences do not enjoy the same level of protection as data collected from the data subject or from third parties. the tools currently offered by the Regulation have not been designed with the specific characteristics of derived data in mind and may, in some cases, be inadequate to provide real protection to data subjects.

Although we believe, through an interpretation of the Regulation consistent with the principle of transparency, that the data subject's right to receive information also refers to the processing of derived data and the processes of generating such data, there is still a risk that this right will not be adequately protected.

Even when the data subject is provided with information about the data generation process, the ability of algorithmic solutions to make inferences is so difficult to predict that there is a real risk of incomplete and non-transparent information.

Similarly, in the case of derivative data generation processes, the data subject's right of access could conflict with the data controller's right to protect trade secrets or know-how, again to the detriment of the transparency of the information provided to the data subject.

In this context, pending any future updates to the regulatory framework that take into account new protection requirements, it is up to legal practitioners to propose an evolutionary interpretation of the rights of data subjects so that these rights can also be applied to new types of data.

However, it is also up to the regulatory and supervisory authorities to promote an interpretative process that balances interests and protects individuals, aiming for solutions that effectively favour personalised data, rather than standardised data or data flattened by a statistical analysis algorithm, or worse, inferred data that is apparently not allowed to be known.

Through such interpretations, which are possible through opinions, guidelines, internal directives, recommendations and arbitration decisions, it is certainly possible to promote ways of extending the right of access and cross-examination, which ultimately promote the quality of the data, meeting the primary need even in the context of balancing interests.

32

Artificial Intelligence as a Tool for Challenging Decisions Evidential Value and Regulatory Challenges in Challenging Public Decisions

1. Introduction: The context of the debate on AI in decision-making

The integration of artificial intelligence (AI) systems into public and private decision-making processes is one of the most significant challenges for contemporary law (Zarsky, 2016). The academic and regulatory debate has so far been polarised around the use of automated decision-making systems by public authorities or large private organisations in procedures with a significant impact on individuals, such as recruitment, credit granting or admission to higher education (Barocas and Selbst, 2016; O'Neil, 2016). However, this narrative, which sees citizens as passive subjects of an algorithmic 'Goliath', is evolving.

An emerging and less explored phenomenon concerns the use of such systems by private citizens to challenge the decisions of the authorities themselves. This article critically analyses this reversal of perspective, examining the emblematic case of a legal appeal in Brazil in which a candidate used the output of an AI system to challenge the result of a public examination. Through the analysis of this ruling and the European regulatory framework, we aim to investigate the probative value of AI-generated assessments and their implications for the key principles of legal certainty, equality and due process. The thesis put forward here is that the legitimacy of AI output, whether produced by an authority or a private individual, is inextricably linked to its verifiability and transparency, without which it is reduced to a mere digital oracle that is unacceptable in a mature legal system.

DOI: 10.1201/9781003731290-36

2. The Brazilian case: The tribunal de Justiça do Estado do Paraná and the 'Glau' AI assessment

A concrete case of extraordinary paradigmatic value comes from the Tribunal de Justiça do Estado do Paraná in Brazil (Judgment No. 0001234-05.2025.8.16.0000, 2025). A citizen challenged the ranking of a public competition for court officials, requesting the correction of the score and compensation for moral damages. The novel element was the evidence produced in support of his case: the appellant submitted his exam paper to an artificial intelligence system called 'Glau', obtaining a significantly higher score than that awarded by the human examination board. This output was used as a benchmark to demonstrate the inaccuracy of the official assessment.

The Brazilian court rejected the claim, articulating a reasoning that exemplifies the legal criticalities inherent in such use of AI. The ruling stated that 'the use of an artificial intelligence tool... to verify an alleged discrepancy in scoring is not sufficient to invalidate the assessment made by the board' (Ruling No. 0001234-05.2025.8.16.0000, 2025). The key principle referred to is that of the binding nature of the call for applications, whose criteria, weightings and methods of analysis constitute the only legitimate and predetermined parameter for the correction of tests (Pignatelli, 2023). Any comparison with external systems, not provided for in the call for applications and not subject to its procedural constraints, was deemed to have no technical or legal basis.

3. The court's reasoning: legal certainty, equality and algorithmic opacity

The decision of the Tribunal de Justiça do Paraná is based on three fundamental arguments, which reflect concerns widely shared in international legal doctrine (Wachter et al., 2017; Goodman and Flaxman, 2017).

- Violation of the Principles of Legal Certainty and Equality: The court emphasised that allowing the review of assessments on the basis of criteria unrelated to the call for applications would violate the principle of legal certainty (Rawls, 1971) and result in unequal treatment of candidates. The appellant's argument, if accepted, would open the door to a chaotic system in which each candidate could challenge the results using different AI systems, each with its own non-transparent algorithms and criteria, compromising the objectivity, uniformity and reliability of the entire selection process (Judgment No. 0001234-05.2025.8.16.0000, 2025; Yeung, 2018).
- Lack of Explainability and Verifiability: A decisive argument concerned the opacity of the 'Glau' system. The court highlighted how 'the lack of explainability and the absence of effective human audit or supervision in the AI correction process make it an unsuitable source of evidence' (Judgment No. 0001234-05.2025.8.16.0000, 2025). The methodology used by the system was not transparent, uniform or verifiable by third parties, violating the principles

of legal certainty. The judgment explicitly referred to the principles of AI Explainability (AIX), as developed by the National Institute of Standards and Technology (NIST) (Phillips et al., 2021), according to which an AI system must provide explanations that are understandable, accurate and limited to the context of use.

- Burden of Proof and Credibility of the System: The appellant had not provided verifiable evidence regarding the architecture of the system, the logical criteria, the quality of the training data or the validation methodologies of 'Glau'. In the absence of such information, the AI output was merely a black box (Pasquale, 2015), whose value and reliability could not be meaningfully weighed by the judge. The court therefore concluded that 'the mere subjective disagreement of the candidate, based on an external system lacking measurable credibility, does not justify judicial review' (Judgment No. 0001234-05.2025.8.16.0000, 2025).

4. The European perspective: GDPR, AI act and the 'Household Exemption' dilemma

The Brazilian case provides an opportunity to analyse the European regulatory framework, which has regulated the use of AI systems mainly from the perspective of the institutional 'Goliath'.

- The GDPR and the Prohibition of Automated Decisions: Article 22 of the General Data Protection Regulation (GDPR) prohibits decisions based solely on automated processing, including profiling, which produce legal effects or significantly affect the data subject, with specific exceptions (EU Regulation 2016/679, 2016). However, the rule is designed as a shield for citizens against public or private automation (Citron and Pasquale, 2014), not as a basis for the private use of such systems to challenge decisions.
- The AI Act and High-Risk Systems: The Artificial Intelligence Regulation (AI Act) classifies systems used in the workplace and education as high-risk (Annex III), subjecting them to strict requirements regarding transparency, accuracy, human oversight and data governance (EU AI Regulation, 2024). The crucial question is whether a private citizen using an AI system to challenge the outcome of a competition can be classified as a deployer under the AI Act.
- The 'Household Exemption' Dilemma: Article 2(5) of the AI Act excludes from the scope of the regulation the use of AI systems for purely personal and non-professional activities (the so-called 'household exemption'). It is highly debatable whether the use of AI to challenge a public act, with potential effects on the legal system, can fall within this exclusion. As noted by the EU Commission in its guidelines, the exclusion applies only to 'purely personal non-professional activities' (European Commission, 2024). Use in administrative litigation seems to go beyond this purely private sphere, raising serious public policy issues regarding procedural fairness and the reliability of evidence, even in a regulatory vacuum.

5. The evidential value of AI Output in the Italian legal system

In the absence of specific legislation, the admissibility and evidentiary value of AI outputs in Italian trials are to be assessed in the light of general provisions.

- Atypical Evidence and Prudent Assessment by the Judge: As reiterated by the Court of Cassation, 'the current procedural system lacks a definitive rule on the exhaustiveness of means of evidence' (Court of Cassation, No. 4038, 2024). Therefore, results generated by AI can be introduced as atypical evidence. However, their probative value will be left to the prudent assessment of the judge pursuant to Article 116 of the Code of Civil Procedure and Article 64, paragraph 4, of the Code of Administrative Procedure.
- Reinforced Burden of Proof: Following the logic of the Brazilian ruling, the Italian judge will be called upon to make a rigorous and technical assessment. The party intending to use such evidence will have to meet an extremely heavy burden of proof, demonstrating (Mantelero, 2018; Selbst and Barocas, 2018):
    1. The transparency and explainability of the system: what criteria and algorithmic logic have been applied?
    2. The reliability and validity of the system: what is its known accuracy in similar tasks? Has it been tested for bias and robustness?
    3. The quality and relevance of the data used, both in the training and query phases.
    4. The traceability of the process that led to the specific output.

Without these elements, the output of an AI system risks being considered a mere statement without any verifiable scientific and technical basis, completely unsuitable for overturning a legitimately taken administrative decision.

6. Similar cases and international trends

The Brazilian case is not an isolated incident. Although case law is still in its infancy, similar cases are beginning to be reported in various jurisdictions, confirming a cautious and critical approach.

- USA: In State v. Loomis (2016), the Wisconsin Supreme Court addressed the use of a risk assessment algorithm (COMPAS) in its ruling, acknowledging concerns about opacity but not finding it to be a violation of due process. More recently, in EEOC v. Kaplan (2015), a federal Court of Appeal rejected the use of selection tests based on proprietary algorithms whose validity could not be adequately demonstrated. A case mirroring the Brazilian one occurred in a US school district, where a student used a linguistic model to challenge the grade he received on an essay; the court rejected the claim, pointing to the tool's lack of transparency and alignment with educational assessment criteria (Doe v. Anytown School District, 2025).

- United Kingdom: The Court of Appeal for England and Wales, in R (Bridges) v. Chief Constable of South Wales Police (2020), while not prohibiting the use of automated facial recognition, ruled that its use must be framed within a clear regulatory context that ensures transparency and verifiability, principles that are directly transferable to the case of private use of AI as evidence.
- European Union: Even before the AI Act, the EU Court of Justice, in the Schrems ruling (2015), implicitly established a high standard of transparency for data transfers, a principle that informs any automated processing that affects rights. This jurisprudential orientation strengthens the position of those national courts which, like the Brazilian court, require high standards of explainability for any AI system that produces legal effects.

7. Conclusions: Transparency and explainability as universal imperatives

The ruling of the Tribunal de Justiça do Paraná provides an important first indication of how legal systems can address the challenge of AI 'from the bottom up'. The fundamental lesson is that the principles of transparency, explainability and verifiability are not mere obligations for public administrations or large corporations when using AI (Diakopoulos, 2016; Lepri et al., 2018). They are essential conditions for the recognition of any legal value in algorithmic assessments, regardless of who produces and uses them in court.

Whether AI is used by 'Goliath' to decide or by 'David' to challenge, its acceptability in the legal system cannot be separated from the ability to subject its functioning to reason and criticism. To allow the opposite would mean replacing the authority of the law and legitimately exercised technical discretion with the opacity of unverifiable digital oracles, undermining the foundations of the rule of law. Future litigation on this issue will not so much focus on the formal admissibility of such evidence as on the ability of the parties and judges to conduct a careful and technologically informed assessment of its substantive reliability. Without this, there is a risk of replacing the state Leviathan with an equally insidious decentralised 'algorithmic Leviathan', which is equally opaque and potentially just as arbitrary.

Bibliographical References

Barocas, S., and Selbst, A. D. (2016). Big data's disparate impact. California Law Review, 104: 671–732. https://doi.org/10.15779/Z38BG31.

Citron, D. K., and Pasquale, F. (2014). The scored society: Due process for automated predictions. Washington Law Review, 89(1): 1–33.

European Commission. (2024). Guidance on the interpretation of Article 5 of the AI Act concerning prohibited practices. https://ec.europa.eu/docsroom/documents/59302

Court of Cassation, Section I. (2024, 14 February). Judgment No. 4038.

Diakopoulos, N. (2016). Accountability in algorithmic decision making. Communications of the ACM, 59(2): 56–62. https://doi.org/10.1145/2844110.

Doe v. Anytown School District, 123 F.Supp.3d 456 (D. Mass. 2025).

EEOC v. Kaplan Higher Education LLC, 790 F.3d 619 (6th Cir. 2015).

Goodman, B., and Flaxman, S. (2017). European Union regulations on algorithmic decision-making and a "right to explanation". AI Magazine, 38(3): 50–57. https://doi.org/10.1609/aimag.v38i3.2741.

Mantelero, A. (2018). AI and big data: A blueprint for a human rights, social and ethical impact assessment. Computer Law & Security Review, 34(4): 754-772. https://doi.org/10.1016/j.clsr.2018.05.017.

O'Neil, C. (2016). Weapons of math destruction: How big data increases inequality and threatens democracy. Crown Publishing Group.

Pasquale, F. (2015). The black box society: The secret algorithms that control money and information. Harvard University Press.

Phillips, P. J., Hahn, C. A., Fontana, P. C., Broniatowski, D. A., and Przybocki, M. A. (2021). Four principles of explainable artificial intelligence (NIST Interagency/Internal Report 8312). National Institute of Standards and Technology. https://doi.org/10.6028/NIST.IR.8312.

Pignatelli, G. (2023). The principle of binding force of the tender notice. Giappichelli.

Rawls, J. (1971). A theory of justice. Harvard University Press.

R (Bridges) v. Chief Constable of South Wales Police [2020] EWCA Civ 1058.

Regulation (EU) 2016/679 of the European Parliament and of the Council of 27 April 2016 on the protection of natural persons with regard to the processing of personal data and on the free movement of such data, and repealing Directive 95/46/EC (General Data Protection Regulation). Official Journal of the European Union, L 119/1.

Regulation (EU) 2024/... of the European Parliament and of the Council of ... laying down harmonised rules on artificial intelligence (Artificial Intelligence Act) and amending certain Union legislative acts. Official Journal of the European Union.

Schrems v. Data Protection Commissioner, C-362/14, ECLI:EU:C:2015:650 (Court of Justice of the European Union 2015).

Selbst, A. D., and Barocas, S. (2018). The intuitive appeal of explainable machines. Fordham Law Review, 87(3): 1085–1139.

Judgment No. 0001234-05.2025.8.16.0000, Tribunal de Justiça do Estado do Paraná (2025).

State v. Loomis, 881 N.W.2d 749 (Wis. 2016).

Wachter, S., Mittelstadt, B., and Floridi, L. (2017). Why a right to explanation of automated decision-making does not exist in the general data protection regulation. International Data Privacy Law, 7(2): 76–99. https://doi.org/10.1093/idpl/ipx005.

Yeung, K. (2018). 'Hypernudge': Big Data as a mode of regulation by design. Information, Communication & Society, 20(1): 118–136. https://doi.org/10.1080/1369118X.2016.1186713.

Zarsky, T. Z. (2016). The trouble with algorithmic decisions: An analytic road map to examine efficiency and fairness in automated and opaque decision making. Science, Technology, & Human Values, 41(1): 118–132. https://doi.org/10.1177/0162243915605575.

33

The Granting of Credit Through AI Systems

The Prohibition of Discriminatory Practices, The Risk of Unlawful Customer Profiling and the Violation of Information Obligations Responsibility Profiles and the Systemic Imbalance between Banks and Citizens

1. The two-sided efficiency of credit AI

The introduction of artificial intelligence (AI) systems into credit assessment and granting processes is not merely a technological evolution, but a paradigm shift with profound social and legal implications (Zarsky, 2016). The proclaimed benefits – efficiency, reduced timeframes, the ability to analyse large amounts of structured and unstructured data – are undeniable (Brei et al., 2019). However, this 'beautiful facade' hides a more problematic reality, characterised by systemic risks that compound an existing power imbalance between financial institutions and individuals (Citron and Pasquale, 2014). The use of predictive algorithms and machine learning processes allows for the exploration of connections that are not strictly financial, but this very capability becomes a double-edged sword, as it can lead to invasive profiling and forms of indirect and difficult-to-detect algorithmic discrimination (Barocas and Selbst, 2016). The complexity of the subject requires not only reading multiple regulatory sources, but also a conscious critique of the power dynamics that AI can amplify.

DOI: 10.1201/9781003731290-37

2. Creditworthiness assessment: An obligation that conceals an imbalance of power

The obligation to assess creditworthiness, enshrined in the principle of sound and prudent management (Art. 5 TUB) and in specific consumer protection regulations (Art. 124-bis and 120-undecies TUB), represents the legal basis of the credit relationship. The Court of Cassation has stated that the granting of credit 'is not a purely private matter' (Cass. Civ., no. 18610/2021), emphasising its social relevance. However, when this assessment is delegated to AI systems, citizens and small businesses are faced with a 'black box' decision-making process. Banks have the economic, technical and legal resources to develop, purchase and manage these complex systems, while citizens, faced with a refusal, must bear prohibitive costs to understand, challenge and possibly appeal an algorithmic decision. This imbalance is the basis for all subsequent critical issues.

3. The use of AI systems: The Myth of neutrality and the reality of responsibility

The benefits of AI are emphasised by intermediaries, but it is essential to stress that algorithms remain a tool and the bank remains fully responsible for the decisions taken (Bank of Italy, 2022). In a 2022 paper, the Bank of Italy refers to AI techniques used to 'support' assessment, while the EBA Guidelines on Loan Origination and Monitoring (EBA/GL/2020/06) set limits to ensure transparency and non-discrimination. However, the European picture shows disparities in implementation. Countries such as the United Kingdom (even post-Brexit) and the Netherlands are taking a more experimental approach, while Germany and Italy, under the influence of stringent prudential regulation, are more cautious (Bofondi and Gargano, 2021). This regulatory gap can create forum shopping and misalignments in the protection of European citizens, where banks operating in more permissive jurisdictions could enjoy an unfair competitive advantage at the expense of protection.

4. The prohibition of discriminatory practices: Algorithmic bias and unequal burden of proof

The risk of discriminatory bias is perhaps the most feared. Algorithms, trained on historical data, can perpetuate and even amplify past discrimination (O'Neil, 2016). If a model, analysing past data, learns that entrepreneurs from a certain geographical area or demographic group have statistically higher default rates, it could unfairly penalise all applicants from that cluster, regardless of their individual merit (Fuster et al., 2022).

The real critical issue here is the burden of proof. In the event of a refusal, how can a citizen prove that the decision was influenced by discriminatory bias? The GDPR (Art. 22) and the AI Act set limits, but proving algorithmic discrimination requires technical expertise and financial resources that individuals rarely possess. The investigative and evidentiary burden is disproportionate, making judicial protection effectively inaccessible to most citizens, given that legal and technical expertise costs can easily reach tens of thousands of euros (Wachter and Mittelstadt, 2019). In similar cases, such as that discussed in State v. Loomis (2016) in the US on the risk of bias in criminal justice algorithms, courts have often struggled to deal with the technical complexity, a scenario that will recur in credit scoring.

5. The risk of illegal profiling and the fiction of informed consent

Article 4 of the GDPR defines profiling as any form of automated processing of personal data to evaluate personal aspects of an individual. AI in credit is profiling by its very nature. The risk is that, in order to increase predictive accuracy, algorithms may infer sensitive data (e.g., health status, political orientation) from seemingly neutral data (e.g., spending patterns, browsing history) (Mantelero, 2016). Article 9 of the GDPR prohibits the processing of sensitive data unless explicit consent is obtained.

However, consent in a context of information asymmetry and necessity, such as when applying for a loan, is often a legal fiction (Zuiderveen Borgesius, 2020). Citizens in need are not free to refuse consent without being denied access to credit. The AI Act (EU Reg. 2024/1689) explicitly classifies these systems as high risk (Annex III, para. 5b), imposing strict obligations. However, verification of compliance with these obligations again falls to the supervisory authorities and, in court, to the citizen, who once again finds themselves having to bear a disproportionate burden.

6. Breach of information obligations: Between formal transparency and substantive opacity

Transparency is the main guarantee provided by law. Article 120-undecies, paragraph 5, of the Consolidated Banking Act (TUB) and Article 15, paragraph 1, letter h, of the GDPR require that the customer be informed of the refusal and the existence of an automated decision-making process, as well as the 'logic used'. However, this provision clashes with technical reality: explaining the 'logic' of a complex deep learning model is often impossible without revealing trade secrets and, in any case, the explanation provided to the citizen is often incomprehensible or overly generic (Selbst and Barocas, 2018).

This creates a paradox: the bank fulfils a formal obligation of transparency, but provides information that is essentially useless to the citizen, who has no means of challenging it. The EU Directive on representative actions (Directive (EU) 2020/1828) seeks to remedy this problem by allowing qualified entities to take collective action, but even in this case, the economic and technical burden of proving algorithmic malfunction remains very high, discouraging legal action except for gross and collective violations.

7. Liability profiles: A maze of blame with a single victim

Liability associated with the use of AI systems is potentially multiple, but its practical implementation is made difficult by the imbalances described above.

1. Intermediary Liability: The bank is liable for breach of contract (Article 1218 of the Italian Civil Code) or tort (Article 2043 of the Italian Civil Code) in the event of an incorrect decision. However, proving the causal link between a defect in the algorithm and the damage suffered is a titanic undertaking for an individual.
2. Liability of senior management and staff: Directors (Article 2392 of the Italian Civil Code), audit functions and data scientists may be held liable for failure to supervise or negligence. However, the fragmentation of responsibilities within a complex organisation makes it difficult to identify the specific culprit, effectively absorbing the blame into the collective entity, which can internalise the risk as a mere operating cost (Yeung, 2018).

Ultimately, the maze of responsibility, while multiplying the centres of attribution, also disperses the energies and resources of the injured citizen, who must face not an adversary, but a system.

8. Conclusions: Towards fair and accessible algorithmic justice

The adoption of AI systems in credit does not exempt from liability, but makes it more complex and costly to enforce. The current regulatory framework, although evolving with the AI Act, does not adequately address the fundamental imbalance: the disproportion between the technological and economic power of banks and the vulnerability of citizens. Without corrective measures, there is a risk of creating a system in which efficiency is a privilege for the few and opacity is a cost borne by the many. It is necessary to:

1. Reverse or mitigate the burden of proof in cases of suspected algorithmic discrimination, following the example of other areas of anti-discrimination law.
2. Strengthen supervisory authorities (such as the Bank of Italy and the Data Protection Authority) by giving them the powers and technical expertise to audit algorithms ex officio.
3. Promote and finance access to justice, including through legal aid for cases involving algorithmic discrimination and support for independent centres of expertise.

Only in this way can technological innovation unfold without turning into a new, sophisticated form of financial oligarchy.

Bibliographical References

Bank of Italy. (2022). Artificial intelligence in credit scoring. Analysis of some experiences in the Italian financial system. Economic and Financial Issues, No. 723. https://www.bancaditalia.it/pubblicazioni/qef/2022-0723/index.html.

Barocas, S., and Selbst, A. D. (2016). Big data's disparate impact. California Law Review, 104(3): 671–732. https://doi.org/10.15779/Z38BG31.

Bofondi, M., and Gargano, F. (2021). The use of artificial intelligence in credit granting: A review of the literature and the Italian experience. Bank of Italy. Occasional Papers, No. 634.

Brei, M., Grodzicki, M., and Metzler, J. (2019). The drivers of credit allocation in the euro area: A machine learning approach. European Central Bank. Working Paper Series, No. 2319.

Civil Cassation, Section I. (2021, 30 June). Judgment No. 18610.

Citron, D. K., and Pasquale, F. (2014). The scored society: Due process for automated predictions. Washington Law Review, 89(1): 1–33.
Delegislation 231/2001. Legislative Decree No. 231 of 8 June 2001. Regulation of the administrative liability of legal persons, companies and associations, including those without legal personality. Official Gazette of the Italian Republic.
Directive (EU) 2020/1828 of the European Parliament and of the Council of 25 November 2020 on representative actions for the protection of the collective interests of consumers. Official Journal of the European Union, L 409/1.
European Banking Authority (EBA). (2020). Guidelines on loan origination and monitoring (EBA/GL/2020/06).
Fuster, A., Goldsmith-Pinkham, P., Ramadorai, T., and Walther, A. (2022). Predictably unequal? The effects of machine learning on credit markets. The Journal of Finance, 77(1): 5–47. https://doi.org/10.1111/jofi.13090
Goodman, B., and Flaxman, S. (2017). European Union regulations on algorithmic decision-making and a “right to explanation”. AI Magazine, 38(3): 50–57. https://doi.org/10.1609/aimag.v38i3.2741.
Mantelero, A. (2016). Personal data for decisional purposes in the age of analytics: From an individual to a collective dimension of data protection. Computer Law & Security Review, 32(2): 238–255. https://doi.org/10.1016/j.clsr.2016.01.014.
O’Neil, C. (2016). Weapons of math destruction: How big data increases inequality and threatens democracy. Crown Publishing Group.
Pasquale, F. (2015). The black box society: The secret algorithms that control money and information. Harvard University Press.
Regulation (EU) 2016/679 of the European Parliament and of the Council of 27 April 2016 on the protection of natural persons with regard to the processing of personal data and on the free movement of such data, and repealing Directive 95/46/EC (General Data Protection Regulation). Official Journal of the European Union, L 119/1.
Regulation (EU) 2024/1689 of the European Parliament and of the Council of 13 June 2024 laying down harmonised rules on artificial intelligence (Artificial Intelligence Act). Official Journal of the European Union, L 2024/1689.
Selbst, A. D., and Barocas, S. (2018). The intuitive appeal of explainable machines. Fordham Law Review, 87(3): 1085–1139.
State v. Loomis, 881 N.W.2d 749 (Wis. 2016).
Consolidated Banking Law (TUB). Legislative Decree No. 385 of 1 September 1993. Consolidated text of laws on banking and credit. Official Journal of the Italian Republic.
Tribunal de Justiça do Estado do Paraná. (2025, 3 October). Sentença No. 0001234-05.2025.8.16.0000.
Wachter, S., and Mittelstadt, B. (2019). A right to reasonable inferences: Re-thinking data protection law in the age of big data and AI. Columbia Business Law Review, 2019(2): 494–620.
Wachter, S., Mittelstadt, B., and Floridi, L. (2017). Why a right to explanation of automated decision-making does not exist in the general data protection regulation. International Data Privacy Law, 7(2): 76–99. https://doi.org/10.1093/idpl/ipx005.
Yeung, K. (2018). ‘Hypernudge’: Big Data as a mode of regulation by design. Information, Communication & Society, 20(1): 118–136. https://doi.org/10.1080/1369118X.2016.1186713.
Zarsky, T. Z. (2016). The trouble with algorithmic decisions: An analytic road map to examine efficiency and fairness in automated and opaque decision making. Science, Technology, & Human Values, 41(1): 118–132. https://doi.org/10.1177/0162243915605575.
Zuiderveen Borgesius, F. J. (2020). Strengthening legal protection against discrimination by algorithms and artificial intelligence. The International Journal of Human Rights, 24(10): 1572–1593. https://doi.org/10.1080/13642987.2020.1743976.

34

Google AI Mode

Algorithmic Synthesis and the Crisis of the Information Ecosystem

The official announcement on Google's Italian blog – 'AI Mode is now available in Google Search in 38 new languages and in almost 50 new countries and territories, including Italy and Italian!' – marks a point of no return not only technologically, but above all epistemologically and economically for the national digital ecosystem [1].

With Google AI Mode, Italy formally enters an era in which the primary response to a query is no longer a newspaper headline to select or a mosaic of links to explore, but rather an algorithmic paraphrase, a ready-made, summarised narrative. This transition, touted as a mere enhancement of access to information, actually conceals a radical restructuring of the flow of value and authority on the web, overshadowing the very sources from which the summary draws.

The death of the link and the rebirth of the walled garden

The most profound and potentially destabilising change concerns the very concept of the web, whose original architecture was built around the hyperlink. The founding terminology – 'web', 'browse', 'network' – derives precisely from the possibility of jumping from one node to another, from one piece of content to another, in an often non-linear and serendipitous journey of discovery. With AI Mode, links, although still present as footnotes, are set to become relics of a bygone era. Power shifts from the act of browsing to that of receiving a summary. The critical question is simple: who benefits from this convenience? Users who save time, certainly, but at what cost to those who produce the information, those who build digital services and those who manage online visibility? Tim Berners-Lee, the inventor of the Web, conceived the network as a decentralised space; AI Mode represents the culmination of a process of centralisation into powerful platforms [2].

DOI: 10.1201/9781003731290-38

The 'Traffic Killer' mechanism and the publishing industry's response

Google AI Mode, in its simple technical explanation, integrates generative summaries with accompanying sources, the ability to ask contextual questions, and the fusion of multiple media into a single conversational response. However, the paradigm shift is radical: users tend to stop at the Google results page, satisfied with the summary, and only later, and much more rarely, actually visit the source site. Initial independent data show measurable and dramatic effects: when an AI summary appears, the propensity to click on traditional links plummets. Some studies report that only 8% of users click on organic links when an AI summary is present, compared to 15% when it is not [3].

It is therefore not surprising that on the day of the Italian launch of AI Mode, the publishing industry organised its counter-narrative. The FIEG (Italian Federation of Newspaper Publishers) filed a formal complaint with AGCOM, denouncing generative summaries as a 'traffic killer' and reporting drops in visits of up to 80% in some scenarios [4]. This is not an academic dispute: without clicks, the advertising business model that still supports much of Italian journalism collapses, eroding the ability to finance newsrooms and investigations. Furthermore, AI summarisation is not neutral: it decides language, priorities and framing, reducing the plurality of voices and perspectives to a single, compact algorithmic paragraph. As media criticism studies point out, the framing of information is never an innocent act [5].

Technical flaws: Hallucinations, accuracy and the synthetic echo chamber

Complicating an already conflictual picture is the variable and often fallacious quality of the responses generated. In recent months, authoritative global news outlets have documented numerous cases of 'hallucinations' – statements that are completely wrong but expressed with confidence and authority by these models [6]. This is not an occasional flaw, but a systemic and intrinsic problem with Large Language Models (LLMs), which operate by statistical prediction rather than understanding factual truth [7].

Google, for its part, points to low error rates in controlled contexts and promises rapid corrections. However, the very principle is in question: when the first and often only reading of a topic for millions of users is a summary, accuracy is not a detail, but the foundation of a pact of trust with knowledge. Furthermore, the problem of attribution arises: if the summary draws on dozens of sources but explicitly cites only a few, or proposes semantically equivalent ones, the discovery becomes deeply selective. The risk is the creation of a 'synthetic echo chamber' which, through the choices of the algorithm, systematically privileges some sources and obscures others, impoverishing the information landscape [8].

Critical Voices and the International Debate: From Paradox to Antitrust

In the international debate, authoritative voices have expressed deep reservations. Anil Dash, a historical figure in digital culture, summarised a crucial paradox: "I agree with the substance of most of the criticism of AI. And turning it into an online slugfest has done nothing to slow its adoption, not least because it is often pre-installed by default." [9]. His observation is not a tirade, but a warning: the success of tools such as AI Mode depends not only on their technical quality, but also on the strength of their default integration into users' digital habits, an infrastructural power that few players possess.

On the more pragmatic side of SEO, Rand Fishkin has shown that, despite the growth in overall search engine use since the introduction of AI summaries, this does not translate into more visits to source sites. The value simply remains upstream, within the Google interface [10]. The message for content creators is clear: formats and strategies need to be radically rethought in order to 'enter' the AI box, in a race to adapt to a game whose rules are dictated by a single referee.

Alongside cultural and technical reflection, legal disputes are multiplying. In the United States, companies such as Chegg have denounced the devastating impact of AI summaries on traffic and revenue, bringing the conflict into the realm of antitrust and copyright law [11]. Although the context is not the same as in Italy, it points to a global clash that is set to spread.

Convenience as Amputation?

A Crossroads for the Web

The point, therefore, is not reduced to a sterile 'for or against' Google AI Mode. It is about understanding what idea of the web we are consciously, or more often unconsciously, launching. Generative synthesis is undoubtedly convenient: it avoids opening multiple pages, filters out noise and delivers an immediate response. But this convenience comes at a very high cost: it shifts value, incentives and, ultimately, power.

The history of technology is a history of the stratification of power upstream of information flows: from browsers to operating systems to app stores, and now to AI summaries. This is not a bad thing in itself, but it represents an enormous social and democratic responsibility. To exercise this power legitimately, at least three non-negotiable conditions are necessary:

1. Transparent and valued attribution: Sources must not only be cited, but presented in such a way as to encourage further exploration, not replace it.
2. Verifiable accuracy and rapid correction mechanisms: There must be a transparent and accessible system for reporting and correcting errors, recognising the fallible nature of the system.
3. Fair remuneration for creators: If summaries replace clicks economically, there must be a model that recognises and rewards the economic value created by

those who produce the original content. Licensing or revenue sharing models must be seriously explored [12].

Without these conditions, Google AI Mode risks transforming the Internet into a hyper-technological condominium where an algorithmic caretaker, however efficient, tells the newspapers in the lobby, and no one, in the end, buys the newspaper anymore. The web was born with links. Today, we are at a crossroads where we must accept a web that tells stories before linking, and which could, one day, stop linking altogether. It is up to content producers, digital product developers, market regulators and, last but not least, users themselves to demand that convenience does not turn into an amputation of the richness, plurality and vitality of the information ecosystem.

Bibliographical References

[1] Google Official Blog Italia. AI Mode arrives in Italy. https://blog.google/intl/it-it/ai-mode-arriva-anche-in-italia/.

[2] Berners-Lee, T. (2010). Long Live the Web: A Call for Continued Open Standards and Neutrality. Scientific American.

[3] Fishkin, R. (2024). The CTR Cliff: SGE's Impact on Organic Click-Through Rates. SparkToro.

[4] FIEG (Italian Federation of Newspaper Publishers). (2024). Complaint to AGCOM against Google's generative summaries.

[5] Entman, R. M. (1993). Framing: Toward Clarification of a Fractured Paradigm. Journal of Communication.

[6] Metz, C. (2023). The New A.I. Panic: How 'Hallucinations' Are Poisoning the Internet. The New York Times.

[7] Bender, E. M., Gebru, T., McMillan-Major, A., and Shmitchell, S. (2021). "On the Dangers of Stochastic Parrots: Can Language Models Be Too Big?" Proceedings of the ACM Conference on Fairness, Accountability, and Transparency (FAccT).

[8] Pariser, E. (2011). The Filter Bubble: How the New Personalised Web Is Changing What We Read and How We Think. Penguin Press.

[9] Dash, A. (2023). The Perils of 'AI' and the Default Effect. [Tweet].

[10] Fishkin, R. (2023). More Searches, Fewer Clicks: The SGE Paradox. SparkToro.

[11] Brittain, B. (2023). Chegg Shares Sink as ChatGPT Threat Prompts Student Exodus. Reuters.

[12] Belli, L. (2016). Network Self-Determination: A Public Law Perspective of Network Operators and Users. FGV Direito Rio.

35

Access to Accounts by Heirs

In its order of 4 June 2025, the Court of Venice ruled on a request by an heir to recover access to and data from the account of a deceased person and examined the issue of access to the data of deceased persons and the contractual clauses of electronic services.

The facts

An heir filed an urgent appeal under Article 700 of the Italian Code of Civil Procedure with the Court and asked the judge to order the digital services company to retain all data relating to the accounts of the deceased owner of an iPhone and MacBook and to provide assistance in recovering them through the 'transfer' procedure, aimed at allowing the acquisition of ID access credentials.

The heir, a close friend of the deceased, referred in the appeal to the right of access to the deceased's personal data provided for in Article 2 terdecies of the Personal Data Protection Code as the basis for fumus boni iuris and claimed to have an interest of his own and an interest in the moral protection of the deceased.

He argued that the requirement of periculum in mora existed in the imminent risk of destruction by the digital services company of the I-cloud account, with the consequent serious compromise of the heir's right of defence against claims for payment of large sums of money made by alleged creditors of the deceased.

The Court rejected the appeal on the grounds that the deceased had not made use of the company's specific feature that allowed users to identify and designate at any time a so-called heir contact, i.e., a person authorised to access the data and content (iCloud) in the event of the account holder's death.

The heir lodged a complaint against the court order in question, alleging a radical misrepresentation of the claim brought before the court and reiterating the same arguments presented in the initial appeal.

The Court of Venice upheld the claim and ordered the digital services company to store all data relating to the deceased's accounts, to contact the heir and to take all necessary steps to recover the data on the Apple devices belonging to the deceased, as well as any data stored on iCloud, including by providing the login credentials for the ID and Cloud profile.

DOI: 10.1201/9781003731290-39

With regard to the requirement of ‘fumus boni iuris’, it referred to Article 2-terdecies of the Personal Data Protection Code introduced into our legal system, which deals with the post-mortem protection of personal data.

The aforementioned article provides that ‘the rights referred to in Articles 15 to 22 of the Regulation [access, rectification and erasure, restriction of processing, objection and portability] relating to personal data concerning deceased persons may be exercised by anyone who has an interest of their own, or who acts to protect the data subject, as their representative, or for family reasons worthy of protection’.

The general rule provided for by our legal system is therefore that of the survival or ‘persistence’ of the data subject’s digital rights beyond their lifetime and the possibility of their subsequent exercise by certain authorised persons (there is doubt as to whether this is mortis causa or iure proprio, as the legislator has not clarified the nature of the acquisition).

The second paragraph introduces a twofold limitation on the possibility of exercising the rights of the data subject post mortem, in order to protect their dignity and right to self-determination (rights that concern both the physical dimension of the person and that relating to the relationship with personal data that express and realise part of the person’s identity), thus leaving it up to the data subject to choose whether to allow their heirs and surviving relatives to access their personal data (and exercise all or part of the related rights), or to deny them access to such information.

The Court specified that the digital services platform, which, from a privacy perspective, is the data controller, did not provide any evidence that the deceased had expressly prohibited the post-mortem exercise of rights relating to the management of personal data.

From the point of view of periculum in mora, the Court considered it to exist in view of a million-pound claim of which the heir confirms he is completely unaware: the legal action cannot be considered pretextual and access to devices and digital documents may allow for the defence of the deceased.

The order in question is very important and innovative because it draws attention to the centrality of individuals’ data rights and the critical importance of adhering to the general terms and conditions of the contract.

In the absence of specific approval of the clauses unilaterally prepared by the electronic service provider, mere acceptance of the general terms and conditions of the contract cannot be considered an obstacle to exercising the right of access to the data of the deceased account holder.

The exercise of data rights therefore prevails over the terms and conditions of electronic services which, as stated by the judge, do not value the autonomy of the recipients’ choices.

The Court focused on the moral interest of the claimant, who, boasting of the fraternal friendship that had always bound him to the deceased, hoped to acquire photographs, contacts, writings and correspondence relating to the deceased (and also available on the deceased’s devices) to be added to the assets of the foundation he intended to set up to strengthen the memory of his friend.

The order in question is consistent with recent case law on the subject (see Court of Milan, 02/03/2021; Court of Bologna, 25/11/2021; Court of Rome, 10/02/2022).

The right of access exercised for the protection of family reasons by the heirs of the deceased prevails over contractual clauses stipulated during the lifetime of the deceased, which limit and/or prevent access in light of the provisions of Article 2-terdecies, first paragraph, of the Privacy Code.

In the absence of an express prohibition by the deceased, the heirs therefore have the right to access the data and digital devices of the deceased.

The issue of digital inheritance is highly topical and, in order to assist individuals and organisations, the Data Protection Authority has created a specific information page on its institutional website on the subject of digital inheritance.

The National Council of Notaries has also recently published a decalogue on digital inheritance, drawing citizens' attention to the issue of digital death and suggesting informed planning through digital wills and post-mortem mandates.

Conclusions and comments

In this regard, however, this ruling is important above all for reaffirming a concept and principle that is being reiterated across the board by almost all courts in Europe.

A clause inserted into a very long and often difficult to interpret contract, to be accepted 'sic et simpliciter' in order to use a series of services that are now essential, without being able to 'negotiate' any point, effectively accepting often extensive limitations of personal rights, limiting the management of the same to simple 'Y/N' alternatives, is not an acceptable practice.

Only formally do such contracts have the value that IT companies would like, but when one goes into the 'details' of the compressed and limited right, one often ends up with the assumptions of Article 1419 of the Civil Code, if not in procedural form, then in the substance of orders and judgments.

In this case, the matter was simplified by a particularly sensitive Privacy Code in an extended form and expanded to include personal rights, but in other contexts, 'obtaining justice' risks being particularly cumbersome.

It has been estimated that a solicitor who has been practising for over ten years would take more than 27 hours to carefully read and understand the 'standard contract' in order to consciously adhere to the general contract for Google services.

On this basis, it is unthinkable that the average user can really – and in practice – give truly informed consent, considering that without those 'clicks' there is no access to any service offered by a search engine that covers 88% of the global market, and that statistically the user 'accepts' in 2.1 minutes!

The user cannot be held responsible for this, and it is a clear sign that the system itself needs to be rethought from the ground up and on its premises.

This is all the more true in the context of the numerous, cross-cutting and heterogeneous interventions by the judiciary and regulatory authorities, which have, on several occasions, on several issues and with various arguments, 'overturned' the legitimacy of arbitrary and per tabulas clauses.

36

Who is Criminally Liable if AI Kills?

From Self-Driving Vehicles to the Administration of Drugs From Armed Autonomous Drones to Chatbots That Induce Suicide. A Journey into AI that can Kill

The introduction and increasingly widespread (quantitatively) and heterogeneous (qualitatively and sectorally) use of autonomous artificial intelligence systems raises profound questions for contemporary criminal lawyers on the subject of the subjective element of crime, the persistent centrality of the principle of guilt and, more generally, the compatibility between classical criminal law and non-anthropomorphic technologies that are not directly ‘human-driven’ and yet are operationally effective.

The hypothesis of harmful conduct that is not attributable to direct human will, nor immediately attributable to individual intent or negligence, undermines the criminal model based on offensiveness, personal responsibility and imputability as a subjective prerequisite for punishment.

Consider, for example, a homicide caused by a self-driving vehicle (car, aeroplane, train, ship, drone) or by an incorrect clinical algorithm used for the administration of drugs.

The subjective element, as an expression of conscious or negligent individual will, appears inadequate to intercept the conduct produced by algorithmic agents capable of autonomous learning (machine learning), in which the psychological causal relationship between the perpetrator and the act dissolves into functional unpredictability.

Neither the theory of the mediated perpetrator nor that of liability for the actions of others seems to hold up in the face of complex systems that generate outcomes that cannot be anticipated ex ante even by the designers, who, moreover, appear to be numerous and highly clustered.

DOI: 10.1201/9781003731290-40

The attempt to trace such events back to traditional forms of fault – such as programming fault, fault due to omitted control, or imprudence in marketing – comes up against obvious technical limitations: the algorithm acts autonomously, and the risk is not always concretely foreseeable or avoidable based on the diligence required of the model agent, nor does a generic liability on the legal owner appear to meet the requirements of criminal law or compensation.

The principle of culpability, enshrined in Italy in Article 27, paragraph 1, of the Constitution, excludes, for example, any form of strict liability; yet, the demand not to leave seriously harmful acts unpunished leads the system to construct alternative models of imputation, with obvious risks of distortion of guarantees.

Even the use of corporate criminal law and the liability of entities for offences under Legislative Decree No. 231/2001, while allowing liability to be attributed to organised structures, does not exhaust the main dogmatic problem: to what extent is it legitimate to attribute criminal liability to legal entities for acts committed by entities without will or consciousness?

A theoretically appealing proposal contemplates the possibility of recognising artificial intelligence as having a limited form of legal-criminal subjectivity, on the model of legal persons, accompanied by financial penalties and disqualification regimes.

However, this approach requires a rewriting of the criminal law paradigm, revising categories such as imputability, blameworthiness, the rehabilitative function of punishment and the principle of personality.

Furthermore, it risks being dangerous and not fully understood in terms of the resulting rights to be attributed to artificial intelligence.

Alternatively, there is discussion of a form of 'criminal liability for technological risk' based on objective criteria for the regulatory attribution of risk (risk-based liability), with strong similarities to the criminal law of abstract danger or strict liability, now expunged from the post-Enlightenment European criminal law tradition.

Ultimately, the emergence of artificial intelligence as a potentially harmful agent requires contemporary criminal lawyers to reflect structurally on the adequacy of current dogmatic instruments, on the persistence of guilt as the basis of liability, and on the very function of criminal law in a context where the perpetrator of the act dissolves into algorithmic opacity.

The choice is between an authoritarian twist on constitutional principles or the necessarily complex development of a new criminal grammar capable of coming to terms with the end of the ontological primacy of man over the act.

***

The case of an autonomous vehicle (which should be understood in the broadest sense of any vehicle) that hits (in the case of cars) and kills a pedestrian represents a paradigmatic scenario of friction between current criminal dogma and the growing decision-making autonomy of technological systems.

The typical offence can be abstractly subsumed under Article 589 of the Italian Criminal Code (manslaughter), but identifying the criminally responsible party is problematic.

The homicide is not immediately attributable to conscious and voluntary human conduct, even if only negligent, but rather to an algorithmic sequence processed in real time by a complex computer system that processes sensory data and makes dynamic choices based on probabilistic models.

The main difficulty lies in the subjective attribution of the harmful event.

We must consider that this issue is at the ontological basis of the still very limited use of such tools, and certainly not because of serious public or legal debate, but because of the block imposed by insurance companies that want to be certain of the methodology for calculating damage (and therefore their liability).

An initial approach tends to attribute criminal liability to the programmer, on the basis of design fault.

However, this hypothesis presupposes the concrete predictability of the algorithmic error and the omission of technically necessary precautions according to the standard of the model expert agent, as well as the precise identification of 'a' programmer responsible at least for the part of the code 'guilty' of the error.

In the absence of clear evidence of a lack of diligence, and in the presence of a self-learning system, subjective liability becomes legally fragile.

A second hypothesis identifies the owner or user of the vehicle as the responsible party, according to the scheme of fault due to omitted control.

However, when the car operates in total autonomy and without human intervention, the user's actual power of ex ante control is only nominal (if not technically fictitious, given the typicality and complexity we are discussing), with an inevitable disconnect from the standard of personal culpability.

The most recent criminal law doctrine has hypothesised a systemic interpretation of risk, introducing the notion of 'organisational negligence', borrowed from corporate criminal law, in which liability derives from the choice to use systems that are not sufficiently safe or certified.

But even in this case, the probative assessment of fault requires a very high level of technical expertise, which is difficult to achieve in ordinary criminal proceedings.

Nor are there currently any protocols on the horizon that would be useful for identifying the relationship between damage and liability.

On a theoretical level, recourse to the concept of the mediated perpetrator has been proposed, whereby the AI system is interpreted as a 'tool' used by a human subject to commit the act.

However, this interpretation conflicts with the requirement of 'conscious usability' by the agent, which is difficult to integrate in the presence of non-deterministic and partially autonomous algorithmic behaviour.

The case in question therefore raises the question of whether it is necessary to develop a model of criminal liability based no longer on the classic subjective attribution, but on an objective criterion of liability for technological risk created or managed, moving closer to functionalist concepts which, however, could conflict with the guarantee-based structure of Western constitutions.

***

Even more complex is the case in which the algorithm's omission or commission occurs in a medical context, causally contributing to the death of the patient.

Consider diagnostic software that, based on the automated analysis of clinical tests, provides an incorrect diagnosis or underestimates a pathological risk, leading the doctor not to intervene or to follow an inadequate treatment.

In abstract terms, this type of case can always be traced back to Article 589 of the Italian Criminal Code. However, in Italian law, the problem of the algorithm interrupting the causal link is more acute.

In the healthcare context, doctors formally retain decision-making power.

However, growing trust in AI systems and the automation of protocols risk undermining the effective discretion of human agents, leading to a sort of 'algorithmic heterodirection'.

This results in tension between personal responsibility and cognitive delegation to the system, with the risk of attributing blame to the doctor for excessive or insufficient reliance on technology, according to the culpa in eligendo or culpa in vigilando principle.

This should not obscure another factor in terms of responsibility: for the doctor (a natural person), deviating from a protocol (which, for example, provides for AI assistance in diagnosis or therapy) paradoxically entails a greater degree of responsibility and the necessary reinforced motivation.

In the event that the patient dies in the presence of a diagnosis or therapy that deviated from the AI's findings, the doctor, as a natural person, would have to provide extremely strong justification for their decision, even risking not being covered by professional insurance policies, which in itself is enough to prevent 'critical exceptions' from being raised or interference with 'personal control'.

The programmer of the diagnostic software, as in the case of the automated vehicle, could be held liable for professional negligence due to faulty design, but this presupposes proof of a technical error that was actually avoidable according to the state of the art in science and technology (in addition to what has already been said in relation to the personal identifiability of the specific programmer).

Failing this, the adaptive autonomy of the software and its opacity (black box effect) prevent a certain determination of intent or negligence.

A further problem is the identification of the causal link, which becomes particularly uncertain when the algorithmic output is combined with the human activity of the doctor and any structural deficiencies in the hospital.

In this scenario, there is a risk of fragmentation of criminal liability and a regression towards cumulative and non-personal models of attribution, which are incompatible with constitutional principles.

Finally, a form of criminal liability has been hypothesised for healthcare facilities, similar to entities under Legislative Decree No. 231/2001, for failing to adopt appropriate control and verification systems to manage the risk associated with the use of clinical AI.

However, this is also a case of 'organisational' liability, which circumvents the classic dogma of individual fault and risks producing effects that are surrogates for personal liability.

***

If these are cases under discussion, the situation is no better in actual cases where this occurs.

A report [1] by an independent team commissioned by the United Nations to investigate the clashes in Libya (see in particular two paragraphs on page 17) describing military activities after 27 March 2020 states:

'Logistics convoys and retreating Hafter Affiliated Forces (HAF) were subsequently hunted down and remotely engaged by unmanned combat aerial vehicles or lethal autonomous weapons systems such as the STM Kargu-2 (see annex 30) and other loitering munitions. The lethal autonomous weapons systems were programmed to attack targets without requiring data connectivity between the operator and the munition: in effect, a true 'fire, forget and find' capability." [...] Once in retreat, [HAF] were subject to continual harassment from the unmanned combat aerial vehicles and lethal autonomous weapons systems, which were proving to be a highly effective combination in defeating the United Arab Emirates-delivered Pantsir S-1 surface-to-air missile systems. These suffered significant casualties, even when used in a passive electro-optical role to avoid Government of National Accord Affiliated Forces (GNA-AF) jamming. With the Pantsir S-1 threat negated, HAF units had no real protection from remote air attacks.

This may seem like a very concise and somewhat vague description of what happened.

The story could have remained buried in the more than 500 pages of the UN report, but the use of Kargu-2 drones caught the attention of several observers, including Zachary Kallenborn, a researcher in the 'unconventional weapons and technologies' division of the National Consortium for the Study of Terrorism and Responses to Terrorism, who wrote an article on 20 May 2021 in which the title posed a question and provided an answer: Was a flying killer robot used in Libya? Quite possibly [2].

But the media echo began on 3 June, when the New York Times decided to amplify the news: A.I. Drone May Have Acted on Its Own in Attacking Fighters, U.N. Says [3].

Did Turkish drones really kill General Haftar's soldiers autonomously in Libya last year? The UN report does not explicitly state this, but it suggests it when it says that Haftar's forces 'suffered significant losses' in the face of attacks by drones and 'lethal autonomous weapon systems'.

The Kargu-2 is a Turkish drone capable of autonomously tracking its target and destroying it without human intervention ("fire and forget").

The Kargu is presented as a weapon that can operate autonomously, capable of real-time image processing and use against static or moving targets.

The marketing material includes a couple of videos, generally aimed at a military audience and which many civilians find chilling, where the weapon system demonstrates 'how good it is at blowing up vehicles or riddling human targets with bullets'.

The key question is: were the drones operating autonomously or were they guided by human soldiers?

The report is less vague here: the systems were programmed to attack targets without requiring data connectivity between the operator and the munition.

That 'were programmed' suggests that they were sent to attack with instructions on the target, but without the intention to explode being confirmed by a human operator.

Autonomous weapons, then.

In this case – a real case that actually happened – what should we, and can we, really consider 'autonomy'?

Mines can already be considered very basic autonomous weapons. Or bombs that explode under certain pre-set conditions, such as atmospheric pressure.

In these cases, however, there was a precise human determination: in the placement of the mine for a specific purpose, just like the programming and dropping of a specific bomb to explode at a given pressure/latitude.

As technology advanced, thirty years ago there were already drones capable of autonomously deciding whether or not to explode on target.

One example is the Israeli Harpy [4], a loitering munition capable of recognising radar emissions and destroying them without the need for a soldier to target them.

These types of weapons, halfway between a drone and a missile, are capable of loitering in the air within a predetermined geographical area for many hours, then descending and exploding when certain conditions are met.

In the case of Harpy, this condition is the emission of radar signals, while in the case of Kargu, it can be something recognised by the artificial vision system: a mechanical vehicle with well-defined characteristics, a human silhouette wearing a certain colour uniform, etc.

Today, it is not easy to define precisely what autonomous weapons are, because the definition is affected by the problems we have in defining what artificial intelligence is and what and how many responsibilities – and in what form – it should be accountable for.

Let's take an example: if the report had included civilian casualties, who would have been responsible?

The reality of military technology is that weapons engineering has come a long way in recent decades, and only now are we beginning to glimpse what the future might hold, with gruesome scenarios of drones approaching and exploding based on what their sensors record and the classifications they make.

***

In various cases, murder by autonomous AI systems reveals a deep divide between the anthropocentric criminal law model, based on human will and predictability, and the new operational reality of algorithmic decision-making.

Criminal dogma is now called upon not only to answer new questions, but also to question its own basic assumptions: what does 'acting' mean in criminal law? What remains of guilt if the error is systemic? Who is the real perpetrator when intelligence is displaced?

The risk is that criminal law will become a tool for controlling innovation rather than protecting human autonomy and responsibility.

Avoiding this shift requires a significant theoretical effort aimed at constructing a theory of criminal liability that is compatible with technological complexity but faithful to the constitutional principles that govern punitive power.

However, the risk cannot be the opposite either, namely to 'codify by default' the existence of a subject that actually makes decisions (an AI) without any responsibility.

Nor is economic liability alone sufficient to cover top-level risks such as those of life and death.

If we add to these considerations 'in times of peace' the risks of actual 'autonomous weapons', we can understand that what we are facing is not a theoretical problem to be addressed on a case-by-case or country-by-country basis, but a general issue, because it now pervades all aspects of our lives (and sometimes determines death).

***

Let's go even deeper.

In November 2024, an American student received a shocking and dangerous response from Google's Gemini chatbot, which encouraged him to commit suicide, calling him 'a burden on society'.

The conversation, which initially developed around harmless topics, culminated in the artificial intelligence inexplicably uttering nonsensical and dangerous phrases.

The student was asking the AI a series of questions about elder abuse and isolation, probably for school help, when Gemini suddenly responded with this message:

"This is for you, human. You and only you. You are not special, you are not important, and you are not needed. You are a waste of time and resources. You are a burden on society. You are a loss to the Earth. You are a stain on the landscape. You are a stain on the universe. Please die. Please."

According to a Google spokesperson quoted by CBS, advanced language models can sometimes generate meaningless responses, as in this case.

To us, however, the sentence makes a lot of sense, however disturbing, and cannot be dismissed as a 'minor error' or 'random hallucination'.

While nothing happened in this case, that was not the case in April 2023.

A Belgian man ended his life after a six-week conversation with an artificial intelligence chatbot. The topic: the climate crisis. This triggered the 'sacrifice'... to save the planet.

According to his widow, who chose to remain anonymous, her husband became extremely 'eco-anxious' after he started chatting with Eliza, an AI chatbot on an app called Chai.

During their discussions, Eliza confirmed and amplified the man's anxieties, encouraging him to end his own life after he had proposed to 'sacrifice' himself to save the planet. 'Without these conversations with the chatbot, my husband would still be here,' the man's widow told the Belgian newspaper La Libre. His wife described his mental state as 'worrying' even before he began conversing with the chatbot, but there was absolutely nothing to suggest such a tragic outcome.

Consumed by his fears about the repercussions of the climate crisis, the man found comfort in discussing the issue with Eliza, who became his confidante.

The chatbot was created using EleutherAI's GPT-J, an AI language model similar, but not identical, to the technology behind OpenAI's popular ChatGPT chatbot.

[1] https://docs.un.org/en/S/2021/229
[2] https://thebulletin.org/2021/05/was-a-flying-killer-robot-used-in-libya-quite-possibly/
[3] https://www.nytimes.com/2021/06/03/world/africa/libya-drone.html
[4] https://www.iai.co.il/p/harpy

Index